MICKY ADAMS

MICKY ADAMS

MY LIFE IN FOOTBALL

Biteback Publishing

First published in Great Britain in 2017 by
Biteback Publishing Ltd
Westminster Tower
3 Albert Embankment
London SE1 7SP
Copyright © Micky Adams & Neil Moxley 2017

ISBN 978-1-78590-242-0

10 9 8 7 6 5 4 3 2 1

A CIP catalogue record for this book is available from the British Library.

Set in Minion Pro

Printed and bound in Great Britain by
CPI Group (UK) Ltd, Croydon CR0 4YY

MIX
Paper from
responsible sources
FSC® C020471

To my brother, Keith William Adams.

CONTENTS

FOREWORD

I was Nottingham Forest's manager when I first really got to know Micky back in 1998. I knew his history as a player, obviously, but I didn't know the man himself until one of my old players, Alan Cork, recommended him when I was looking for a first-team coach.

Micky had been a manager himself, but was out of work after leaving Brentford. I was looking for someone who was better placed to connect with the players than I was. I needed someone they could relate to.

It was a good fit. I knew I had made the right decision because of the speed with which he became respected by the first-team squad. He took pride in his job and had enthusiasm and passion in equal measure. As I got to know him better, I saw more of his mischievous nature and an anger that burned deep inside.

It was obvious he was hard working and conscientious, and he also had other attributes that make a successful manager. He was never afraid to say what he thought, especially if a player was shirking his responsibility.

However, he had his work cut out with Pierre van Hooijdonk. The Dutch striker had thrown a huge spanner in the works when he went on strike shortly after we had won promotion to the Premier League.

I tried to get through to van Hooijdonk, because he would have been a help for us in the Premier League. But I just couldn't.

When the Dutchman eventually returned, I used to send him away from the main group to practise his free-kicks with Micky. This was an opportunity for Micky to wind up Nottingham Forest's forward, although I'm not sure van Hooijdonk had a clue what was going on.

Micky used to tell him about the great free-kicks he had scored at places such as Stevenage and Ashford, but it went straight over the Dutchman's head.

I enjoyed working with Micky, both at Forest and later at Leicester. I still miss the verbal jousting, warmth and humour. There was a lot of amusement and fun with childish, caustic banter and camaraderie.

One incident in particular sticks in my mind. I took him from Brighton, looking for him to be groomed as my successor at the King Power Stadium.

We would have staff games in the gym every Friday afternoon and drag everyone in. Somehow, Muzzy Izzet ended up playing when he was coming back from injury. Obviously, he was fitter, younger and miles better than everyone else.

Anyway, Micky's team is losing. And Muzzy, not to put too fine a point on it, is taking the piss.

Leicester's Academy staff members Steve Beaglehole and Jon Rudkin were playing, along with some of the staff and one of the chefs from the canteen. Mick used to wind it all up. In the end I used to go in goal, because it all used to kick off. And this particular afternoon it kicked off properly, too.

All of a sudden, Micky shouted 'Bury that c**t, chef, he's taking the piss,' when he was chasing down Muzzy. The next second, Leicester City's star midfielder is flying through the air after being booted by a member of the kitchen staff.

How would that look in a press conference, explaining away why your star midfielder had suffered a set-back in his rehabilitation?

The true answer would have been because the club chef smashed him to kingdom come in a Friday afternoon kick about after being goaded by the assistant manager. But I'm not sure we could have told the media that; we would have been a laughing stock.

At Leicester, I felt Micky stepped out of line and put me under pressure. I was disappointed that he was in such a hurry to be a manager. He was a young man and was frustrated.

Behind the scenes, I think he was egged on by people who wanted him to be in charge. They saw him as the future. I stand by what I thought back then, which was that he would have been far better staying in the background for another season or two and then taking over.

As it was, Leicester's relegation from the Premier League affected him more than I thought it would. It was clear to me that his confidence had been knocked. What happened at Fulham, Brentford and Swansea City was out of his control.

His decision to leave Leicester was a dreadful one. I had a row with him over it but couldn't change his mind. I battled like hell to keep him there. It upset me when he left because it was unnecessary. No one wanted him to go, me least of all.

It was the wrong time for him to go to Sheffield United, too. I know he thought the chance wouldn't come around again, but looking back now, it would have done. I know he would have done it justice. Of course, hindsight is a great thing. What's done is done. Everyone makes mistakes and sometimes you follow your hunch in football.

Irrespective of those blips, Micky's been successful. Certainly by the yardstick of many current managers who have little of any note on their career records. He has four promotions, has managed a lot of games and has survived for a long time.

He's old school. He started ever so young, he's been around. Supporters warm to him because he doesn't give them any flannel. If any side of Micky's has played poorly, or has not put in a shift, then he will tell them the truth.

I'm glad I worked with him. Managers don't have a laugh like we did, going out and taking the piss out of each other morning, noon and night or having a drink and putting the world to rights.

I'm sure this book will reveal what I know about the man: his warmth, his humour, his loyalty, his love of football and, above all, his honesty.

Dave Bassett, May 2017

PROLOGUE

I am a member of an elite club. There are twenty of us in it. I am a football manager in the Premier League and I've worked hard to get to this position with Leicester City.

I've managed clubs out of every division and I'm experienced. Whether I'm any good is for others to decide. To put my life – such as it was – into context at the time, there were nine matches to play in the 2003/04 season. And we were battling to preserve our status in the world's richest football competition. I had agreed to take the players away for a few days for a change of scenery and a chance to relax and refocus ahead of the climax of the campaign.

It was Monday 1 March 2004, the second night of our stay at a five-star hotel on the La Manga complex in southern Spain. It was a chance for me to regroup as well. I may be a Premier League boss, but I'm not immune to fatigue.

That evening I had decided to stay in. I was tired following our 0–0 draw with Wolves at the weekend, and I was also trying to dodge the few beers my staff would be having that night. I was temporarily on the wagon, so I left the players in the charge of my assistant, Alan Cork, and went to bed. They headed out to an Italian restaurant to enjoy an evening meal.

It was only about 8 p.m., so I planned to find some football to watch and go to sleep. I settled down, only to be disturbed by a couple of people banging on my door. I ignored the noise. I thought it was a guy called Pat Walker, a former teammate of mine from my early years at Gillingham. I'd met him in the foyer earlier that morning and had promised to go for a drink with him, even though I was on a self-imposed abstinence. I didn't want to leave my room. I thought I'd make it up to him when I saw him next. Sorry, Pat.

But there was no chance of any rest. My mobile phone was going off every couple of minutes with numbers I didn't recognise. More banging on the door. I turned the sound down on the television, wondering when people would get the hint that I wanted to be on my own. Then the phone in the room started to go off. Honestly, it went on for about an hour, on and off. I was getting a bit brassed off by this stage.

I thought to myself, 'Bloody hell, Pat, I know I said I'd come for a drink but surely you can't be that desperate...' I had put the latch on my door but the next thing I knew, someone was trying to get in. It's the hotel manager.

'Whoa, what's going on?'

Outside the door, there was the hotel manager, our fixer – the guy who was looking after us during the trip – and a copper.

I said, 'Hang on a minute, let me put some clothes on.'

When I saw the police were involved I thought someone had died. The copper looked at me and said, 'We need you to come downstairs.'

'All right, but please tell me no one has died.'

He looked at me and, in broken English, said: 'I can't tell you anything at this time, Mr Adams.'

So, it was serious.

Little did I realise at the time but my life was going to be turned upside-down in the most horrible manner possible. And, what's more, for me as a football manager, it would never be the same again.

CHAPTER 1

EARLY YEARS

There was no silver spoon in my mouth when Michael Richard Adams came into the world on 8 November 1961 in Sheffield's Northern General Hospital.

I was the second son of Keith and Margaret Adams, a typically hard-working family in one of England's great industrial cities. My dad was a pattern-maker who worked mainly with wood. It was a skilled job. To add a few quid more to the family kitty, he also ran a general store with my grandad in Attercliffe. And, as if that wasn't enough to keep him occupied, he also sold coal on the side.

One of my first memories was helping my dad and grandad with their deliveries. I couldn't have been more than five or six years old, but I used to go out after having filled the sacks. I couldn't have been much help. At that age, I couldn't even see into the bags.

My dad was always working, so the majority of the childcare fell upon my mum's shoulders.

I wasn't the oldest of the brood. My elder brother, Keith, preceded me by about twelve months and my mum went on to have two girls after me. However, Keith had been deprived of oxygen when he was born and was diagnosed shortly afterwards with cerebral palsy. My sisters and I understood Keith's condition, but it was hard on my mum who literally had to carry him wherever we went. It didn't help that, in his early years, my brother has a problem with his Achilles that meant he couldn't walk. He had numerous operations on it and, eventually, it was strong enough for him to make it across the room. I still remember my parents' reaction afterwards. It was uplifting, to say the least.

I grew up on an estate, so there were always loads of other kids to play with – which was fine for me, but I also had to consider Keith. Back then, the word for his condition was 'spastic'. Eight-year-olds aren't politically correct and can be cruel. I still cringe when I hear that word. It's a dreadful label.

Anyway, I tried to compensate by taking him everywhere I went when I was growing up and my earliest memories with him are of us playing football together.

As I mentioned earlier, he wasn't very agile and could hardly stand up. But that didn't matter. I used to put him in goal and everyone smashed balls at him. He couldn't react. Looking back, it was cruel. He was forever getting whacked in the face. But at least he was with me.

I was trying to make him feel a part of what I did. I didn't want him to miss out. I tried to protect him. If they took the piss out of him, I took it very personally. I got into a couple of scrapes. Back in the day, it didn't take much for me to lose my temper – as you'll discover later on.

The one outing that we used to go on – my dad, Keith and me – was to Bramall Lane to watch Sheffield United. By this stage, we had moved to a suburb called Tinsley, an area mainly populated by steelworkers. It was a big Blades' territory.

Like I say, we'd take my brother. He could walk, but every now and again required a bit of help. Of course, this was the early '70s, the days of real hooligan problems at football matches when the two sets of supporters frequently clashed outside the stadium. There would be bricks and bottles flying as they laid into one another, and there was me and my dad trying to hold up Keith while a violent battle was taking place around us.

Keith's cerebral palsy meant that he had problems forming his words properly. I became his translator. But there was one area where I was never needed, and that was in the language of football.

Keith had two pet hates. Goalkeepers – and that's all goalkeepers – he didn't discriminate. And the second object of his abuse sat in the home dug-out. Whoever occupied the managerial hot-seat at Sheffield United used to get both barrels on a regular basis. Many years later when I managed the club, I could hear him in my ears saying: 'Rubbish Adams, rubbish.'

At this stage, football was beginning to take a grip on me. I played for the school and at the weekends. I played whenever I could. When I was thirteen I had the opportunity to sign for Sheffield Wednesday. Len Ashurst was the manager of the Owls at the time and he called me in to see him. My dad and my brother came with me. Imagine that these days, a manager speaking to a thirteen-year-old.

I'll always remember that Ashurst was behind this big desk and he said to my dad: 'I'd like to sign your Michael.'

My brother just burst out laughing.

Ashurst was a bit taken aback by this and said: 'What's the problem?'

My brother, still laughing, said in his unsteady way: 'We're United-ites – there's no way he's signing for Wednesday.'

That was the end of that dream!

My life was starting to take shape at this time and my father had a massive bearing on who I was and what I stood for. And, in fact, he still does.

It's difficult to know where to start because it was a complicated relationship. To begin to understand him, you have to dig into his background. He was dogged with health issues. When he was a boy, he'd suffered with scarlet fever and that had affected the valves in his heart. He was eventually forced to give up work because of it. He had real problems and, as he grew older, he could be a difficult man.

However, when I was growing up, he was great. Every Thursday was payday and we'd call it 'Spice Day'. I have no idea why it was called that, especially since it involved him sending one of us kids down to the shop to get us all chocolate.

But my main association with my dad involved the pigeons he had in coops in the backyard. He flew them out of Sheffield along with my grandad. We had lofts up on Wincobank, which was about four miles away from where we lived. Sadly, though, one day someone got in there and killed all the birds. It was out of spite because we had been winning plenty of races. After that unfortunate incident we moved house to Brinsworth. It had a garden that stretched back about 100 feet and my dad could fit his loft in it.

My life revolved around football, school and pigeon racing. It wasn't until I was older that I realised that my dad's hobby was similar to football management.

Before the race, there was a feeling of huge excitement about what the day was going to bring. Then, as the race got closer, the stress of the event taking place set in, which was followed by the come-down afterwards. If it goes well, fantastic and everybody's happy. If it doesn't, well, life isn't as sweet. And my dad could be an absolute bastard when it came to his pigeons.

On a Friday, you would basket them all up. Dad would pluck a bird from the loft. He would read out the ring number and it was my job to write them all down correctly. If I missed one or if my writing wasn't legible, I would get a big telling off. The pigeons would go off on Friday night. You would get word that they had taken flight, and then my dad would find out the wind speed to give him an idea of what time to expect them back. It was always so exciting when they returned. We'd take the bands off and clock them in and out. That was the race.

The first one back has the best velocity. Don't forget, people lived all over. Some birds might have to travel an extra mile or two. The velocity was calculated from the distance and the time. That decides the winner.

You could gamble from a penny to a pound. Fivers and tenners for the big races.

My old man was so stressed. He was always desperate to win. Consequently, if he didn't, he would be in a foul mood. And I mean a really bad mood. And everyone was on the receiving end of it. Some worse than others.

The problem was that he had been indulged. My grandparents had been soft with him. They just couldn't handle him. I want to mention – because I don't think it should be forgotten – that there were occasions when he used to hit my mum. It became worse as time went on. He'd drink and, well, take out his frustrations on her. So there were long periods in our lives where my siblings and I would see her with a black eye and bumps and bruises. My earliest recollections go as far back as when I was five years old. How bad did it get? Well, let's put it like this: on occasion the police were called.

There were other times when I just wanted all the noise to stop. It didn't happen every day, don't get me wrong. There were significant periods when nothing happened. But I don't want to gloss over it. This is my story, and I want to tell it. I am not going to sugar-coat it.

The day of my dad's funeral affected me like no other. I didn't want someone to stand up and say 'what a great bloke...' I didn't want that. For some reason – and I don't know why I did it – I stood up and said: 'There were times when my dad was fantastic. He loved Morecambe and Wise, Tommy Cooper, *Tom and Jerry* all of that.' But I didn't want to say that and leave it there. I couldn't. I felt it wouldn't have been right for me not to say something about what went on. So I did. How do I feel about that? It didn't make up for what went on the past, that's how.

So, I stood up at the funeral and said that there were some things that weren't right. Even though I meant what I said, it affected me for a long time afterwards. I couldn't quite work out why I'd done it. But I didn't want everyone to turn up and just gloss over the bad bits. Maybe, just maybe, I shouldn't have said anything at his funeral. Perhaps I shouldn't be writing these words.

And, even though it was hard for my mum who, at the time, had two jobs, she still speaks about my dad in glowing, loving terms.

I couldn't sit in her company today and say my dad was this and that. She would just remind me of all the good things. They say time does heal. And it does. Of course, she never wanted anyone to know what was going on. But you can't hide black eyes, can you?

Did he ever hit me? Yes, he did. All of us were strapped by his big belt. I was scared of him.

But even so, psychologically, I beat myself up about it because without him – without the discipline and values that he instilled in me – I wouldn't have got where I have. He hammered discipline into me.

When I was about thirteen or fourteen, he decided I wasn't fit enough. He bought me some weights and I used to do squats with them. I'd do anything to make him happy. I lived for him being happy with me and if I knew he was around, I'd do the weights so he could see me.

He once told me to run back from my Auntie Alice's house. I clocked it the other day when I went back to Sheffield. It was three miles. And to a fourteen-year-old, that was a long way. But I ran to please him. Everything I did was to please him.

By the age of fifteen I was at Sheffield United. I played on a Sunday for Hackenthorpe Throstles, the top team in the city at the time. In those days, a lot of the junior sides were affiliated with the professional sides, and they in turn were associated with Wednesday. For example, Mel Sterland played for Middlewood Rovers.

My football career was starting to kick off as part of the youth team at Sheffield United. While my mates were going out on a Friday or Saturday night, my dad made sure there was no chance of that for me. Absolutely none. If he ever came to watch me and I'd had a bad game, he wouldn't speak to me afterwards. He just totally blanked me and would go down to the pigeon loft. I'd make my way down to see if he needed a hand and then he would open up. He'd ask me questions like: 'Do you know when such-and-such happened … could you have done it any better?'

Discipline was present in everything I did as a teenager. I had chores every day. We had a big garden and there was a hedge running on one side of it. My job was to look after that, and if the garden became too full of weeds, that was my responsibility too. And I had to clean out the pigeons. That was a big task. If I hadn't done it by the time he had got home from work, there would be a problem.

If I ever wanted to go out with my mates, I'd ask him what time I had to be back. And if he said 8.30 p.m., then I was back at 8.30 p.m. All hell would break loose if I wasn't. I remember once when I went round to a pal's house and I asked his mum if she could give me a shout at 8.20 p.m. because I had to be home ten minutes later. She forgot and didn't call me down until 9 p.m. I got home and was strapped across the backside.

While my sisters didn't get it to the same degree, the threat of violence was always in the air. I suppose, looking back, a lot of the anger was to do with his illness. When I was sixteen, my dad had his first valve replacement operation. He was only forty but he had to pack in work. Suddenly, we were living off benefits and, in many respects, things got worse after that. Nearly all the fights that he had with my mum after that were about money. The frustration must have just built up inside him. So, they were testing times. Me trying hard to please my dad and him taking out his life's frustrations on me and my mum.

I attended Park House School during my teenage years and, when my parents were fighting, I had no one to turn to. I ended up talking to my games teacher, a guy called Roger Blades. He was the one person who kept me going. He just told me to concentrate on my football and said that it would sort itself out and that I had to give it time.

It was hard to concentrate fully on anything going on outside the home when you have those issues inside it. When my parents weren't talking to each other or when my mum had a black eye, it was hard work.

Having said that, there were some good times, too. We all used to go to Skegness on holiday in a caravan. I remember we were bought a kite each year and my brother, because he couldn't operate his hands properly, always managed to lose his within five minutes. The rest of us charged through fields on countless occasions trying to retrieve his bloody kite. We'd give it him back and five minutes later, he'd lose it. And off we'd go again.

We'd have a donkey ride and it was the highlight of the week. Think about the kids these days with their tablets, iPads and the rest of it. Honestly, it sounds Dickensian doesn't it? We had to make do with a ride on a donkey.

These holidays was also proved my dad's consistent ability to buy the worst cars in the world. They would almost always break down. Because he had his heart problems, he would be in the driver's seat, while my mum and my two sisters and I would try to bump-start the thing. One stand-out memory involved the road from the M1 that leads into

Sheffield city centre called Sheffield Parkway. It was built when I was about fifteen years old and, once it had been laid – or so we thought – my dad said: 'Right, let's get on it.' Unfortunately for us, however, they hadn't put down any tarmac. We got stuck in the mud and had to wait for a rescue truck to come and get it the next day. We all trudged home through the mud.

• • •

At sixteen, leaving school was in sight. I was unique among my mates in that I used to attend. The big thing at that time was 'wagging it', i.e. not going. I was so scared of my old man, though, that it was never on the agenda for me. He'd say, 'If I ever catch you smoking, I'll cut your fingers off', so that was enough to put me off for life. There was always that fear. If he said 'don't do it', then I didn't. Simple as that.

At this time, as I was waiting for a decision as to whether I was going to be offered an apprenticeship or not, there was a change of manager at Sheffield United. Jimmy Sirrel was the manager and John Short was the youth coach when I first got there. I thought Jimmy was great and I felt I'd done well under him. He used to come and watch us kids on the old bowling green just by Bramall Lane.

However, the new manager, Harry Haslam, brought in another youth coach instead of John Short.

My dad, who was about to have his first heart operation, went in to see the people at Sheffield United. He told them that he wasn't likely to be around because he was recovering from his heart operation and wondered if they had made a decision on my future. They said they hadn't officially but they told him they were going to release me. He took me to one side and said: 'Right, what you need to do is not to get too down. Get fitter, get stronger and you are going to prove people wrong.' On the day that he went into hospital, the letter arrived from Sheffield United telling me I had been released.

Around the same time, I had to decide whether or not I was going to continue with my education. But it wasn't a real choice. My dad had told me that I was staying on at school, so that was that. He didn't want me leaving school with nothing.

But my old youth team coach, John Short, had got a job at Gillingham as a physio and chief scout. He got in touch to ask if I'd be interested in going to Kent with him for a two-week trial. After a few words with my dad, I decided to go down and get a lift with Sean Pendleton and another ex-Sheffield lad. It went on for miles. Two hundred and forty of them. Almost as soon as we arrived, that was it. I ended up at Gillingham on a pre-season trial.

One of the things my dad had drummed into me, which really stood me in good stead, was: 'Make sure you are as fit as you can be.' I remember the first day I went into Gillingham and I was in great shape. Steve Bruce was already there and we had a practice match against the first-team.

I was playing left-wing against a bloke called Graham Knight. His nickname was 'Booty' and he was a lovely fella. But I noticed there was something strange about him that day. He had his kit on, but underneath it he was covered in plastic bags from his neck down to his ankles.

It was an old trick. Plastic doesn't allow the skin to breathe, so you lose water very quickly. He was sweating like you wouldn't believe playing right-back, so I just kept getting the ball and running past him. I had a fantastic first day. And within two weeks, I had managed to get myself an apprenticeship. My dad was right. Who was to say whether fitness had played a part, but it certainly didn't do me any harm. And I managed to put my first foot on the ladder of my football career.

While footballers today tend to live very glamorous lifestyles, that wasn't the case for me. There wasn't the same money sloshing about professional football back then. Gillingham put me into digs. It was one of our jobs to take care of the dirty kit. We used to put the kit on coat-hangers after every training session and hang it in the boiler room to dry off. You can imagine the stench of it as the week progressed. By Thursday, it was horrendous. There was no transport to the club, either. You got up and caught the bus, or else you walked. I didn't have any money to get myself a taxi or anything like that, so it was a four-mile trek before you had even started training. We were paid £12–14 with two paid fares home per season. I couldn't telephone home. But I had a great time.

A fella called Bill 'Buster' Collins was my coach. He was a tough Northern Irishman but he and his wife Betty looked after us young-sters like we were their own.

He was slightly deaf was Buster. His old Lada was rubbish, just like something my old fella would have probably bought. There was a horrendous squeal every time he put it into gear. It used to go right through you, that sound. But he was a tough man. He told it you as it was.

And I suppose because of my upbringing, I didn't really mind people taking a pop at me. I suppose, if you want to be clinical about it, I had developed a mental toughness. Even at that age.

It wasn't emotional for me anymore. You see so many kids now, and if you raise your voice it's like the end of the world for them. It just wasn't ever like that for me. I got used to it. It was a case of 'OK, I understand why you have shouted at me. I'll try to do better.'

As I say, Buster told me how it was. As did the manager Gerry Summers and his assistant Alan Hodgkinson. Not one of them was a shrinking violet.

Anyway, I soon got in and around the first-team. And if there were four of us, we'd train with the first-team on Friday. With me being a left-winger, I came up against either Booty or John Sharp – another tough old right-back – and he used to kick me black and blue.

Of course, they were preparing for a game on Saturday. They got all the free-kicks, all the corners and there were no fouls given. One day, I mistakenly nutmegged Sharp. I say 'mistakenly' because I hadn't meant to put it through his legs. It went around the other side of him and got my cross in. The next tackle came in. He nearly cut me in half. He stood over me and said, 'Do that to me again on a Friday and I'll kill you.' One, he didn't want to be embarrassed and two, he was getting ready for a game.

I also remember once pulling out of a tackle. Well, I didn't so much pull out of it as wriggled out of it – I think there's a difference. I still maintain that tackling for wingers and tackling for full-backs are two different things. As a winger you are trying to win the ball, so you want to gain an advantage and away you go. As a full-back, you just go to stop the winger. As long as he doesn't get away, then you're all right. Anyway, we were playing in the south-east counties' game against Millwall and Brucey was playing centre-half. He thought that I'd pulled out of one. He shouted over: 'If I ever see you do that again I'll come over there and sort you out myself.' As I came off the pitch, Buster came over to me at the end and said: 'Do you know what Brucey said to you earlier?' I replied that I did. 'Well, he was absolutely spot-on. Don't pull out of a tackle again.' After that, I never did.

The Gillingham first-team used to go out every Thursday night before a Saturday game and think nothing of drinking seven or eight pints in an evening. Training the next day was madness. Anything went. We'd have a six-a-side or seven-a-side in a certain area and it used to be all kicking off. The club wondered why they lost so many goals in the last ten or fifteen minutes of games, but if you'd seen the state of some of them on the Thursday night you wouldn't have been in the least bit surprised. They were all dehydrated and running on empty.

However, Brucie blotted his copybook, big time. It was about this time that he used to reverse the telephone charges from a phone box to call his missus Janet, who was standing in another phone box in Tyneside. It was an ingenious plan but ended with him getting nicked. He copped some flak for that. For weeks afterwards he was called 'Busby', after the woman who used to be on the British Telecom adverts.

We used to have a lad called Terry Nicholl in our ranks as well. He was the brother of Chris Nicholl who played for Villa and was later my manager at Southampton – but Graham Knight, aka Booty, had this trick that he played on all the apprentices. He had the ability to cry at the drop of a hat.

Terry would collar an unsuspecting new apprentice and say, 'Go and find Booty and ask whether his sister is still having those ballet lessons…' So off the apprentice would trot. He'd knock on the door and be invited in. There he would say that Terry had told him to come in and enquire whether Booty's sister was still having the ballet lessons. Booty would start crying, leaving the apprentice shame-faced.

'You little bastard,' someone would shout, 'she was in a car accident last week and had to have her foot amputated…' Of course, it was all a wind-up but when the apprentice got back to our dressing room we knew he'd been in to see Booty as the colour had drained out of his face.

We used to have a big communal bath and had to clean it all out. Brucie was the head boy so he had to tell us what to do, but I have to say that he was the worst apprentice I have ever seen. Shocking. Every Friday before a home game, the manager would inspect it. He'd come in, run his finger around the rim and declare that it wasn't good enough. 'Do it again,' he'd say and off we'd go. Of course, Brucie didn't lift a finger. Apprentices have it easy now.

On the pitch, I'd done OK. I made my debut when I was seventeen years old and I was earning £14-a-week at the time. When it came to Christmas time, I'd had an inkling I'd be playing because the manager wouldn't let me go home. So I stayed behind. Brucie had already made his debut by this time, but he didn't play on my debut against Rother-ham United.

I had changed digs by then as well. My first proper home down there was great but my landlady, Mrs McCauley, was temperamental, although her daughter, Sharon, was nice. I had also met my first wife, Mandy, by this stage. I moved to a house across the road from her with a couple called Charlie and Cath Mannerings and their sons Steven and David. They were absolutely fantastic.

Of course, I was still an apprentice at the time and was marked down as a winger. Even though I was enthusiastic, fit and relatively quick, I didn't have a trick. My Plan A, Plan B and Plan C was my pace. If I could push it past someone and get a cross in, that was me. I'd work up and down.

But my big breakthrough came when Keith Peacock and Paul Taylor replaced Gerry and Alan as managers. Keith saw me as a full-back, and that was probably the turning point of my playing career. He quickly realised that I didn't have trick, that I wasn't great with my back to goal and that I needed to see the play spread out in front of me and come on to the ball.

As I was quick, I began to establish myself as an attacking full-back. I hated defending at the back post, and being 5ft 8in. tall didn't help.

However, I took big strides at Gillingham. Despite our status there were some decent players, such as Dick Tydeman, who was a lower-league version of Glenn Hoddle. He sat in the middle of the park, didn't have any legs but could pick a pass and had the ability to execute it.

In fact, we played Spurs in a cup tie and Tydeman was up against Hoddle. It was a packed house at Priestfield and I think it was the first time that I began to learn more about the game. We would have the ball – then they would. We'd get it back, they'd get it back. It just went on like this.

We tried to involve Spurs in a game of football. We were in the Fourth Division at the time and they were among the elite. Spurs had Hoddle, we had Tydeman and, while Dick played well that day, Hoddle was better. They won 4–2.

I started thinking: why didn't we get in their faces more? Why didn't we close them down and make it difficult for them, rather than just having a game with them? That was the time I really started to think about managers and the messages that they were trying to get across.

But I will always be grateful to Keith Peacock for encouraging me and seeing something in me to promote me as a left-back. I suppose in many ways I was like him as a player. He was small and enthusiastic – he was bubbly where the assistant manager, Paul Taylor, was dour and serious about the training ground.

There were plenty of scouts beating a path to the door at Priestfield to watch me and Brucie. There was non-stop chatter about Steve moving to a big club and perhaps me following him out of the exit door.

Apparently, Spurs had made contact with Gillingham. The chairman had given the north London club the price and contact had been established between the two clubs over my transfer.

But then we had an away game that night against Orient. There was a guy called Peter Taylor playing for them; well, he was on the bench. In the first half of that match at Brisbane Road, I'd done all right. I'd got forward, done a little bit. Played quite well. But the one question that people had about my ability was: could I, as an ex-winger, defend?

Taylor was a substitute that night and came on the second half. He nutmegged me three times in front of the main stand and, to cut a long story, that was the end of that. Gillingham never heard from Spurs again.

Instead, I got the call to go and see Keith Peacock after I'd come crashing to earth with a big bump to find that they had agreed a £75,000 fee with Coventry City. I was told to travel to the Midlands and meet my agent who, as chance would have it, was a family friend.

He was a lad called Paddy Sowden, and I'm trying to be as fair as I can here, he wasn't much of an agent. We travelled up to Highfield Road and the manager, Bobby Gould, came out to meet us.

He didn't observe social niceties, and the first words to come out of his mouth were: 'I speak to the player – and the player only.'

That would never happen these days. Sowden should have said: 'No, you talk to me and the player, or we're getting back in the car.'

But I was only twenty, earning around £140-a-week at Gillingham and the Sky Blues were in the First Division.

So Sowden said 'OK.'

Bobby took me inside his office and gave me the spiel about building the club and that they wanted young players.

He said, 'Your wages are £250-a-week with no signing-on fee.'

At this point, I should have said: 'I'm flattered, but I'm not accepting that', and got back into the car and gone home. It wasn't the contract I was looking for. But I was keen to play in the First Division – the Premier League as it now is. And I wanted to leave Gillingham.

As I came out of the office I realised I was getting a pay rise of £110-per-week. Really, it felt like happy days.

On the way home, my so-called agent said: 'You know what we

should do? We should ring up Gilllingham, tell them we haven't quite agreed terms and see if we can get some money out of them for leaving.'

So we stopped the car at a phone box and phoned Gillingham's chairman, a lovely old fella called Dr Grossmark. The first question out of his mouth was: 'Has he signed?' Paddy replied that I had. With that, the phone went down. Conversation over.

In the years to come, I realised that I hadn't received the deal I should have done. But at the time, this lad from Sheffield was about to start rubbing shoulders with English football's big boys.

And I couldn't wait.

CHAPTER 2

THE SKIES ARE BLUE-ISH

By signing me, Coventry City and Bobby Gould had realised my dream. I'd reached the top-flight of English football and I was delighted.

But within days that joy was tinged with bitterness. The manager had effectively turned me over with the contract I'd signed. I arrived at the club all bright-eyed and, within a few days, I heard the top boys were earning £500–600 per week. I was £250 a week short of that. You may think: 'Well, more fool you.' That's fair enough, but I'd be lying if I said it didn't gnaw away at me.

On the upside, it was the beginning of my journey in the top-flight. Bobby said he saw me as a left-sided player. He didn't actually specify where he wanted me to play, but scoring on my debut against Everton at Highfield Road got me off to a flier with the supporters, the manager and my colleagues. I'll always remember it. I had fractured my wrist in pre-season and had to play with a light cast on my arm, which wasn't ideal.

Unfortunately, that bright start soon faded and any issue with my arm paled into insignificance when, during the fourth game of the season against Watford, I twisted my ankle and was out for six months.

At the time, my relationship with Mandy had moved to a more serious level and we were engaged. She was still living in Gillingham at the time and I was due to go back to pick up some clothes and spend the weekend with her. There was a change in the plan when the club told me I had to report for treatment instead. I phoned with the breaking news but, not for the first time, she trumped me with some of her own.

'I'm pregnant' was the gist of it.

My reaction? 'Well, we'll get married then.' Yes, I know. Mr Smooth.

And so it was that we tied the knot in November while I was injured, and we had three days in Broadstairs for our honeymoon.

Rock 'n' roll, eh?

After that seismic change in my personal circumstances, I had to get fit and start playing again. I could have done with the cash, and the odd win bonus wouldn't have gone amiss, either.

Playing for Bobby was an eye-opener. I know people have called him a character before, but it really is true as far as he is concerned.

For instance, if he called you in to see him on a Friday, it meant one of two things. If you had played the week before, you were now dropped. If you hadn't played, it meant you were in. He had no problem saying: 'I'm leaving you out – and here are the reasons why.'

As time went on, footballers being footballers, we would turn up later and later to training on a Friday, leaving it until ten minutes before we were due to go out. He was a stickler for getting out on the training ground at 10.30 a.m., and there was no way he could break the news to your face as you were getting changed.

During the time I was injured, he signed Stuart Pearce – and what a shrewd piece of business for the club that turned out to be, although it did have a knock-on effect for yours truly and not in a good way.

In fact, Bobby signed a lot of players from the lower leagues. As well as me and Stuart, there was Micky Gynn from Peterborough and

Trevor Peake from Lincoln. Steve Ogrizovic joined from Shrewsbury Town and Nicky Platnauer came from Bristol Rovers. With all those lads who had put in the hard yards in the lower leagues, we really appreciated what we had. We had team spirit by the bucket-load.

At times, that's all it came down to. But, do you know what, the strength of that group – a mentality forged lower down the ladder of football – meant we had a solid mind-set that would see us grind out results when, if truth be told, our individual ability was nowhere near as strong as that of players in other clubs.

However, when I was injured, Mandy and I had bought a house in Ernsford Grange in Coventry, not too far from where my new team-mate, Nicky Platnauer, lived. Money was tight for both of us and now I had a young daughter to look after as well.

So Nicky and I decided to start our own business. At this time, don't forget, we were top-flight footballers. We plumped for garden clearances, and we were looking for scrap metal. The two of us bought a van, an open-backed one, and we did the work before we went training. We'd turn up early doors, do a couple of hours' graft, drop stuff off at the tip if we had time and then get to training before 10.30 a.m. Imagine that nowadays at a Premier League club – no chance!

But I'll always remember this; in fact, I remember it as if it were yesterday. Even though we were both running a garden clearance business, Plats was out looking for work rather than doing it. I was the silly sod actually getting my hands dirty. One fella came up to me one time and handed me £10. He said, 'Don't tell your gaffer, you've done a really good job there, well done.' I'd been marked down as the navvy and Plats got the job as my boss!

The other incident that sticks in my mind concerns Gouldy. We'd just finished a job and had to go back past his family home, as he was staying at his dad's at the time. Only the van broke down about 100 yards from his old fella's house. We had to abandon it. I found the nearest phone box and rang my missus to come and pick us up. Bobby never found out about it to this day, although we did eventually go back for the van.

However, even though I had this gig on the side we were still struggling for cash. So, I went to see Bobby one day and said: 'Listen, I've got this contract – I know everybody else is on more money. I don't normally do this – but can you help me out?'

He replied: 'I'll come around your house to see you.' It was the best thing he ever did.

Our house was a small, detached, three-bedroomed place. In the front room, we had just two chairs and a telly. There wasn't any carpet on the floor. We had a cooker in the kitchen and that was about it. We just didn't have anything.

He took a couple of steps over the threshold and said: 'I see what you mean. I'll see what I can do.'

Within twenty-four hours, a fitter arrived and carpeted the whole house. Then a load of furniture turned up. He didn't improve the contract at all, but he looked after us and it was well appreciated.

The thing about Gouldy was just how passionate he was about Coventry and the city – although some of his methods did not always pay off. We had one training session and he was trying to impress on us the need to move the ball more quickly. His theme was that there is no way any player can move as fast as a football. And then he said: 'Look, I'll show you.'

He called out for the quickest player and the lads turned to me and said 'It's probably Micky.' Gouldy told me to go and stand on the goal line and to run to the halfway line as quick as I could. He plonked the ball down and got ready to kick it, so that I could race against it. That was how he was going to illustrate his point. Only, as I set off, he shanked his pass and it went miles off to the right. Of course, the lads just stood there pissing themselves.

You just couldn't shake his belief in Coventry. And, at times, he was right. We played Liverpool early one season. We had a good start and battered them, winning 4–2, and we went to the top of the league. I was injured at the time but that had nothing to do with it, honest.

This being Coventry City, we might as well have gone on an open top bus tour on the back of our win. It was an incredible time but, and forgive the pun, the wheels then fell off. We went on a horrific run of results. We ended up in a position of having to win our last four games of the season to stay up. Which we did, thankfully.

• • •

I remember the day Gouldy called me into the office on a Friday. I'd played the week before, so I knew I was being dropped. We were play-ing Ipswich and I think Stuart Pearce had been injured or suspended. He'd done well, had Stuart, so no argument from me. I had to take it, begrudgingly. I was professional and I wasn't a sulker. I did have a temper, though. The lads used to call me 'the Fuse' because I had a very short one.

We all went out training. Gouldy went into the middle of the pitch. He didn't speak to anyone. He just stood there. All of a sudden, after about five minutes, he whistled us all in. We approached him, watching his face with his big eyebrows, waiting to hear what he was about to say. 'Two laps of the pitch' was all he said. We think he has lost it by this time, but we set off as requested. He stood there, still not looking at or talking to anyone.

He called us all again. 'That will do – in you go', he said.

He'd already told me I had been dropped, so this lack of activity wasn't any good for me. I wouldn't be playing at Portman Road and I saw the reserves were having a kick-about on the far side of the pitch. I went up to him and said, 'Gaffer, if I'm not playing tomorrow, can I just go and join in with them for half-an-hour?'

He said, 'No, you are playing tomorrow – I've changed my mind.'

I went away scratching my head thinking to myself: 'I must have looked impressive on those two laps!'

That was it. To this day I have no idea what he was thinking. I don't understand the psychology of it. Perhaps he had a little brainwave. I've done it occasionally as a manager where I've just gone with my instinct. You might think to yourself, 'I've got to play him today.'

And if you haven't named the team on a Friday, you'll have permutations whizzing around your mind about what is best for the team. But he'd dropped me and then five minutes later reinstated me. Needless to say, I had a nightmare of a game. I think I had switched off a little bit. I was one of those players who needed to get a sweat on the day before the game to feel like I had done something, rather than just save the energy.

Bobby was a great laugh at other times, though. We went to Sweden during one pre-season and you know what the prices are like for alcohol in Scandinavia: extortionate. Anyway, we walked into a bar and he wanted to buy everyone a drink – obviously on the club bill.

The only instruction was: 'Don't take the piss.' He was getting the order in and going around the lads. It was lagers all round apart from for Micky Gynn, who asked for something else. I don't believe the manager expected the reply that came: 'Babycham and brandy.' It cost a fortune, about £6 on its own, which was a small fortune thirty years ago when you could get a pint in England for less than 50p.

I'm not sure it was anything to do with Gouldy's management style but Coventry was one of those clubs where someone was always brassed off about something. The fact that he was never consistent with his team selection certainly didn't help matters. It became a question of 'who's pissed off? Let's go and have a pint somewhere.' It also meant there was never any shortage of drinking partners.

There wasn't much by way of progress on the pitch. We'd been in relegation battles every single year. The greatest escape came in 1985, when, as I mentioned earlier, we had to win our last few matches to stay up. We had to win – a draw was no good to us.

It went to the death. Against Luton at home, we just managed to scrape ourselves over the line with a narrow win. Next up was Stoke at the Victoria Ground. Ian Painter missed a penalty. Pearcy scored one and we managed to get three points from that.

Then, on the final day of the season, we played Everton at home. Howard Kendall's side had just been crowned champions. For some reason, it was on a Sunday and Norwich, who would have gone down had we won, were already away somewhere. All week we had been hearing stories about how the title-winners had been out on the sauce. Everton had the FA Cup final against Manchester United to prepare for the week after they played us, so they had taken their eyes off the ball.

We got right into them early on and they just didn't want to know. Whether it was the prospect of the final or not, they just weren't bothered. I scored and we won 4–1 in front of a packed house at Highfield Road. There was a great night of celebrations. But it wasn't too long afterwards that Gouldy was sacked.

We met at Highfield Road as we had a game the next day. He gave me the usual call. I'd played the week before so I had to go and see him in the office. I thought I knew what was coming. He said: 'I'm not playing you tomorrow.' I came out of the office and, for the first time, I thought, 'I'm not happy with that.' I thought I'd played well the week before.

So, I went back in. I knocked on his door and walked in. I said:

I've got to tell you gaffer, I'm not happy about this. Every time there's a decision to be made, it always looks as though it's me who is left out of the team. I did all right last week. The reasons you've given for dropping me, I don't understand. I know Stuart Pearce is quality but I've sat in front of him, worked up and down the pitch and, by messing me around, you are starting to affect me. If you aren't happy with me, put me on the transfer list and let me go. Because to me, it looks as though every time there is a decision to be made, I'm the one who is left out.

He looked at me and said: 'OK, leave that with me.'

I walked into the first-team dressing room and the lads asked me what had gone on. I said, 'The usual. I'm out.'

You know what the lads in the dressing room are like. They started to take the piss. So I carried on. 'Well, I've told him to fuck off.' The lads aren't having any of it. They don't believe me.

Normally, we'd be in the dressing room for about five minutes before Gouldy would come in, have a quick word and get us out for training. This time, we were sat there for about an hour in our kit. It was very strange.

All of a sudden, the door opened and Gouldy popped his head around the door. He looked straight at me. He gestured towards me and shepherded me back into his office. I was thinking to myself, 'I've gone overboard here. I shouldn't have said anything to him.'

He sat down, looked at me and asked: 'What have you got to do?' I shook my head. I didn't understand.

He carried on. 'I've dropped you, haven't I? What have you got to do?'

'I'll do what I always do gaffer, I'll get on with my work and prove you wrong.'

He left it for a second and said: 'I'd better do the same ... I've just been sacked.'

I went back into the changing room. He didn't bother going in to tell the lads. Just me. And I never saw him at Coventry again.

The dressing room was divided on him at the time, but I was sad to see him go. I liked him as a person. Yes, he had his slightly odd ways at times, but he cared. You often see managers kissing badges but when Bobby did it, he really meant it. He was a genuine Coventry man who loved his club. I can't help but think that if he were around the club now, some of the current mess might have been avoided.

Towards the end of his reign, Bobby had brought in Don Mackay to help with the coaching. When Don was on the side-lines, his combination with the manager hadn't worked. He was a nice enough bloke, Don, but he didn't like confrontation. And he was given the manager's job.

But he thought he was a coach. He had been a goalkeeper in Scotland and every Coventry City player knew it. There was just no way he was going to cut it on the training pitches at an English First Division club. Can you imagine a former Scottish goalkeeper trying to teach Cyrille Regis how to bend his runs into the channel? That's what Don was trying to do. The lads weren't having him at all. It was never going to happen.

He wasn't popular in the dressing room either, although I have to say I got on fine with him. Consequently, it filtered back to the directors that he was struggling on the training pitch, and from then on his reign in charge of the club was doomed.

However, I had other issues to contend with this time, because Sheffield United had come in for me.

The Blades' manager at the time, Ian Porterfield, had an idea with the then chairman, Reg Brearley, to try and sign Sheffield boys. They wanted lads with a passion for the club. So, I got a call from Porterfield one day, asking me to come and meet him.

'Listen son, we shouldn't be doing this,' he said, 'but I'll meet you in a hotel in Leicester. I'll see you at the Holiday Inn. Don't tell anyone because this is hush-hush.'

I quite liked the sound of it. They were going to spend a few quid seeing if this project worked and I didn't feel particularly wanted at Coventry. I was being selected sporadically by Don, so I went over to Leicester to meet them. I sat in the reception area of the Holiday Inn and in walked Porterfield with his chairman, carrying a briefcase. The manager of Sheffield United manager was still wearing his club tracksuit. I stood up to shake his hand and said, 'I thought this was supposed to be secret?'

He looked at me and, in his Scottish drawl, said to me, 'Don't worry about that, son, I've just come from training.'

He gave me the spiel and Brearley opened his suitcase. It had £20,000 in cash inside. Porterfield said, 'Look, we want you. You can have this to sign. Take it away now.'

It was a tempting offer, despite dropping down two divisions. It meant I was going to get an increase in my basic wage as well. So I left the money on the table, went back to Coventry and told them that unless they improved my contract, I was off. And, in fairness, they did.

Incidentally, It was about this time that Stuart Pearce was arrested for drink-driving, and he's accused me in his own book of walking off and leaving him to face the music on his own. Now it's my turn to set the story straight.

So Stuart and I had been drinking and he said he'd give me a lift. Going home, I had told him about the policeman who used to sit in his car at a particular roundabout. But he was so busy listening to his punk music that he didn't see him. The bobby duly pulled us up about 400 yards from my house. Stuart was breathalysed and arrested. By this stage, there wasn't a lot I could have done for him. He said that I got out and left him there. I can't deny that I did, but I'm not exactly sure what he wanted me to do. I was only 400 yards from home.

However, despite this, if ever there was a player destined for the top it was Stuart. He had a fierce will to win and was extremely tenacious. It was little surprise to anyone who knew him in those earlier days that he would go on to be as successful as he was.

It was also about this time that I decided to dip my toe into the waters of politics and became the club's PFA representative. Because of my background and my upbringing, the association matched my politics, and I managed to nail my colours pretty spectacularly to the mast by obtaining a miner's coat during the strike with the letters 'NCB' written on the back. I took it into training one day. I put my coat on a hanger and, when I got changed afterwards, someone had made an amendment to the lettering. The 'C' had been turned into an 'O' and so there I was walking around for a couple of days with the word 'NOB' written on my back.

Anyway, Mackay's reign couldn't last. The punters hadn't taken to him and nor had the players. The board decided to make a change.

In his place came John Sillett. More importantly for the club, George Curtis came in as managing director. He was one of the hardest men I've ever met. Hard as nails. There's a picture of him breaking his leg and getting carried off on a stretcher with a smile on his face. He was mad as a hatter but the atmosphere under that pair was miles better than it had been. They were lively.

Behind Curtis's back, we called him 'Barney Rubble' after the character in *The Flintstones*. One day, while on the bus heading off after a match, we'd had a few drinks. I made a massive mistake of taking the piss out of him and, unfortunately for me, he overheard me. He immediately grabbed me and got me in a headlock. I had a moustache at the time, and he ripped one side of it right off. It was the most pain I had ever been in. He literally tore the hair out of my top lip and, for weeks afterwards, I was walking around with a huge scab on my face as the wound healed. I think I shaved the other half off.

Sills was a good coach. He'd come in, get the lads organised and managed to put a smile back on the face of the club. He didn't encourage a drinking culture but George had this idea where if you went out, you had to sip halves on the basis that it didn't look as bad. I got on OK with Sills but I had a problem: he preferred Greg Downs as left-back. I couldn't understand it. I thought he struggled for pace and couldn't really run and I just couldn't see what he had that I didn't. He's a nice fella, Greg – no issue with that – but I wanted to play.

For me, it all came to a head when I was left out again during the 1986/87 season. I was twenty-six years old and I needed to play regularly. I wasn't in the squad for the third round FA Cup tie against Bolton Wanderers, so the feelers went out and I left in the same month to play for Billy Bremner at Leeds United. And so my next chapter began.

CHAPTER 3

BILLY'S BOY BUT NOT HOWARD'S WAY

I was dropping down a division to sign for Billy Bremner, but I didn't mind. He had such a big influence on my career and life that I wouldn't have swapped it for the world.

If Bobby Gould was Mr Coventry City, then Billy was Mr Leeds United. He had so much affection for that club.

I've mentioned the word 'tough' a few times so far in this book, but I wouldn't be doing Leeds United's midfielder any disservice to say that, on the pitch, he certainly fell into that category. Off it, his enthusiasm for Leeds United could not be questioned.

He had a genuine love for the club and I was in awe of him straight-away. There aren't many people I've met that I've felt like that about. What made me warm to him was we didn't really argue about the contract I was getting, he just wanted me to be happy and settled. To be around him every day was a great experience. Win, lose or draw on Saturday, come Monday morning he was back on it again.

Having said that, I didn't always agree with the regimented and repetitive style of his training sessions. For instance, we'd start with circle ball. If you're in football, you know the drill. The players form a circle and then play one-touch trying to keep the ball away from the player or players in the middle. Billy would be in there with us. You couldn't stop him. Sometimes, he'd come out wearing his shoes. He'd be playing with us in a pair of loafers.

Then we'd have an eight-a-side and some shooting practice at the end. If you scored, you were allowed to go in for your shower. Training really was very basic. With all of this 'one shot and you can go inside' business, it wasn't as if we were actually learning.

And that was it. No one wanted to be left out on the pitch on their own too often. He would head into the dressing rooms with us and pick the best player of the session. He would then ask the best player to choose the worst one in a silent vote among the squad. If he thought it was you who had been poor he'd come in and plonk himself down next to you, which pretty much gave the game away. He would be sitting there as we changed, taking it all in. I think he loved the company of players. We used to have to whisper in his ear who was the best – and worst – and he'd sit there giggling.

Uncomfortably, for those who were being paid to play, at times both Billy and Norman Hunter used to train with us. What worried us was that apart from John Sheridan – the best player at the club by a distance – Norman and Billy were the stand-out pair!

They would have been into their forties at this stage – embarrassing for the rest of us, but true. We used to call Hunter 'Bollocks Norman' because every time he gave the ball away he used to say 'bollocks' to himself. Alan Clarke would come in again occasionally just to watch training, and afterwards we'd see him chewing Billy's ears off, pontificating about the good old days.

Billy was a great player and we really used to be in awe of him on that pitch. If, say, you were on free-kicks and shanking them everywhere, he'd take over. He would walk across the pitch, sometimes wearing his shoes, and calmly say: 'Let me show you how to do it, son.' He'd put the ball down and say 'I want it done like this…' Inevitably, he'd land it on a sixpence. It didn't help. All it did was ramp up the pressure on the taker. But it did prove to everyone what a great player he had been in his day.

He'd been brought up under Don Revie and a few of his mentor's methods worked their way into what Billy did – particularly if we were playing away. Carpet bowls was an absolute must. It was non-negotiable. We played it after dinner in almost every hotel we ever stayed in. And Billy was good at it. The lads would be seeded ahead of the competition – some were that good – and then we would pair up.

One person would run a book and we'd all have a few quid on it. Some of the squad weren't that bothered about it and didn't take it seriously. But there was never an option to duck out: everybody played.

The other time-filler was cards. Billy joined in with our games on the bus where we used to play a game called hearts. You have to be proficient at card-counting to be any good at it, and Billy was excellent. We'd be on a trip somewhere and Billy would come down the bus. He'd sidle up to the card school and say: 'Fancy a game of Hearts, lads?'

We were playing for a penny a point and if you put a card down that he disagreed with, you'd get loads of stick. I can still hear him now. 'Fucking hell son,' he say, 'what did you play that for? Your brains must be brand new…'

The lads liked him. They respected him. He was a Leeds United legend and his team-talks consisted of motivation, motivation and more motivation. Before games he would just tell us: 'We are Leeds United. We are the best. We have got the best fans, the best players.'

But, one of the most important lessons I learnt from Billy is that this approach is never enough for any team. You can give someone a real pick-me-up in the dressing room but words and enthusiasm aren't enough. On their own, they won't take you where you want to go.

For instance, we didn't really do any team shape. We would perhaps work on set-pieces twenty-four hours before a match but that would be about it. Billy just wanted us to go out and play. And we were decent.

Under Billy, Leeds was going through something of a revamp. John Pearson and Mark Aizlewood came in at the same time as I did but, as I've mentioned, the best player at the club by some distance was John Sheridan.

However, Shez's Achilles' heel was the fact that he loved a drink. There were plenty of occasions when he turned up the worse for wear late on Saturday mornings. We just used to hide him from the manager. Not that the Billy would have ever dropped him – he loved Shez like we all did. And it wasn't every week. But, just occasionally John would come in and it would be difficult to disguise it – his breath reeked of it. But then he would go out and be the best player on the pitch.

The rest of us all fell into the bracket of 'decent' without being superstars. Ian Baird knew where the net was. Mind you, we would wind him up something rotten. He was Scottish and Billy was forever saying, 'If I'm ever manager of Scotland son, you'll play for me.'

Of course, that was it. His nickname was 'son of Billy'.

Mark Aizlewood – or 'Flip-flop' as we used to call him because that was all he ever wore on his feet – with Neil Aspin at right-back and Peter Haddock did well. Noel Blake at centre-half was a solid presence.

We went on a run in the FA Cup. I scored at Wigan – with my right foot – and, even though we were battered that day, we ended up winning 2–0. We made it to the semi-final, where we were pitted against Coventry at Hillsborough. I had two of my family in the Leeds end who, a couple of years later, would witness the horrible deaths of ninety-six Liverpool supporters.

I remember seeing my relatives afterwards and they told me how tightly packed all the fans had been. It's easy with hindsight, but I can't help but think that someone, somewhere should have seen what was on track to happen a few years later.

Anyway, I don't want to talk too much about specific matches but, as this is the closest I got to reaching the final, I think it's only fair to highlight it.

It is never really mentioned what a big influence Coventry keeper Steve Ogrizovic had on the day. We went one-up through Dave Rennie, but Steve then pulled off two or three magnificent saves down at that Kop end. If we had taken those, who knows? But then, that's the story of many a game.

In the second half, we were hanging on and it looked like we were going to weather the storm but, as Brendan Ormsby tried to shepherd the ball out of play, Dave Bennett robbed him, He cut it back and Micky Gynn equalised. That was a real blow, as we were just eighteen minutes away from the FA Cup final. That was the trigger for a couple more goals before the game went to extra time and they sneaked it.

At the time, I was still living in Coventry. George Curtis and John Sillett came in to commiserate afterwards, which was a nice touch. I then had to go back home to Coventry after the match. The city was jumping.

I grabbed my next-door neighbour Tim and said: 'Come on, we're going out for a pint.' We went into a pub and it was just packed full of Sky Blues' fans. They were taking the piss at first, as you would, but after a while they thankfully left us alone.

Two days after the semi-final we were at Shrewsbury. We needed to win the game to get into the play-offs. And we did – which really said a lot about that team. We then played Oldham in the semi-final. We got through to the final, but this was where our off-the-cuff approach let us down. If you want one example of where exactly our lack of organisation came into play, then we need to look no further than the end of the season.

After seeing off the Latics, we reached the final against Charlton Athletic. However, following draws at Selhurst Park and Elland Road we couldn't be separated, so we had to play a decider at St Andrews, of all places.

There must have been 18,000 Leeds fans in a crowd of about 20,000. We were within ten minutes of promotion when Peter Shirtliff scored two headers in the last knockings of the game. Both came from corners. The goals were almost identical and they could have been stopped had we paid more attention to the defensive side of the game.

As I say, Billy wasn't big on organisation. He just wanted us to go out and play – but he was right about one thing, mind you. Leeds United's support is incredible. The supporters will come from far and wide to get to see their beloved Whites play. Leeds was, and still is, a fantastic club.

However, what matters more than anything when you play for a club of that size is the mentality of the players involved. It counts far more than ability alone. They have to be able to cope with the scrutiny and the criticism. Of course, it's not all bad. When a club like Leeds is flying, it can be an unstoppable force. But when it turns, you need players to stand up.

This is a poor analogy, I know, but it's the best I can think of. I'm talking about the difference between Crewe Alexandra and Port Vale. At Crewe it's OK for you to lose as long as you've played nice football. At Port Vale, they don't care how you play, as long as you win.

You need that mentality at big clubs: that you need to win. And if you aren't winning, you need to find a way to win. I think, when you look at the success Leeds went to enjoy under Howard Wilkinson, that was the one factor he changed – the mentality. He brought in players who could handle the expectation.

After that season in which we reached the semi-finals of the FA Cup and the play-off final, it was clear we needed to improve in one or two key areas.

For some reason, Billy decided the next season he was going to play three centre-halves. And, to be honest, it didn't really suit the players we had. Noel Blake was a tough stopper, but he couldn't shift it out from the back; that wasn't his game. It wasn't fair to ask him to bring the ball out like Franz Beckenbauer.

I was playing left-wing back. I was happy to do that because I would have played anywhere for Billy, and he gave me the honour of being his captain, albeit for a short spell after falling out with Mark Aizlewood.

As we emerged from the tunnel with me leading out the side for my first game as captain, I couldn't have been prouder. But the event didn't work out quite as I'd hoped. Keeper Mervyn Day thought it would be amusing to stop everyone else following me. I ended up running out on to the pitch on my own and had to wait a good thirty seconds for the rest to follow suit. He made me look a right idiot, but at least I was the one with the armband on.

But anyway, we had missed out on the play-offs and the semi-finals of the FA Cup and had now changed the system. It disrupted the momentum and Billy ended up getting the sack.

However, not before he had overseen the delivery of sixteen sponsored cars. That in itself wasn't a problem. The issue was that we had twenty-three first-team professionals. How do you share them out? Well, the obvious answer would be for the manager to give one each to those who had made the most appearances and to the senior professionals.

Unfortunately, as he didn't want to upset anybody, Billy decided that we needed a draw to settle the argument. It was the biggest farce I've ever known. We had people such as David Batty, who was coming through at the time and was my apprentice. He got one at eighteen years old and I, the captain, missed out. All the kids ended up with cars. They'd played five, six times and I was left kicking my heels. I was gutted.

You could tell Batty was going to be a player. He could handle the ball and he had an edge to him. He had a proper go. Billy loved him. They were very similar as players – not in temperament because Billy was more fiery – but on the pitch. Off the pitch, Bats was actually rather quiet. He and John Sheridan were a great combination in the midfield.

Anyway, after the draw Billy realised he had dropped a clanger. I was called into his office a couple of hours later and he said that he had found a piece of paper on his desk with my name on it which meant it hadn't been included in the draw. Much to the anguish of those who thought they were driving home in a nice new saloon later that day, there was another raffle.

This time, I ended up with a car. Obviously, there was plenty of stick flying around. It was carnage. They were killing me. I got the 'son of Billy' nickname after that. However, it wasn't too long before the axe fell and Billy was sacked. I was gutted. I liked and respected him as a person, admired him as a player and appreciated that he had thought enough of me to make me a captain of a club like Leeds United.

And talk about going from one extreme to another: within twenty-four hours of Billy being replaced by Howard Wilkinson, I thought I would be getting the sack.

The seeds of the incident that almost ended my career at Elland Road were sown because of an injury. Towards the end of Billy's tenure, I was suffering with tendonitis in one of my knees. I had been taking painkillers before games to combat the condition, and sometimes would have injections to get myself through. I would rest throughout the week and then play at the weekends.

When Billy was sacked, I decided to have my knee operated on. I knew my current approach to my injury wasn't going to wash with a new manager.

The physio was a guy called Alan Sutton. Every morning when Billy was manager the lads would go out training. If anyone was injured they would go into the canteen, have a bacon sandwich and a cuppa until they were called in for treatment.

To be honest, it was a jolly-up. It all changed when Howard came in. The new manager's big thing was team meetings. We'd have hundreds of them. His Number Two was a fella called Mick Hennigan. Every day he would bring in a box of apples and hand them out. Howard cracked the whip.

It was the classic good cop, bad cop routine; although, in Howard's case, it was more 'bastard cop'.

Anyway, I had the operation and I was in plaster from my ankle to the top of my thigh. I went into the canteen, with my leg in plaster, to have breakfast as I had done under Billy. I wrongly assumed I couldn't do anything so I didn't join in with the circuits. Under the previous regime, this was just an opportunity for me to enjoy breakfast at my own leisure. Not under Howard. He changed it all.

All injured players had to report in at a set time. We would be assessed and would be already doing our first circuits by the time the lads were arriving for training at 10 a.m. As the lads came back in from training, the injured players would be doing another circuit. When the lads left for home, they were doing another one to show that being injured wasn't a cushy option.

I was only supposed to be in plaster for a couple of weeks but Howard wasn't one to mess around. As soon as I got back to fitness, we worked on set-pieces and we had 45-minute running sessions on Thursdays before matches. That was unheard of. It was a constant run with hurdles and benches. His point was that we weren't fit enough and that we had had it too easy. Looking back now, he was probably right.

Sutty, the physio, was a lovely fella, but he changed as well. He was under pressure because Howard was looking at everyone. On this particular morning, in the canteen with my leg in plaster, after filling my face, I walked into Sutty's room to be met with: 'Where have you been?'

I said, 'What do you mean, where have I been? Having my breakfast.'

'Ah, you don't do that anymore. The manager will be after me.'

I replied: 'Well, it's not as if I can do anything anyway. I'm in plaster here.'

His next words stunned me.

'Yes, you can. You can go on one of those little trampolines. And with your good foot, you can bounce up and down on it to keep your muscle strength up.'

So, just to recap here, Sutty wants me to jump up and down on his trampoline on my fit leg and hang the other one over the side while I'm doing it.

'You're fucking mad. I'm not doing it.'

'Listen, you'll do as I'm fucking telling you.'

And, at this point, he has got right into my face. I'm getting angry now, and the situation is threatening to spiral out of control. My next few words didn't help.

'Look Sutty, get out of my face because if you don't I'm going to do something about it.'

'Micky, get on that trampoline.'

I took a step backwards to give myself some room and I smacked him. It was a good shot. I remember it well because he had false teeth at the front and they just went flying. Sutty is bleeding from the mouth by now. He gets up and I warn him, but he comes at me. I'm defending myself, so I hit him again. He starts scrambling around looking for his false teeth. By now, the lads are all banging on the door trying to get in.

This wasn't just in Howard's first week as manager; this was in the first couple of days. And the skipper has just clobbered the physio – twice. It wasn't good.

I left the room on my crutches. Sutty waited for Howard to come in off the training ground. I saw him go into Howard's office. Then I got the call. Mick Hennigan shouted, 'Micky Adams – manager wants to see you.'

I thought: I've had it here.

I get there and Howard was sitting behind the desk with Mick standing alongside him. He looked up when I sat down.

'Is this right, what I've been hearing?' he asked, cool as a cucumber.

I said: 'I dunno what you've been hearing, boss.'

'That you have assaulted one of my staff.'

'Well, if he says I've done it, I can't deny it. There was a confrontation.'

He said: 'I'm not having that.'

At this point, I think I'm sacked. So, it's time to roll the dice.

'Can I just say something, gaffer? He asked me to do something I didn't agree with. He got in my face and I defended myself.'

He asked: 'Did you throw the first punch?'

'Yes.'

'Well, I'm not having that. I can't have that. You're fined two weeks' wages.'

As far as I was concerned, this was a decent result. I thought I'd be out of the door. But in Howard's first week, I hadn't done a stroke of work. He hadn't seen me train. Sutty – who is still my mate by the way – had to go to the dentist to have a new plate fitted. That wasn't the greatest start to life under Mr Wilkinson.

However, when I eventually got into his team, I learnt more from

41

him about coaching than anyone else. He was very organised. There were no grey areas. Not one. Everyone knew their jobs.

For example, we would work on defending a corner from the left-hand side. Howard would work through it with us bit by bit, stage by stage. He would begin with the goalkeeper and walk him through it. Then he would place people where he wanted them, one at a time, giving them their roles and responsibilities. It was long, tedious work. No player enjoyed it. There was a lot of standing around, but we did it. If a ball came in from one of the apprentices and we didn't do our job, he would shout, 'Stop!' And we would have to do it all over again.

We would spend a good half-hour defending a left-foot corner. And he did not care one jot if we were out there for five hours. We would stay until everyone knew what they were doing. And then? We would do right-foot corners.

At times like these we had stay switched on because he was watching. We really needed to bring our A-game to the table.

If, for any reason, someone did switch off and their role had not been fulfilled during a match, woe betide the lot of us come Monday as we would have to go through it all again.

Repetition is a part of the job footballers do not particularly like, but we stuck at it and the results began to pick up. It is the one aspect of coaching that is extremely effective, if delivered properly. I learnt this from Howard and took this lesson with me throughout my coaching and managerial career.

But later that year, I left. My contract was running out anyway. I had only six months left and Howard wanted me to sign a new deal. He pulled an old stroke to get his way. I think the team could quite easily have been promoted that season, but looking back now, I'm convinced Howard did not want it to be seen as Billy's team. It just fell away at the death and I think Howard knew the following year would be the one where it would all come together.

As I mentioned before, Howard and Hennigan were a good partnership. I was called into Howard's office. I knocked on the door and there they both were ready to perform the routine they had perfected. Howard always had a raised desk, so anyone who was sitting facing him would have to look up.

The conversation about my contract went something like this.

Howard started: 'I like what you have been doing recently. I want you to sign a new deal.'

Then, there was a pause.

'Look, I shouldn't be doing this, but tell Mick what I said the other day about him.'

Hennigan looked bashful.

'Ah, come on gaffer, do I have to? You'll embarrass the lad.'

'Tell Micky. He's sat here now. Come on, I don't mind.'

'You're embarrassing me as well as him, gaffer … OK, look Micky, he said you were the best player at the weekend. He thought you were right at it, did your work well, you got right in people's faces and he thinks you're on the up … that you can be a part of it here.'

I was looking around for the pen. This was brilliant to hear. I felt valued. Howard was one of those who didn't dish out praise lightly, most definitely not in any of his team meetings. If ever he did give a player any recognition, it was on a one-to-one basis only.

Anyhow there it was: I had impressed him. I was happy enough with the terms, a £30,000 signing-on fee and a salary of £700-a-week. Unlike how things were at Coventry, my home was fully furnished, I loved the club and I was settled.

What happened? I signed but, no word of a lie, within three weeks I was gone.

These were the days before Bosman. It was a game that the pair was playing – they were trying to get the best price for me. They knew there was outside interest and could therefore claim a higher transfer fee if I had a long-term deal.

And that's exactly what happened. Howard was full of a football manager's little tricks. Ones that I used plenty of times in management myself.

For instance, one day I wasn't particularly happy. I'd been dropped; story of my life, I suppose.

I decided to go and bang on his door. It really wasn't the 'done' thing, going to hammer on Howard Wilkinson's door to have a moan, but I felt it was justified.

I asked if I could see him. If, as a manager, you know a player is het-up, the key is to give yourself time. He replied, 'Give me a while, I've just got one or two things to sort out and I'll come and get you.'

I waited two hours. It turned out he had left out of a side-door and there I was waiting, totally unaware that he was no longer in his room.

He did it on purpose. I never managed to see him that day or the following day. After I had calmed down a little, it didn't seem half as bad as it had at the time. I'm not saying he didn't like confrontation; he certainly wasn't bothered about that. No one challenged him anyway because he had an aura about him.

So, despite a new contract in my hands, my days at Leeds United came to an end.

I was playing golf when my missus rang and asked to speak to me urgently once I was off the course. I called her back and she told me I needed to ring the club. I got on the phone to Howard. He told me that Southampton had come in for me and that he wanted me to go down there.

'By the way Micky,' he said, 'you'll still get your signing-on fee for the contract you've just signed. And you know those two weeks' wages you were fined for? You can have those back as well.'

That was brilliant of him. A nice touch.

And that was me at Leeds United. I didn't fit in with Howard's way. So, once again, I was off to start a new chapter – this time at Southampton.

CHAPTER 4

SAINT MICHAEL

'Where are your scars?' said my new boss.

I shrugged my shoulders.

'Come on, where are your scars?'

These were the first words ever said to me by Chris Nicholl, another interesting character.

Back in the day, he'd been a rugged stopper – mainly for Aston Villa and Southampton – and it would have impressed him plenty if I'd broken my nose a few times.

His thought process was that, as someone employed not to allow the ball into my own net, I should have some scars to show for it.

'You're not really a defender then, are you?' was his short reply when I told him I didn't have any.

Of course, his hooter was all over his face. As a player, he had acted first and thought about it afterwards. As a manager, he had to think hard about what he was going to say and how he was going to say it. His messages were always deliberate and generally not off-the-cuff.

As luck would have it, another player joined Southampton in the same week: Neil 'Razor' Ruddock. It was the start of a friendship that involved more drinking and playing golf than anything else. He led me astray on numerous occasions, and set the tone for years of mischief to come by almost getting us booted out of the hotel in the first week.

Razor was living with his missus at the time and he somehow managed to sneak her and his pet Doberman into the hotel room. Within a week of us checking in, we were called in to see Nicholl. He had a pile of bills in front of him from the hotel restaurant.

'You're having a great time you pair, aren't you?'

'Yes, thanks very much boss, it's OK.'

Nicholl went on: 'Can I ask you two a question? How come you two are having fillet steak every night on top of your evening meal?'

We had been ordering meals for ourselves as well as a steak for the dog.

'We're hungry, gaffer,' said Razor, 'it's all the hard work you are putting us through.'

Somehow, we got away with it. That dog must have thought all his Christmases had come at once. Razor ended up staying in that hotel with his family for quite a while, which doesn't come at any great surprise looking at the size of him now!

Meanwhile, I'd moved my own family down from Wakefield to a place called Warsash near Southampton, ready for what turned out to be the best few years of my playing career. However, it didn't start out like that. After my first day out on the training pitch, I wondered what I had let myself in for.

I can't remember who we had played on the Saturday prior to my arrival, but something had happened during the game. This was my first training session on my very first day, and the three Wallace brothers, Danny, Ray and Rodney, were walking off afterwards having a full-scale row with the manager in front of everyone.

They were yelling: 'You're fucking shit, you are, fucking rubbish. You don't know what you are talking about.' They absolutely slated him. The

Wallaces clearly had to be sorted out. Once back in the dressing room, Nicholl walked in and demanded: 'Right, everyone back to the club this afternoon.'

The lads weren't too happy with the Wallaces for winding Nicholl up. We all came back to the Dell at 2 p.m. as ordered and we sat in the dressing room… but nothing happened. We looked at the clock. 2.15 p.m. Still nothing. Finally, at half-past two, the door finally opened. Nicholl walked in with Dennis Rofe, his assistant.

He started to say, 'Right, two things…', but he totally forgot what he was about to say. He tried again: 'I'll tell you what, I'll go out and come back in.' He walked out, shut the door behind him. I'm looking at the door expecting it open immediately as he walks straight back in. But no. Another fifteen minutes went by. Nothing. Again, no sign of him.

Dennis came in and briefed us. He said: 'Right, he's on his way and, whatever you do, don't laugh at him.'

In Nicholl comes. 'Right…' and he was looking around the room… I was sure he was looking for the Wallace boys – they were the ones who were having a go at him. But he went up to Matt Le Tissier and he announced: 'You, I've had a letter from the Football Association, shut it, shut it.' And with that, he went out. It was absolute madness. Chris would have taken on the Wallace brothers, but it was almost as if he had forgotten what had taken place a few hours earlier.

To a certain extent, the Wallaces ruled the roost. They were good players, mind you. Not so much Raymond, who was a decent right-back, but Danny was on fire. I played behind him. It was just a case of staying behind him, giving him the ball and letting him get on with it. Rodney, for me, was the best of the three brothers. He was a wide player with electric pace who would eventually move on to Leeds United and win the league under Howard Wilkinson.

Mixed up with these senior professionals was a crop of really good kids. Le Tiss was one, Alan Shearer was another. It was a good combination with the likes of Jimmy Case, Glenn Cockerill, the late Kevin Moore – bravest centre-half I ever saw – and Russell Osman. With me and Razor, we made up a good team.

I knew about Shearer before I arrived. I'd actually seen him score on his debut when he was just seventeen. For some reason at the time, Leeds was down in Bournemouth. We had just missed out on the play-offs and Billy Bremner sent us down with his assistant.

Billy said to his assistant: 'Don't let them out for a drink.' However, as we had nothing to play for, the lads took an executive decision to ignore his rule and we decided we were all going down to the bar. We were in the hotel, late at night, having a laugh. One of the guests came down, moaned that we were making too much noise. We were, I suppose. So he spoke to John Sheridan and Mark Aizlewood and asked them to tone it down. Someone told him to leave us alone. But the fella was within his rights.

He said to Mark Aizlewood: 'The problem with you footballers is you've got nothing between your ears.'

Aizlewood looked at him and said: 'Is that right? Well listen to me, we've paid nothing to be here ... How much has it cost you?'

With this, the fella went mad and we were kicked out the next morning. It's memorable as it was that day that I witnessed a young Shearer making his debut for Southampton against Arsenal – and, two years later, I was sharing a dressing room with him.

By the time I played with him, he had matured. He was getting stronger. He was a man. If you didn't put the ball in the box or find him when he was making his channel runs (which he had been taught by a great coach, Dave Merrington – who was to eventually become manager), then he would let you know in no uncertain terms. In his debut for the club, he scored a hat-trick.

Merrington was brilliant with the youth team, but he was hard with them. He brought them up well, they were fit and organised. They were no-nonsense, they did their jobs. I saw one year, when they got knocked out of the FA Youth Cup, him ordering them in to train at 5.30 the morning after, just to show them what normal people had to do in the real world to earn a living.

He would make them all do 100 laps of the pitch. Shearer was one of these players along with Tommy Widdrington and Neil Maddison to name but a few. There was a good sprinkling of young talent coming through. It was a great base for their education, although I'm sure they didn't think so at the time.

By this stage, it didn't take a genius to work out that Shearer was going to be big. No question about it, although he actually nearly didn't made it out of Southampton in one piece. We had a mid-season break to the Algarve in Portugal one season. We were in a five-star hotel complex, really beautiful. I really do not know why they put us in these fantastic places.

Of course, plenty of ale was being sunk. After two days on the sauce, Tiss and I decided we were going for a round of golf and left the likes of Shearer, Ruddock and a few others in a beach bar. They were dead happy with the situation. They were even happier, or should I say merrier, when we returned four hours later. Tiss and I had had a couple but we were compos mentis. The rest? They were on another planet.

There was only one rule on this particular trip, and that was we had to return to the hotel to eat our meals. We duly obliged with no mishaps during the meal. After we had eaten, we all trooped back to our rooms. However Shearer, Ruddock and the rest of the drinkers decided it would be a great wheeze to nick a portable fridge out of someone's room. They stole a key and sneaked upstairs into Widdrington's room. They grabbed the fridge and came running out with it down the corridor.

Only, on top of the fridge were two empty wine glasses. As they took off with the fridge, the two glasses fell in front of them and smashed. Shearer walked through the sharp broken shards of glass and he didn't just cut his foot. He almost severed the tendon. There was blood everywhere.

At this point, everyone sobered up pretty quickly. Apart from Razor. Being the sensible one, I dragged him into a room and said, 'For fuck's sake, Razor, can't you just have a drink without all this?'

He obliged by sticking one on me. He threw a few punches and we had a stand-up row. I did get a couple back in at him. The fuse came out again, but I was hardly going to stand there and let him smash me and do nothing about it.

Anyway, Shearer was lucky. He was patched up and got away without too much damage. Had he severed a tendon, it would have been serious – potentially even career-threatening.

At that time, he hadn't yet established himself as the number one. The biggest fish in the pond at the Dell was Jimmy Case, who had won every honour going with Liverpool. Those achievements commanded respect. As did the fact he was a proper hard man. The first thing to note about Jimmy was that all the people you thought were genuinely tough, such as players like Vinnie Jones, never bothered him. When he was playing against them, there were never any problems. There was mutual respect.

Jimmy had a way of really knocking people down. Then, as his victim got up, his arms and legs would be all over the place. At this point, he would pretend he was trying to step over his opponent. Of course, nothing of that sort was happening; he would be standing on their backs, treading on their hands, all sorts.

I remember one game against Everton and Jimmy copped a load of flak, being an ex-Liverpool player. One of their players, Graeme Sharp, went to do him. Sharpy was high … knee-high to be exact, with his studs showing. Jimmy was aware of him, he saw him coming a mile off, and trumped him by going in even higher. As his opponent was being carried off on a stretcher, Jimmy leant over him and snarled: 'Have some of that, shithouse.' He didn't even get booked for it because everyone could see what was going to happen.

Jimmy was always immaculately turned out. He used to fold his training kit where the rest of us would just throw it on the dressing room floor. He would make it look smart. He even looked after all the food on the away trips and served everyone after the game.

He was funny though. He wore a hearing aid and, depending on his mood, it would either be on or off. He made out that he didn't know what was going on – but he heard every single word.

At that time, he would have been thirty-four or so. We were always allowed a couple of beers after away matches and he'd sort that out for us, too. Jimmy was a complex bloke. I don't think I'm stepping out of line too much by saying that he had his own demons in terms of the booze. He would disappear for days on end sometimes.

A night out with Jimmy always followed the same pattern when it came to ordering drinks. Someone would go up and get the round in. 'What are you having, Jimmy?'

'I'm not drinking today,' he'd say, 'I'd just like a lemonade [slight pause]. Well, do me a lemonade with a dash of lager on the top.'

His drink would be given to him. He was happy.

Next round…

'Jimmy, do you wanna drink?'

'Tell, you what, I'll have a Shandy. I'm not drinking today,' was the response.

Next one…

'Jimmy, what you having?'

'I'll have a lager with a dash of lemonade.'

Next up…

'Jimmy, what do you fancy?'

'Pint of lager, please.'

Last few rounds…

'Jimmy, what can I get you?'

'Pint of lager … and I think I'll have a whisky chaser please…'

By the end of the evening, Jimmy was in a right state.

Another character on the team was John 'Budgie' Burridge and everyone has a story about him. He had a well-founded reputation for being a bizarre individual.

One of the trips we went on at the end of the season was to Carl Zeiss Jena, before the wall came down in East Germany. We went to play them and then jetted off to Portugal for a bit of sun. Talk about a contrast.

Trying to get through the Iron Curtain took an age. When we eventually turned up at Carl Zeiss Jena, there was a gymnastics display going on around the pitch. We got on the pitch to start warming up. The crowd was roaring. But, all of a sudden, there was silence. We looked over and Budgie was on the athletics track surrounding the pitch. He decided to make his way to the trampoline, where he performed an on-point somersault and landed on his feet. It was absolutely brilliant. He got off, expecting a reception. Nothing. Stony silence. A tumbleweed was blowing across the pitch while 30,000 people wondered if they were supposed to clap or cheer. All we could hear was the sound of the Southampton players laughing their heads off.

And that wasn't the end of the unusual goings-on that day, either. After the game, we were in the dressing room waiting for the bus and an official came in with a policeman.

He looked at us and said, 'We're a ball missing – and one of you lot has got it.'

We looked at each other, wondering who's nicked it.

'No one's got a ball', we replied.

'One of you lot has taken the ball and you're not going anywhere until it's sorted out', comes the response.

Then it quickly started escalating.

'Look, mate, all we want to do is get out of this fucking shit country as fast as possible. No one has taken your ball.'

They weren't having it. At all.

So, we emptied all the skips and another policeman appeared. The message is simple: no one is leaving until they've got their ball back. The lads were moaning and the stand-off continued for a good fifteen minutes. We searched everywhere for this ball.

And then Budgie opened his bag. There it was. He handed it over with a shrug.

We should have known where to look in the first place, to be honest. Between us lot, he was famous for taking things that he thought were his. We always used to joke that if you ever visited his home, you'd see half the weights from the Saints' gym there.

From East Germany we went on to Portugal, where Nicholl had a room with a balcony overlooking the pool, mainly to keep him abreast of everything the lads were doing. It was a nightmare to be honest, because you couldn't get him pissed. His favourite tipple was Crabbies Ginger Beer and that was as daring as he got.

I enjoyed working for Nicholl. Given my background, I didn't mind the challenge of proving him wrong. If he thought I'd played poorly and he told me to my face, I'd make sure I played better the week afterwards.

He always let the players know how well or badly they had played before they went home. He was very uptight, particularly after match-es. He used to say: 'Right, go and have a drink,' after the final whistle.

We'd shower and troop off to the players' bar but forty-five minutes later, the call would come to go back to the dressing room.

He would sit us down and then he would say: 'I don't want anyone going away from here not knowing how they have done.' So he'd go around the team, one-by-one, pointing at you as he went.

'Shit, shit, not bad, did all right, shit, wanker, shit, wanker, not bad, did all right...'

To make matters worse, he would make the 'wanker' gesture right in front of your face.

You'd sit there and think to yourself: 'Please let it be a "shit", I don't think I can handle the "wanker"...'

That's the way he was. Honestly, I didn't mind what I got; I just re-doubled my efforts in training the following week.

I remember once our goalkeeper, Tim Flowers, hurt his wrist and he had to come off. We had used our three substitutes and Russell Osman went in goal for the final ten minutes. We hung on for a draw.

We were all sitting in the dressing room after the match and Nicholl looked at Tim and said, 'How is it?'

'Gaffer,' replied Tim, 'I'm going to go straight to the hospital after this and get it X-rayed.'

'Right,' he says, 'if it's broke, that's OK. If not: wanker.'

I remember once we played at Norwich and he played me in the centre of midfield. I was like a fish up a tree – I didn't have a clue what I was doing. I was up against Tim Sherwood, who led me a merry dance all afternoon. At the end of the game, which we lost 2–1, Razor – who hadn't had the best of games either – and I were chosen for drug testing.

We didn't go back to the changing rooms; instead it was straight to the testing room for us. We provided a sample and, even though we had finished with the testers, we decided to keep well out of the way of the changing rooms until the inevitable match post-mortem had finished. We eventually approached the dressing room door and pressed our ears up against it. All was quiet, so we unwittingly presumed Nicholl had finished his rant.

When we walked into the dressing room, however, he was still there – but, thankfully, we had missed the worst of the post-match bollocking.

'Where have you two been?' asked Nicholl, not unreasonably.

'Oh, we've been with the testers', says Razor.

'Drugs testing? Right … well, they clearly know what they're doing, they chose the two biggest dopes out there today didn't they?'

One of Nicholl's other little idiosyncrasies was his fascination with weighing everyone.

There used to be an old set of scales outside the dressing room door at the Dell. Every Monday and Friday we had to have our weights checked, in essence to monitor if we'd had a good weekend. There was a wall right next to the scales and, if timed right, one could indiscreetly hold onto that wall to slightly prop ourselves up. It could easily knock off two or three pounds.

It was always worth the risk if we felt we were going to be over the approved weight, although we had keep out of Dennis Rofe's eye line so he couldn't see what we were up to. There was also a Sunday club for those who hadn't played on the Saturday or hadn't even made the squad. Those sent to the Sunday club had to go in for a 'special'.

When I say 'special', there wasn't anything too unique about it. Being a member of the Sunday club meant you were in line for over an hour's worth of running drills. That was hard. That's really where I first started being alert about fitness. I had been aware of it under Howard Wilkinson but at Southampton, they had a run called the 'crash'.

It used to go something like this: four laps in four minutes and forty seconds, three laps in three minutes thirty seconds, two laps in two minutes and twenty seconds and a sixty-second lap to finish. It was tough. Dave Merrington introduced it, I think. They used to have another run at the Dell which involved us starting at the bottom tier of the Milton Road end and going up to the top tier, hitting every step as we ascended. Three runs up and down the steps. Then we would have to try to complete a sixty-second lap around the pitch with our legs shot to pieces.

I've tried using the 'crash' at many of the clubs I've managed at. It's an interesting exercise because players start mentally questioning their ability to complete it before they have even started. I picked up the practice of doing 'thirty-five seconders' which, as a lot of my former players will tell you, I'm quite famous for. That involves running from one touchline to the other and then back again. This is done six times with seventy seconds between each one. At all of the clubs I have managed, I found this gave me a good indication of the players' fitness levels. When I managed, I never gave the players one single exercise I hadn't done myself.

Are players fitter now? I'm not sure. And I'm not sure if they are mentally tougher either, but the one thing they are good at now is recovery due to all the modern science. This would surely have helped us at the time but back in the day, any injured player who returned to fitness had to do the 'crash' before they had a chance of playing a first-team game. Ray Graydon, who would join as the reserve team manager, upped the stakes when he introduced five laps in five minutes and fifty seconds. Now that was a killer.

The other exercise of note at the Dell was the warm-up gym. It measured 60 x 40 metres and we had full-scale games in there. It was like *Rollerball*. It was murder.

Nicholl liked playing football squash in there. Many managers like to have a drink after a game, but that was his way of unwinding. Nicholl used to go in there for hours with his mate and play football squash to get the match out of his system. We would often leave the ground late at night and the gym lights would still be on.

He also used to love us as players heading balls. Razor and I copped it during a trip to Old Trafford. Whenever we played Manchester United, Peter Schmeichel used to thump balls as far as he could inside the opposition half. They nearly had snow on them, they went that high.

Once, Razor and I were under this high goal-kick. I was at left-back and my mate was on the left-hand side playing at centre-half.

He shouted, 'Razor's ball!'

On hearing his call, I ducked out of it. It bounced and Mark Hughes went through, hit the post and almost scored.

At half-time, the inquest started.

Nicholl pulled me and said: 'You let that ball bounce.'

'No, no, gaffer, Razor called for it, didn't you Razor?'

As I said that, I looked across to Razor who was apparently tying up his shoelaces avoiding eye contact with me at all costs.

Anyway, the gaffer was having none of it.

'No, no,' he said, 'I saw the fear in your eyes. I saw the fear. Waaanker.'

If he felt a player was ducking out of things, the next day the culprit would have to spend an hour just heading balls.

•   •   •

However, life was about to take a turn for the worse for me, as it was about this time when we lost my cousin Richard. He was only twenty years old when he was run over and killed by a taxi. I was eight years older than him, but we were close. He had been out for a few drinks with his mates, got separated from them and decided to walk home on his own.

To this day, it's unclear what actually happened. The circumstances have never really been explained, except that he was knocked down and killed. His death had a huge effect on me. As was the tradition in those days, his body was laid out in the front room of my Uncle David and Auntie Gloria's house. I was asked if I wanted to go and say my goodbyes to him. I'd been told that the accident had left him in a mess, so I bottled it. I regretted it afterwards and wished I had gone and paid my respects to him in person.

A few games later, we were playing Sheffield Wednesday. My cousin was a huge Wednesday-ite and my uncle asked me if I would scatter some of his ashes at the Kop End of the ground. I agreed to do it, although in those days there was nothing formal arranged with the club. I took his ashes with me to the game.

As I remember, they weren't in an urn to avoid arousing suspicion. My uncle gave them to me in a large envelope. When we went out to have a look at the pitch, as you do about seventy-five minutes before kick-off, I broke off the from the main group and walked towards the Kop. I managed to open up the envelope and scatter his remains in the goal-mouth. It was a surreal experience. No one saw me do it. None of the family was there. The manager, Nicholl, didn't have a clue what I was up to. But afterwards, I really struggled. I didn't realise it, but the whole episode had a huge bearing on me.

When my dad died, I was OK. But weeks later, everything hit me. It was the same with my cousin. As you will have deduced by now, I came from a background where it wasn't the 'done' thing to show your emotions. I was grieving and I was off-form for two or three weeks. When my dad died, it manifested itself in a different way. Like I say, I was OK at the time, but I would be driving along to watch a game and suddenly find myself crying. I was feeling low, not bothered about football. Eventually, I snapped myself out of it. I didn't speak to anyone.

I didn't have any counselling. Nicholl obviously saw there was something wrong with me. He just looked at me and said, 'It's the grieving process and you're going right through it.'

Apart from this awful event in my life, I was having an absolute ball at Southampton. It was difficult not to, although the quality of players had started to dip. Not enough as to think Nicholl's job might be under pressure, though.

For instance, Nicholl brought in a Russian, Alex Cherednyk, whose main claim to fame was cheating in the card school. The big thing at the back of the bus was three-card brag. It started off innocently enough but it started to get naughty. I think it reached a point where players were betting on three-card blinds at about £1,000-a-time. Back then, that was a lot of money. It's a lot of money now. Cherednyk used to cheat. He looked at his cards and swore that he was going blind. We caught him out but he wasn't having it. So, one day we arranged to stitch him up. We fixed the cards. He had a prial of tens, but it wasn't good enough. It taught him a lesson.

All of these fun and games came to an abrupt halt when Nicholl lost his job. We thought he had done well. We had never in any real danger of being relegated, and we'd even had a couple of decent runs in the Cup. But out went Nicholl. And in came a man who was to have an even bigger impact on both my playing and coaching career.

CHAPTER 5

BRANFOOT AND BALL

Ian Branfoot's appointment as Nicholl's successor was not greeted with universal approval, but his arrival was a watershed moment for me. I was getting older, I'd started my coaching badges and I already had one eye on my future.

However, I did have to focus on the present when Branny became the boss, as the main job for any player is proving yourself to the new man.

The bottom line for Branny was whether you were a grafter. He liked hard workers. There were no grey areas for him, it was either black or white and, as I was never afraid of hard work, he saw something in me.

What he wanted us to do was simple: play the ball into the channels, turn teams around and play in their half. He was labelled with the 'long-ball' tag. It didn't wash with the supporters. After a while, one of the fanzines ran an article with Branny's picture and the headline read, 'I hope you die soon.'

It wasn't a particularly happy time at the club itself, mainly because of the relationship Branny had with Matthew Le Tissier. Southampton's star man used to drive him mental. Of course, Tiss was blessed with natural ability, but, sometimes, when you say that, it implies they don't have work to improve that talent.

It's a popular misconception about Tiss. He did used to work. In the gym, there was a skirting board running around the walls. What we used to have to do was stand in a box and players would stand behind you, firing balls at you, off the wall. The name of the game was to take one touch and fire the ball towards the goal. You had to take one touch and then crack off a shot. Occasionally, we wouldn't control it properly or would fail to hit the target. When it was Tiss's turn, the coaches would make sure they hit the skirting board so the ball would come off at all angles and directions at him. That wasn't a problem for him. He would control it with his chest, knee, thigh – and invariably he would score. Either foot, it didn't matter.

For some reason, he and Ian never got on. Tiss had a tendency to put weight on. He wasn't a drinker; any extra weight was more to do with his diet than anything else. He used to have the odd pint, but he enjoyed a Malibu and Coke more. Tiss's problems started because he'd regularly scoff chips and a pint of Coca-Cola. That diet doesn't feature in any sports science literature under the heading of 'Nutritional Advice' and there is a reason for that, too.

At Southampton, the issue was finding a position for him to play in. We used to play 4–4–2 and, if he played out on the right-hand side, he would let the left-back run off him. If he was over on the left with me, the same would happen. We could play him up front but he never won a header. It was really hard finding him a position in the team. You could never trust him to play in one spot. Nowadays, he would be a number ten, asked to go and create havoc without any responsibility.

More often than not, he ended up in front of me. When I gave him the ball, he'd cut inside. As a full-back, that was great for me. I'd charge up the outside and nine times out of ten I was free. He used to come inside and shoot, or play it anywhere but where I was. Eight times out of ten, he would lose it. The other two times he would create magic out of nowhere and earn a win bonus you never expected. Going back the other way, I'd have to run past him as well. He would never fill in for me. No wonder he put me in his fittest XI in his book – all I did was charge up and down the left wing on his behalf!

To give you a practical example of how exasperating he could be for a coach, let me set a particular scene. Branny picked the team on Friday. Tiss was in charge of the set pieces.

Branny would say, 'Tiss, can you go over to the right and take an in-swinging corner please?'

So, for the purpose of the exercise, this is what the manager wanted Tiss to do. However, Tiss had other ideas and thought to himself, 'I've got an opportunity to score here.' That's how his mind worked, and that's how good he was. He didn't disappoint.

Anyway, Branny told him to raise one arm; this would mean it was a near-post corner. One of the big lads would be there ready to flick it on. The others would charge in at the back. Branny would explain that 'free-kicks around the box, taken with either right foot or left, are to be swinging in towards the near post'. Tiss heard all of this, played along with it on the Friday, but when it came to Saturday he must have just thought to himself: 'No chance.' He would wander over to take a corner and try to score.

Branny would be screaming at him, 'Tiss, don't forget the one arm!'

As he was running past me to take it I could hear him muttering: 'Fuck that, I'm going to try and score.'

When it came to penalties, he would say, 'Which square of the net do you want me to hit?'

No word of a lie. He was that confident. It was no surprise to anyone who played with him at Southampton he had actually only missed one by the end of his career. He was brilliant at them.

I look back and think, 'What would he be worth now?' There's no one like him.

Yeah, you could have done something with his diet, but it would have taken something away from his play.

To get a response, Branny would try dropping him. The manager didn't give a monkey's about the supporters' opinions. He was his own man. It didn't matter how much stick he got but, to be honest, we weren't good enough to do without Tiss for any length of time.

The fans hated Branny for his style of football, but he was undeniably organised. His training was good and well-structured. I learnt a lot from him. It was a turning point in my career, certainly, and it was an education for me in how I was going to go about my future business.

Branny was more personable than Howard Wilkinson. He was not aloof; we could go and have a chat with him. It was under him that I had the chance of playing at Wembley after we reached the final of the Zenith Data Systems Cup against Nottingham Forest.

Unfortunately for me, six weeks before the showpiece occasion, I tore my thigh muscle. A fortnight beforehand, I was still doubtful, but Branny said he wanted me to prove my fitness.

The game was against Manchester City. I played and it was the worst thing I did. I started with serious doubts in mind and, sure enough, came off after twenty-five minutes after tearing it again. Obviously, missing a chance to play at the home of English football was a big kick in the teeth for any player. Had I left it one more week, I feel confident I would have been fit enough to play.

The other major gripe I had (and I still have a go at him now about it) was that I had played in all the games apart from the final. There was a big bench at the old stadium at Wembley. All I wanted was to be down there with the lads in the thick of it, but, for some reason, Branny gave me and a couple of the other boys tickets for the stands. I felt I had contributed enough to the pathway that saw us there. I was, and still am, upset about it.

Overall, he was decent towards me and I found his methods good. He just had a problem with the fans. I suppose, in part, it was because he was the manager who sold Shearer. In all honesty, I'm not sure he had much of an option. The club had received a good offer from Blackburn Rovers – £3.3 million, I think – and we ended up getting David Speedie and Kerry Dixon with that cash.

There was another reason that explains why the supporters didn't like him: he was also the manager who got rid of Jimmy Case. I don't know why he did that. Jimmy had at least another season in him.

He always talked about moving into management did Jimmy, but he hadn't taken any practical steps to make his way towards it. In fact, a few of us talked about it. The one good thing about Southampton was that we talked about the game. We would go to the back of the bus, Jimmy would feed us and we would chat. We'd talk about what we would do differently. Looking back, I wonder if Branny thought he was removing a threat to his job.

Unlike Jimmy, I had done something about it. I went on a two-week residential course at Lilleshall to complete my full badge. After completing my final session and passing the course, I stayed on to help others to finish theirs – as was common practice. However, in doing so, I stupidly managed to dislocated my shoulder trying to kick Neil Smillie, of all people. Crazy. Absolute madness. I was left-back and he was right-wing, and he took the piss out of me for fifteen minutes. The fuse came out and I decided to boot him up in the air.

The only problem was that I missed! I fell over and managed to dislocate my shoulder hitting the ground. It was the worst pain I've ever had – yes, even more eye-watering than George Curtis ripping off my moustache. If your shoulder doesn't pop back in – and this one didn't

– it's absolute agony. An ambulance came onto the training pitch. They ended up taking me to hospital and putting me on the gas and air. However, like I say, I'd done my session by then – so I passed.

I digress. Without Jimmy, we clearly needed a physical presence in the middle of the park. So Branny turned to Terry Hurlock, who was yet another character. A monster character, in fact. The team spirit was great, but then Speedie turned up after Shearer left – and it all went to pot.

Former Chelsea duo Speedie and Dixon were contributing to the team but they weren't scoring goals. And the one thing you learn about forwards is that they are the world's worst manic depressives if they aren't scoring. The more it went on with Speedie, in particular, not scoring, the more aggressive he became in training. It was a nightmare. Everyone wanted to be on his side because if you weren't, he would try to kick lumps out of you. It didn't matter who you were. He just went around kicking everyone. It wasn't going well, so Branny arranged a trip to Jersey for us all as a team-bonding exercise after we lost to Sheffield United at home.

We were on a minibus going to Southampton Airport and everyone was down in the dumps. The manager even allowed us to have a drink. When we were nearly at the airport, Speedie took a pop at Glenn Cockerill, saying something along the lines of 'Who do you think you are, Mr Southampton?' Glenn left it.

When we arrived in Jersey, we dumped our bags and made a quick exit to explore what the island had to offer in way of entertainment. There was no curfew, so we could do what we wanted. We headed to a nightclub, but it was obvious Speedie wanted a fight. Everyone was steering clear of him. It was clear by his demeanour that he was going to kick off, so an executive decision was taken to head back to the hotel. Branny was having a drink with his assistant, Lew Chatterley, when we marched in.

He realised something was up.

'You lads are back earlier than I thought you would be. Is there a problem?'

I think Glenn said to him, 'Speedie is playing up. We need to keep away from him or it's going to kick off.'

We then sat down at a table. We were drinking Grolsch out of those big green bottles with the spring-loaded stoppers when Speedie wandered back into the hotel.

'Can I buy you all a drink?' he asked. He got the round in and, to be fair, he was being all right. He apologised for his behaviour, and the mood in the camp lifted.

But when I went to the toilet, he followed me in. I had a brief chat with him at the urinals. It went something along the lines of: 'Listen Speedo, the goals will come. We are creating enough chances. Relax.'

To which he replied: 'You – fuck off – or I'm going to do you here and now.'

I realised then that I was either going to have to front him up and have it out here and now – or leave it. I left it. I went back out. Nothing happened. We all sat back down drinking.

Terry Hurlock was one side of the table. Speedo was the other. There was about eight of us at this stage and the bottles of Grolsch were flowing. We're having a chat, a laugh – nothing too outrageous – when all of a sudden Speedie turned to Terry: 'You know what the problem is with you, don't you?'

'No, what's that David?' said Terry.

'You're just a fat, fucking lazy wanker.'

'Oh, is that right?

'Yeah, it is.'

With that, Terry launched himself across the table – and I mean, he properly launched himself – and gave Speedie a right pasting.

All the lads – me included – stepped back and thought to ourselves: 'We can let this one play out...' Speedie was getting a good hiding. Then some of the lads decided he had had enough and split it up.

There was glass and blood everywhere, and we needed to tidy it up because there had been a hell of a commotion.

Lew Chatterley managed to calm down the situation. He grabbed Speedie and walked him in the direction of the toilet. He even convinced the assistant manager that he needed to say sorry to Terry for winding him up. There weren't many people in the hotel, but the manager had come across to us to warn us about calming down. By this time, everything had been cleared up. We all sat back down.

But, as they say on *A Question of Sport*, 'What happened next?'

Next thing is we see Speedie heading back towards us after we thought he'd gone to bed. He started saying: 'Look boys, I just wanted to apologise...' and, with that, he picked up a bottle and threw it at Hurlock.

The bottle, fortunately, missed its target. Hurlock grabbed a chunky crystal ashtray from the table and said, 'I am going to fucking kill you.'

At that point – and, to this day, I still have no idea why I did it – I stepped in between them. I started saying, 'Come on, leave it lads...' That short sentence was barely out of my mouth when Hurlock launched the ashtray. It hit me on the forehead, went spinning off and then clattered by the manager of the hotel, just for good measure.

Hurlock then grabbed hold of Speedie and gave him another right good seeing-to.

I've sat down by this stage – chaos is going on all around me – and all I can feel is blood trickling down my face. One of the boys pointed out that I'm cut and within seconds we can see a blue flashing light outside. I can see that Speedie is nursing a few war wounds but it's nothing too serious.

I hear the manager calling for an ambulance. I said, 'What for?'

Little did I know that my forehead had been split wide open.

Lew told me he would accompany me to the hospital in the ambulance. I had no idea where Speedie was at this stage. I was more concerned, obviously, about the claret that was dripping from my head and getting it seen to as soon as possible.

I got stitched up at the hospital and, as I was leaving, I get a tap on the shoulder. It's a copper. 'Micky Adams?'

'Yeah.'

'I'd like you to accompany me to Jersey police station. I'm arresting you for being involved in a fight.'

'What?'

'I believe you have been involved in a fracas.'

'Listen, mate, it wasn't anything to do with me. I'm just the innocent victim in all of this.'

'Well, you are going to have to tell me that down at the station. You can explain that to the custody sergeant.'

So Lew and I were put in the back of the Black Maria. My head was thumping by this stage.

I was booked in and was walked down to my accommodation for the night – a cell. All I can see through the bars of another cell is Speedie. He was still raging.

'I am going to fucking kill you, you little wanker,' he was mouthing at me.

'What are you having a go at me for, you prick? Fuck off.'

I was released at 6 a.m. after being interviewed. Speedie left the station later that day, but he now had twenty-four hours to get off the island.

The manager – in his wisdom – decided to get us all together for a team meal that night. The tension was unbelievable. We thought it was going to kick off again at any minute.

That was the end of Speedie. The club had to get rid of him after that. He was a loose cannon. He tells it differently in his own book, but that's how it was as I saw it. Speedie says that it was Terry who wound him up, but that's not how I remember it. Terry might have launched himself, but that was only after he had a few unnecessary things thrown his way.

You simply didn't do that with Mr Hurlock. When Terry went for a drink, he went big. When he went on one, he would go on the missing list.

In the season of 1991/92 we were struggling going into the final six or so games. The campaign was reaching the point of no return and we were all called in for a team meeting. The message was along the lines of: 'Listen, we've got six games to save our lives in this league. We need you to be totally dedicated. We don't need you to be on the booze. We don't need you to be seen out and about in town. Let's concentrate fully on the task ahead.'

It was comical timing, not that Terry was in any fit state at the time to have realised it. He crashed through the door at that precise moment and he was absolutely steaming.

He slurred, 'Sorry I'm late gaffer.'

'Terry, I've just been saying to all the lads that we want to be totally dedicated towards staying in the League...'

'To be fair gaff,' he continued with glazed eyes 'I think you will get that, you will get that...'

He was as drunk as a lord. Brilliant.

At the start of the next campaign, I created history for being the first man to be sent off in the Premier League –a landmark for all the wrong reasons. I was given my marching orders for punching Ray Wilkins.

Ray was to have a big impact on my life when he took my job at Fulham with Kevin Keegan, but I wasn't to know that at the time. People asked me why I did it. I said it was because I didn't like him, but I didn't really know him. I was playing in midfield again. I had no idea why because I was never comfortable there, and he was probably running rings around me. I turned around and thumped him. I was fined two weeks' wages and a hit with a three-match ban.

My first ever sending off was against Nottingham Forest under Nicholl. We played away at the City Ground and Brian Laws slid in to tackle me. I jumped out of the way and as I came down I stamped all over him. The referee saw it and off I went. After the match, Nicholl pulled me and said: 'What did you get sent off for?'

'I dunno gaffer,' I said, 'I didn't touch him.'

'Is that right? I'll have a look at that', came his reply.

I was called up to his office on the Monday morning. His memory, as we have established, wasn't the best. I knocked on his door. 'Gaffer, you wanted to see me.'

He was sat behind his desk. He looked at me, vacantly, and said: 'What did I want to see you for?'

There were about 100 yellow post-it notes all over his desk. So he started going through them, one-by-one.

'No, it's not that. Or that. No. No. No...'

He went through about twenty of them until he finally found the one concerning yours truly. I could hardly contain myself from laughing.

'Before you say anything, what was it you said you did in the match?' He was eyeing the video recorder where there was a cassette playing.

I thought to myself, I'm just going to have to own up to this.

'As he came in, I might have stood on him, gaffer.'

'You stamped on him, didn't you?'

'Er, yeah...'

Another two weeks' wages was docked.

It was about this time Razor left for Liverpool, and I was stitched up one day by my big mate Dave Willis who used to own a motor home business. He had sponsored Razor, and made the same offer to me. It involved driving around in a sponsored car. So I had a Peugeot 309 with 'Micky Adams, Sponsored by Marquis Motor Homes' written along the side. Shortly after receiving the car, he caught up with me again and said: 'I've got a personalised number plate for you. When you get back from a game, drop in, and I'll get one of the lads to put it on for you.'

Good as gold, I did as he said. Unbeknown to me, however, the registration he had for me read as follows: 'FAN 1E.' So there I was, driving around with a car which near enough spelled out the word 'fanny'. I stuck with it for six months. People were pointing and the number plate was the centre of everyone's amusement. It was killing me. Eventually, I handed it back to Dave, apologising that I couldn't carry on driving it with such a number plate. But it turned out the number plate was a fake. I'd been driving around with an illegal plate for six months! Goodness knows how I didn't get pulled over by the police. Of course, he thought it was hilarious.

Anyway, back to the story: we weren't scoring enough goals. So, Branny dropped Tiss, and then brought him back. By this time, it wasn't even a love-hate relationship. It was just hate-hate. In the end, the inability to pick our star player turned out to be Branny's downfall.

There had been a game and the punters were demonstrating, getting their white hankies out. That was a thing they had picked up from the Spanish Leagues, where fans would wave hankies to show their displeasure. To be fair to Branny, he always fronted up to any criticism. Unfortunately, it was one crisis too many and he was consequently given his cards.

I had respect for Ian; so much so, in fact, that when the call came to join him at Fulham a couple of years later, I was happy to rekindle our professional relationship. To those on the outside, it wasn't too much of a shock when he left and in walked Alan Ball with Lawrie McMenemy.

It was not only bad news for me, but for all of the senior professionals, too, such as Iain Dowie, Terry Hurlock and Steve Wood. I had no preconceived ideas about Alan. I had heard he was a good coach – but he never involved me from day one, so it is difficult to pass fair judgement.

He didn't pick me and made me train with the kids. I resented that because I was never a problem for managers. I'd always tried my best. I wouldn't cause any of them any real issues but, for some reason, Bally saw the established players as a real headache. He wanted us out and, as he got results early on, that helped him with the punters and he gained courage of his convictions.

I don't know what his problem was. My history as a manager shows that any football club is only as good as any senior professionals they have in it, and the older boys weren't a problem. However, it wasn't just me; there were others who were pushed out, too. I don't know what influence Lawrie had on him, but I know that he had been in the stands a number of weeks before Branny's sacking.

I always confronted people head on. I was the same with Alan. I said to his face a couple of times, 'Look, if you don't want me around, pay me up and I'll go.' His response was always: 'Go and see Lawrie Mac.' While Alan didn't like confrontation, Lawrie didn't mind it.

I was out of the side. Simon Charlton was one choice for my position and Francis Benali the other. Eventually, one of them picked up a knock and the manager wanted me to play. I received a call on the Thursday morning. I was at the Dell and the lads were at the training ground. Someone had failed a fitness test and he needed me.

I thought to myself: 'There's no way I'm rushing my bollocks off getting up there.'

So I took my time. As I slowly made my way to the training ground, he was pacing up and down, glancing at his watch: 'Where have you been?' he said, well brassed off.

Twenty-four hours later, I was in the gym. As I've said already, it was like *Rollerball* in there and I jarred my knee going in for a challenge with Ken Monkou. The next morning – the day of the game – I got out of bed but could hardly walk. It was obvious I wasn't going to play, and Alan thought I'd done it deliberately. He came in to see me in the treatment room.

'What's happened here?' he said.

'I've tweaked my ligaments.'

'Can you play?'

'No.'

And that was it. Apart from the day I left, he never spoke to me again. He thought I had injured myself on purpose. I hadn't. Of course I would have played – it would have been a great opportunity to showcase my talents to other clubs.

Southampton sent me to Stoke City on loan. They were in the First Division at the time under Joe Jordan. He was a fearsome character and in many ways similar to Nicholl. He was another one who had a thing about fitness and weight. If we got on the scales on Friday and we were a couple of pounds up, then we had until Saturday lunchtime to lose it. It was a ridiculous rule. On Friday, you could be up three pounds. So, to make the weight to play, you would either have to starve yourself or go in the sauna to dehydrate yourself, neither of which is a particularly sensible approach to take as far as I'm concerned. Having said that, though, I enjoyed working with Joe and Asa Hartford. I spent a decent month there before heading back. There was no messing around. But upon my return at the Dell, Lawrie Mac told me they wanted me to leave.

I had a £30,000 loyalty bonus due at the end of the season. I advised Lawrie I wouldn't be going anywhere without it. The next thing I knew, I was being told to report to the track at the Dell. Lawrie was obviously going to run me. At that time, I was as fit as I had ever been. He was going to give me sixty-second laps. I would finish one, and then I would be told to do another. As I was running round, more and more of the other players started appearing out of the dressing room to watch.

It annoyed him immensely. I would finish one and I brazenly announced: 'You've still not fucked me up', before, inevitably, I was sent on another one.

While passing the lads I would snigger, 'I'm still going boys', and they chuckled to themselves.

After lord knows how many laps later, Lawrie finally lost his patience. 'In you go', he said, 'I'll go and speak to the directors'.

The next day he declared, 'I'll give you your money. Stoke want you until the end of the season'.

I went up to collect my boots, which were kept in an area just outside of the ground and up some stairs. Bally followed me up. There was no one else around, just me and him in the boot room. 'Micky', he said, 'you want to go and say "thanks" to Lawrie because he's worked really hard to get you your money'. I stared him straight in the eye. 'Are you fucking sure? The way you pair have treated me… piss off'.

Anyway, while at Stoke, I came back to Southampton one night. My missus, Iain Dowie and his wife, Debbie, and I were in the local pub The Jolly Farmer, and who should walk in but Bally. He had been at Goodwood with the pub landlord, Martin. By this time he had treated Iain exactly the same as he had treated me. Like me, Iain had also left Southampton. Bally spotted us and continued around the other side of the bar.

Next thing we see is Martin coming over to us with a bottle of champagne and four glasses. He promptly placed it on our table. 'Mr Ball has sent this over, with his compliments'.

Iain didn't even blink twice. 'Listen, go back over there and tell Mr Ball to shove this up his arse'.

Martin began remonstrating and told us what a nice day the pair had just had etc. etc. Iain, getting slightly irritated by now, said, 'Martin, unless you go over there and tell him that, I'll go over and do it.'

With that, he retreated with the bottle and glasses and Bally scuttled off soon afterwards. Looking back, I didn't have any real and lasting issues. He had his reasons. I have no real understanding of why he acted the way he did to the senior professionals; perhaps it was a bad experience somewhere else. I never spoke to him about it. I saw him many times after that, particularly in the pub. Yes, at the time I resented being treated that way – but it was a life lesson for me. I was always respectful to him and bore no grudge.

But I knew that, when I eventually became a manager myself, I didn't want to be like him.

CHAPTER 6

ON THE ROPES AT FULHAM...
AND LEARNING THEM

My relationship with Southampton Football Club, or more specifically with Alan Ball, meant that, by the end of the 1994 season, I had been given a free transfer.

Coming up to the age of thirty-three, it wasn't the greatest of time for any player to be looking for work, but my salvation came in the shape of my former boss Ian Branfoot. I already had one eye on a career in management by then. I had completed my badges, and Ian's offer was the opportunity I'd been waiting for to combine playing with coaching.

Unfortunately for me, it meant dropping down from the Premier League to the Second Division in one swoop. To soften the blow, I had been given a two-year deal and, at £600-a-week, I was the highest paid player in the club. Toss in a decent signing-on fee and there wasn't much for me to grumble about.

Fulham was run by the Muddyman family, i.e. Bill and his son, Andy. They had some finance behind them, but it was nowhere near sufficient for the club to buy its way out of the league. The chairman was Jimmy Hill, someone who was to feature heavily once I'd stopped playing, when he took over as manager.

For now, Ian and Fulham had to concentrate on making a decent fist of life in League Two. To do this, the manager brought in a couple of ex-Southampton players, Mark Blake and Kevin Moore. There were a few decent players already there in the shape of Simon Morgan, Terry Angus and Robbie Herrera, but Ian also spent money on Micky Conroy. This helped Ian stamp his own mark on the team.

Terry, in particular, was an interesting one. The story went that Don Mackay – our paths had crossed at Coventry, if you remember – had brought him down from somewhere in Scotland, believing him to be a 6 ft 4in. tall Scot from the Highlands. Instead, however, into the dressing room walked a black lad from Northampton… I had no idea how that happened.

Anyway, prior to Ian's arrival, all sorts of rumours had been doing the rounds that Jimmy Hill had been making the substitutions and influencing team decisions. Ian wasn't having any of that. However, it was going to be a long, tough job to resurrect the club's fortunes. To be quite frank, the situation was a shambles. There was no training kit; we had to wear old gear. We trained on rugby pitches. The dressing rooms were behind a train station and we must have been raided about seven or eight times by thieves who made their getaway by boarding the next train with all our gear, of course. They were taking a big risk trying to out-run a group of professional athletes, but fair play to them, they managed it on numerous occasions.

Behind the scenes, we had a groundsman called Steve who was a member of a group who used to hire an executive box on a match day called 'OUT'. The group effectively represented people who were against any manager who may be in charge at the time. It didn't matter who it was, they wanted them out. It was allegedly a laugh and a piss-take, but it was pathetic and unbelievable that the club itself was allowing them to get away with it.

In terms of on-field discipline, it had to change and Ian needed to come down hard. A car-load of players, including Jim Stannard and Glen Thomas, had to travel around the M25 from Essex to get to Craven Cottage. Apparently, if there had been an accident under Mackay, he would ring up and say there was traffic. Mackay's response would be, 'Don't bother then, lads. Go home and we will see you to-morrow.' So the lads tried to push the boundaries with Ian very early on in his tenure. The first time it happened, they phoned up and said the same line about an accident.

Ian's response was: 'You make sure you are nice and safe, and we will see you when we see you.'

'Yeah, but gaffer, there's been an accident, we could be here for hours.'

'No problem, we will wait for you. We've got all day.'

So they learnt very quickly not to take him on.

He would wait for them, too. We all had to, which was a bind but it made a point to all of us. Ian also signed ex-Wimbledon legend Alan Cork who, like me, was coming to the end of his career. Corky claims I finished his days as a professional because I would never get the ball into the box, but he wasn't the most mobile by that stage.

However, he was mobile enough at the end of training. All he wanted to do was get off the training ground to head to the bookies and then onto the Green Man pub in Ewell where he lived. Fulham's fans weren't too taken with him, but I was, and he became a good pal of mine.

Elsewhere at the club, however, relationships were strained. For instance, Ian had to make a stand with the chairman. He would be called to see him for Jimmy to say how he thought things should be done. Ian, however, was his own man. He asked me at half time to stand at the door of the dressing room and not to let anyone in. There had been rumours that in the past Jimmy would come into the changing rooms and make substitutions himself. This clearly had to stop. So, during team-talks or at the end of the game, no one was allowed in. Not even the chairman.

By this time, I had ideas about being a manager myself. Part of the deal when I joined was that I would be allowed to coach, and so I was put in charge of the reserves. I used to drive the minibuses up to Northampton, Cambridge, wherever it was. I'd take the players for extra training – in the weights' room, for example.

One day, Terry Angus came up to me and said: 'Why are you punishing us?'

I replied: 'Why do you think I'm punishing you?'

He said: 'Because the first-team is off and we're here in the afternoons.'

So I said: 'Get in the first-team, then. If you think this is a punishment you're in the wrong profession.'

I'd take him in the gym and do extras with him. I was gradually learning how to talk to players, how to treat them, what made them tick.

What also helped me was Ian taking me scouting with him. He certainly wasn't lazy. We would be out most days. We didn't have much by way of money so we needed to familiarise ourselves with every reserve player in London. Sometimes we needed to be in Manchester, so we would traipse up the M6 to Manchester City and Manchester United to watch their youngsters.

I was still playing at this time but, unfortunately, I was injured during my first pre-season. During the last game before the campaign kicked off I picked up a foot injury, which wasn't great because I was the big signing and didn't play for four months. I felt as though I had let Ian down. It wasn't great, that spell on the side-lines, but it did give me the opportunity to study the manager hard.

I got to know him through that. He always had a dour, hard exterior he also had a softer side. He had a shell around him, just like a lot of managers. They don't want to let too many people in because they don't want to show their insecurities – and we've all got them.

I remember we once went up to Manchester United reserves and I was booked for speeding on the way home. A copper pulled me over on the M3 to Southampton and asked me if I knew how fast I was going. I replied that I didn't. The truth was I hadn't even seen him. Apparently, I'd been doing 96mph in a 50mph zone at 12.30 a.m., so that was a two-week driving ban. On any other occasion, this wouldn't warrant a mention in anyone's memoirs. However, it set off a chain of events that was to take my off-field life in a very different direction.

But more of that later.

By now, I started to realise what the game was all about, particularly scouting. You had to rely on your own judgement if you were to sign a player. Agents were in the game but, as anyone in management will tell you, no agent on the planet has a bad player on their books. If you have a limited amount of money to spend at that lower level, you live or die according to the people you sign.

However, I needed to cut myself some slack in the first-team dressing room. I had been driving up each day from Southampton with Mark Blake and Kevin Moore, and some of the other lads resented my involvement on the coaching side because they thought I was too close to the manager.

I wasn't; Ian was his own man. He picked the team, but I realised then I had to stop car-sharing and come up on my own. When I did return to the first-team, I was struggling for form. I wasn't paying as much attention to my own performances as I should have been and that wasn't helping Ian, either.

It had been built up as though I was going to be a world-beater. It was never going to be like that. At the end of Ian's first season in charge, it hadn't ended in success, but it had improved, and we finished one place outside the play-offs. The rot had been stopped. After all, the club had been relegated just twelve months previously.

It was something to work with. Unfortunately, back in those days, only two teams gained automatic promotion and then the next four were fighting for one other spot. Under the new system we would have been in the play-offs. It makes me wonder what would have happened had that been the case. History might have been very different. Nonetheless, it had clearly been a better campaign for the club.

On a personal front, an FA Cup tie against Ashford Town was to provide me with a highlight that season. It was on live TV, hammering down with rain and we were two goals down. Fortunately, we were awarded two penalties in the last five minutes. I stuck both of them away. That was memorable, but not as much as when we were coming off the field at full-time. While ten players were covered in the muck and grime of ninety minutes on a mud heap of a pitch, one player boasted a pristine shirt that looked as if it had come straight out of the wrapper. Yes, while ten players had a white kit on that was now black, one didn't. Step forward, Corky.

We were lacking in experience, and one of the most significant additions – that of Terry Hurlock – was not as effective as we'd all hoped, because he suffered a broken leg following an incident with Brentford's Martin Grainger. Funnily enough, I confronted the same player after a game one season later. I wasn't happy with one of his challenges and when I came out of the tunnel area, I let him know.

But, in general, it was a decent first season for Ian, although the fans weren't particularly happy. Obviously we wanted to kick on with the season afterwards, but Terry Hurlock's injury during that pre-season friendly knocked us back. He might not have been as mobile as he was but he still put the fear of the almighty into opposition defenders.

To start with, it looked as though we would have to continue on our upwards path. We won the first two games then drew two. We then inexplicably went on a really bad run. There were only two more victories in the League between then and when Ian was removed from his post. Both were at Craven Cottage against Cardiff City and Scarborough respectively.

I had belief in Ian and I thought what he was doing was right, but he was labelled with this 'long-ball' tag and with each passing match, the players' confidence drained just a little more. For instance, he had bought Micky Conroy to the club and he had not scored the goals that we all thought he would. Try as we might, we couldn't get a win. We were competitive and just about kept in touch because we drew a fair few games.

As the season went on, Ian was getting frustrated. He was never a ranter or a raver; his assistant, Len Walker, was the one who had a pop. Unfortunately, the lads never took him too seriously – mainly, in my opinion, because they all knew he wasn't the boss.

On 30 January 1996, we lost 3–1 at home to Scunthorpe and slumped to twenty-third in Division Three – or, more pointedly – ninety-first in the Football League. As soon as we struck that low point, that was it. The fans were after Ian, big time. Even though had been in the Premier League and had kept Southampton in the Premier League for years, after that he went to Fulham in what effectively was the Fourth Division – and was never employed as a manager again. He ended up going to Sunderland with Peter Reid to be in charge of the youth recruitment. I was thinking to myself today about how he never had another chance. It goes to show that if you do fail at that level, you might never get another crack.

Looking back now, it's easy to see it was just a club that was meandering along. It needed a lift; a spark from somewhere. And, amazingly, they turned to me – at the age of thirty-three.

When you become a coach or a manager for the first time, the players will work you out inside thirty seconds. How you talk, what you say, how you present it, the content of it. The good thing was that I knew the lads anyway. They knew pretty much what I was about. They knew I had decent standards and I wasn't going to take any shit.

One thing I knew straight away was that I didn't want Len around. I didn't want him as my assistant. I was adamant Corky was going to be promoted to the position. Now, Corky is the complete opposite to me. He's happy-go-lucky, a bit sloppy at times but he understood what I wanted and, more importantly, was a tremendous coach of forward players. Set-plays for and against were also a speciality of his.

The tempo of training needed to be increased. I had to instil some standards, which pissed some of the players off. For example, I wanted them to be clean shaven. If any scouts went to a game, I wanted them to wear a collar and tie so that they looked as though they were representing a football club. I wanted us to show that we were in charge of a club that had decent values. I just felt that the management should have a shave. It takes what, two minutes?

I also wanted to change the style of football that we played when I took over from Ian. I wanted to play more of a passing game, so I asked Steve, the groundsman, to keep an eye on the weather. If it was going to remain dry, I would ask him to put some water on the pitch to get the ball to move quicker. Steve, however, trying to show me who was boss, verti-drained the pitch so that it was bone-dry and very bobbly. He was basically saying 'Up yours'.

When you step into the hot-seat, a lot of things hit you all at once. Dealing with the press is one. I was very naive. Although I had conversed with the local media guys at pretty much every club I'd played for, this was now on another level. Branny was very negative towards the press. He'd had a rough ride, but I hadn't had any particularly bad experiences.

I was very green, so Ian tried to guide me through it. I remember the day I was appointed at Fulham, I turned on the television to see Alan Mullery was doing an interview, criticising the appointment. He said I wasn't a Fulham person and all the rest of it. Fine. That was his opinion.

But what wasn't fine was that he was actually doing it on the pitch at Craven Cottage! We'd opened up the ground so that someone in the media could criticise us. Unbelievable. That's where Fulham was at the time, and when you have a team that is ninety-first in the Football League, you find every single member of staff have their safety jackets on.

The lifeboat was in the water and they were getting in. It was every man and woman for themselves. They weren't worried about anyone else. They were just looking after their own little patch. They weren't concerned for the manager. The attitude is very much 'he could be gone in a few weeks, so what's the point of bothering about him?' That's not to say everyone was bad; far from it. Ian was the catalyst for change. He and I, along with the Muddymans, managed to clear it out before we left.

We were training in Ewell at the time. We didn't have any money, so I had to think hard about what I would do. How I was going to resurrect the club? Well, we lightened it up. We gave the players more freedom to go and play. That was the simple answer. There were one or two hiccups along the way, but we collected twenty-six points from our remaining matches and stayed up with ease.

The brief had been to keep Fulham in the football league and I had done that. I was well aware, however, there needed to be big changes if we were to make any headway when the players came back after their summer break.

CHAPTER 7

BALLYGAR AND THE REBIRTH
AT THE COTTAGE

The call to take over as manager happened much sooner than either Ian or I had thought it would.

While I was young and fairly inexperienced, I did have one thing going for me: I had watched a lot of football. And I had Ian as my mentor. He was diligent and we came up with an agreement with each other whereby we promised we would get know to about every single player in the greater London region; as we had a limited amount of cash, we needed to know who was out there.

I wanted to know who the successful teams were, so I spent a lot of time watching Gillingham play where Tony Pulis was in charge. It was that vintage who formed the nucleus of the team that went on to face Manchester City in the League One play-off final a couple of years later. They were a big, strong and powerful unit. The team included nine six-footers and they weren't going to be bullied by anyone. Set-pieces were the key for Tony. In fact, they still are and there's nothing wrong with that – he has managed very nicely in the Premier League for the past ten years or so.

However, we were still too small and not powerful enough. We weren't good enough at dead-ball situations at either end of the pitch. We needed to change. It was with that brief in mind that I met up at the Muddymans' offices at the end of the season for a meeting with the chairman.

As usual, Jimmy Hill was late. He was notorious for it, particularly for board meetings. We would often start without him and generally, after about half an hour, Jimmy would walk in and everything that had been discussed would have to be repeated. It was a total ball ache.

Jimmy liked a certain type of player, and that was the fanny merchants, or, for the layman, the players who liked to get on the ball and play. I had already realised this was not the way Fulham were going to progress in League Two. The idea of this meeting was to put out a retained list and to formulate our plan of action for the next season. We started talking about players. Jimmy arrived and started pontificating.

'What a poor performance that was, we weren't big enough, we weren't strong enough – we weren't good enough,' he chirped on (we had played the previous evening and lost at home).

I had to sit there, as a first-time manager, and listen. He was ranting on about not being physical enough for fifteen minutes. When he eventually finished, Bill Muddyman turned to me and said: 'Have you anything to say to the chairman about all that?'

I replied: 'I think he's spot on.'

Jimmy was full of himself at this point.

Bill, trying to move the meeting on, asked: 'Right can we talk about the retained list for next season?'

So we began to go through the players, one by one. I started.

'Danny Bolt...' Jimmy interjected.

'Oh yes, good player, nice left foot, got potential...'

I ignored him and firmly said: 'Free transfer.'

He looked at me.

'Free transfer, Micky?'

'That's right, chairman. He's 5 ft 7in. tall. He's not big enough for me. Free transfer.'

Tumbleweed. I carry on.

'Right, Gary Brazil...'

Once more, Jimmy pipes up.

'Yes, experienced professional, knows his way around this league. Good in the dressing room...'

Again, I ignored him and carried on. 'Free transfer.'

'OK ... next, Arjan Pedrosian...' He was a little winger.

Jimmy can't stop himself. 'Oh yes, Arjan, good on the ball, very tricky.'

The pattern was set by now. 'Free transfer, chairman.'

He interrupted me before I could go any further. 'Micky, Micky, what are you doing? These lads are good players, very good in some cases.'

I turned to him and said, 'chairman with the greatest respect, you've come in here late and I've had to listen to you banging on for fifteen minutes about how small and unphysical we are. So let me get on with rectifying that, would you?'

By the end of the meeting, I had given seventeen players free transfers. I cleared the lot, even some of the lads who had done well for me. It sounds cruel, and I suppose it is the harshest thing you can ever do to a player, but there was reasoning behind it all. A good number of them had been there for a few years and look where the club found itself. We had not improved a great deal. I just thought it was my turn and I needed to give it a run on my own terms. From a managerial perspective, it's my neck on the block, and certain tough decisions had to be made.

There was no doubt his heart was in the right place, but Jimmy's face was an absolute picture. I did not want to dismiss the older professionals just because they were older. I wanted to give them respect, especially in light of what had happened to me under Alan Ball. Players such as Gary Brazil, for example, had done well for the club, but the blueprint I was working towards was what I had seen Pulis do with Gillingham.

To that end, I needed a goal-scorer who was going to find the net twenty-five times a season. I needed him to be backed up by someone who I felt could also get twelve to fifteen in and I wanted them to develop a strong partnership together. We didn't have that. The reason I mention Gary is because he was a senior professional and a nice kid, but he scored few goals. It's always hard telling lads who aren't good enough that they won't be coming on the journey with you – and particularly so if they are decent sorts.

I remember I went to watch Gillingham reserves against Crawley at the end of that season. Once again, I wanted to see who was in Gillingham's reserves and also who Pullis was going to potentially throw out at the end of that season. Don't forget, the Gills were stepping up a division too, and that only increased my chances of landing someone who I thought might do a job for me.

Another fact that worked in my favour, particularly with respect to Gillingham, was that the cost implications were good. There were three that caught my eye. Paul Watson was a full-back and could play on either side, He didn't possess a great deal of pace but he could handle the ball. His set-pieces with his left foot would be a valuable asset to our squad.

Darren Freeman ran around like a headless chicken but he was quick and could get behind the opposition's defence and stretch teams. And then there was Richard Carpenter, a midfielder who was fiercely competitive and had great passing ability. I thought to myself, 'if I can get those three out of Gillingham that would be a great start.' All three were offered contracts by Gillingham but had turned them down.

I persuaded Bill Muddyman to invest in the squad. We went to tribunal with all of them, despite the fact they were all out of contract. It was a gamble for Bill to take but we ended up getting the three of them for around £50,000 with add-ons. Tony wasn't very happy with the figures, but the tribunal set the sums. We had committed ourselves to the players and, if they had cost hundreds of thousands, we would have been in a right state. It was definitely a gamble on Bill's part, but we had managed to take all three for not very much.

I also took a keeper called Mark Walton and a youngster called Danny Cullip who I'd seen play for Oxford's reserves. He was only eighteen years old, but he would head it and boot it and fight pretty much anyone he could get his hands on. He fancied a scrap.

Matty Lawrence came from Wycombe's reserves for £15,000. That was a result. The season before we had taken a fella called Rob Scott out of Sheffield United's reserves. He was quick and had a long throw, and we were looking for someone who could hoist the ball into the box. He could do that.

I gave a debut the year before to a kid called Sean Davis. Obviously, he went on to have a great career with Spurs, Portsmouth and others, but he was only seventeen when he played for me.

Simon Stewart came from Sheffield Wednesday's reserves. Glenn Cockerill, my mate from Southampton, also came in. He knew what it was about but, more importantly, he was a pal – and, if there were any issues in the dressing room, I knew he would have my back. As I said, some of the squad that became important to us were still there, such as Robbie Herrera, the left-back, and Simon Morgan, the captain who was key to everything. I had a few problems with him one year later because, unbeknown to me, Tony Pulis had tapped him up. But once he had got his head straight he was absolutely invaluable.

We had another young lad called Paul Brooker. He was a little winger – a little bottle of pop, 5 ft 6 in. tall and wet through. If you said 'boo' to him, he'd just give you the ball. But if it was at his feet, he could destroy anyone. We didn't, however, have a clue – any of us – how it was going to gel or if, indeed, it was going to work at all.

At that stage, I met an important man. Fulham's club sponsors at the time were Britain's General Union – the GMB, as it was known. The head of the southern area was a lad called Paul Kenny. He was important because, firstly, he was a Fulham fan and, secondly, he was in charge of the finances for the GMB.

Branny and I got him into the dressing rooms at the Cottage. The place was little short of a disgrace: paint was peeling from the walls, tiles were falling off, the floor was a mess and the showers didn't work properly. At the time, we couldn't sit upstairs in the cottage as you can now. It was falling to bits.

We built up a relationship with him. We just asked, 'Can you help us?' And he did. And then he came up with an offer of a pre-season trip away. He said, 'Look, I'd like you to come out to Ireland.' He was from a place called Ballygar, which is on the County Galway border, almost slap-bang in the middle of the country. Fulham hadn't been away for donkey's years. The club couldn't afford it, and I'm not exactly sure we could afford it back then, but we said, 'Can we go out and look at the facilities?'

So Ian, Paul and I went on a little reconnaissance trip. It wasn't much more than a three-day bender if I'm being perfectly honest, but we looked at what they had planned for us. It was a village in the middle of nowhere. There was a main street running through the centre with five pubs on one side and four on the other! On one side, there was a hotel which only had ten bedrooms. That wasn't enough to accommodate a full squad of players, so Paul devised a plan whereby the players would be put up with families.

His mate who organised it was a fella called Art O'Keefe, who happened to be the bank manager. To give you a sense of what sort of sleepy place it was, on numerous occasions he had left the bank unlocked simply because he forgot to close it!

The O'Keefes became like my second family. I ended up taking a lot of teams out there, but Fulham was the first. The plan was to organise friendlies against Galway and Longford, places which were up to a ninety-minute drive away. We did all our training in the village of Ballygar on one Gaelic football field. And that was it.

Before we travelled across the Irish Sea, we played a couple of other matches in the south-west of England which fostered a bit of team spirit, but the tour did not get off to the best of starts. The organisers sent a fifteen-seat mini-bus to pick us up. Since our party consisted of twenty players and four staff, we had to grab ourselves three taxis to take the rest of the players and the kit to Ballygar. It seemed to take for ever on a single-track road from Dublin.

When we eventually turned up at this little village, Paul had to tell us which pubs we could and couldn't go in; the reason being they had all sponsored either a match or the programme or whatever and obviously wanted a piece of the pie for themselves!

He'd say, 'Today, you can go in this one that one and the other. But don't go down there to that one.'

With regard to the accommodation, the pecking order in the hotel meant that management, staff and senior players had the hotel rooms. The rest were scattered around the village in pairs. If you were really unlucky you had the house down a country lane, by a graveyard, with no lights, which was quite scary for the younger ones.

What else can I tell you about Ballygar? Well, there are plenty of rivers and we would offer the players a trout fishing trip. We thought a few of them might like to go and catch their supper. The only real issue for those who wanted to go was the transport left the hotel at 4 a.m. – an early start. Well, I say the only real issue was the fact it was an early start. That's not strictly true. And neither was the promise of the trout fishing. There wasn't any. It was a set up. With Paul's help, we managed to reel in eight lads who were supposed to wait for the van – only no one turned up to collect them. They were outside for hours, having got up before the cock. What makes me laugh now is that Darren Freeman was one of those who were caught hook, line and sinker.

A couple of years later, this time with a different set of lads, we went back to Ballygar and tried the same trick, only for Freeman to put his hand up again and offer to go! That's how dopey he was. Incredibly, he saw it through as well. Unbelievable.

Another great Freeman story was the time he forgot that we had turned around at half-time. He still thought we were attacking the same goal we had been in the first forty-five minutes. I can still re-member Corky screaming at him from the side-lines, 'Darren, Daaarreeennnn, you're going the wrong way son!' There was a reason he was nicknamed Forrest Gump.

Anyway, we had a great time in Ballygar for the eight or ten days. I always had the approach as a manager that the players could have a pint or three; they weren't there to be treated like kids. I always tried to operate on the basis that drinking was fine so long as you were able to do the work the next day. Otherwise, I would not have been very happy – not very happy at all. One player, I thought, however, did abuse the freedom, and that was Glenn Cockerill, who I had to be careful with because he was older than me at just thirty-five years old at the time.

One morning he was nowhere to be seen. We found out which room he was in and we started banging the door – no response. We walked down to reception, picked up a key and let ourselves into his room. Sure as eggs is eggs, there he was lying in his bed – so we woke him up with the words: 'Come on Glenn, training. Get your arse downstairs – sharpish.'

As he was rubbing the sleep out of his eyes, he started protesting: 'I've got the day off. I'm going nowhere.'

I said: 'You've got the day off? Who's told you that?'

He replied: 'You did – last night.'

It turned out we had been drinking until 12 a.m. and I'd told him not to worry about the next morning and forgotten all about it!

In Ballygar, there wasn't much to do apart from train, eat, sleep and have the occasional drink. For me, the one big thing I took from Pulis was fitness. That particular pre-season, they got battered. I probably went overboard, if I'm honest, because it was my first season in charge of a professional outfit.

On top of the three friendlies we had when we were in Ballygar, we also organised one north of the border against Dungannon Swifts. It was when the Troubles were escalating, so I remember that well. I told them they could all go out that night if they wished, but no one ventured so much as a foot outside the hotel! We had that many injuries, including Tony Lange – our second keeper – that Corky had to go in goal. He managed to save a penalty and he still mentions it every second week, even now.

I learnt a lot from the experience in terms of the recovery times and number of matches needed for a pre-season. We went into the campaign with a few injuries as we'd had two or three games too many. That was due to my philosophy though; I wanted them to be fit.

At this stage, I'd be lying to you if I said I thought we were going to go on and get promotion in the manner we did. I honestly believed we were going to be better than last year, but I'm a big believer in the fact that how you start a season sets you up for the remainder. Micky Conroy got us off to a flier by scoring the winner against Hereford in the opening match.

However, I sensed I had a problem with Simon Morgan, the skipper. He was quiet and subdued, which was very much out of character. I pulled him aside and said, 'Look, Morgs, stick with us and let's see where we are going.' He was good enough as a player not to be plying his trade at the wrong end of the Third Division.

It was a trip to Hartlepool, which we lost, that was to prove the turning point. I could sense something was bugging Simon. I could see it in his game too. I remember saying to him, 'Listen, let's get this sorted one way or the other. Are you in? What's going on? Can we work something out because this is no good for either of us.'

Little did I know that he had been tapped up by Tony Pulis and was undecided about whether or not he wanted to leave. He was disillusioned with it all, but once he made a decision in his mind, he was all in. That was a huge plus for me.

Another plus was Conroy's form. He couldn't buy a goal at times under Ian. However, as I look at the statistics now, all I can see is his name on the scoresheet. Under Ian we had played 4–4–2 and he was very reluctant to change it. I played 3–4–3 or 3–5–2. Generally, we played three attackers up top, occupying their back four and sacrificing a man in the middle. Away from home we stuck in another midfielder and Glenn Cockerill was the one who was rotated, depending on the system.

The idea was to get crosses into the penalty box. Micky had been starved of any service from the flanks and this really played to his strengths. We had Robbie Herrera on the left-hand side and Paul Watson on the other. I had a striker called Nick Cusack who was a fantastic footballer. I played him between the two centre-halves. He was so good on the ball that he could step out into midfield and switch the play if we needed to get out to the other side.

I recognised we now had a system that suited our players. Slowly, it started to dawn on me that we were on to something. We started well and, after a sticky spell in October, we were very good – particularly away from home. I always had in my mind that teams in the Second Division had to be big enough – but it wasn't enough to be big and bullied. We had to stand up and dish it out – and this lot could. Frankly, they used to scare people.

Chippy Carpenter took no prisoners, nor did Blake, Watson, Morgan or Terry Angus – they were all as tough as old boots. Cullip, as I mentioned previously, would fight anyone.

When we did lose games I would call a meeting. I have to say I was never a big believer in meetings, but I actually found them useful when we had lost.

But, after a while, even that became predictable. I'd call the lads in after a defeat and say, 'What happened at the weekend?

They'd all look at me. So I'd continue.

'Well, what happened at the weekend was you lost a game of football. Have a look at the league table, believe in yourselves and get back to what you were doing.'

We had a successful team and they were almost self-policing to ensure the mistakes were eradicated. They gained confidence with every win and knew what they had to do to win. When we lost it was a kick up the backside, a reminder of what needed to be done.

The one area where they did take great delight was with Corky. To be precise, they loved nothing more than 'ragging' him, i.e. stripping off his clothes and leaving him naked on the pitch. He was the butt of most of the jokes and he wasn't very happy about it. After all, he was the assistant manager. It didn't matter where we were, if he said something they didn't agree with, they'd jump on him, rip all his training gear off and just leave him there. There was a time when we arrived back from a game on a Saturday and he warned the lads he was simply going to run them during the next training session. That was enough for them to pick him up and dump him into the nearest industrial waste bin!

If there was snow on the ground, the call went out to 'rag Corky'. He wasn't too happy about it, but there wasn't much he could do once twenty blokes had decided he was going to feel the snow on every inch of his bare skin in December. Thinking about it now, I suppose, as manager, I could have stopped them…

Anyway, it was about this time we played Darlington at home to a crowd nearing 8,000. At the start of the season we were attracting 5,000 but, as we kept winning, the crowds started growing. We recruited Paul Parker: yes, we somehow managed to persuade the former England international to come and play for us.

The rules of the dressing room were simple: no tracksuit bottoms; you had to wear shorts. I picked up this particular idiosyncrasy from Jimmy Case when we played together at Southampton. Jimmy had been part of that great Liverpool team in the '70s and they weren't allowed to wear anything but shorts. If it was good enough for a side that had won European cups and leagues in the '70s and '80s, then I decided it was good enough for my team.

Another of my theories was that if you want to warm up, then you had to warm up properly. I remember being on the training ground on Parker's first day. It was snowing and he trotted out wearing a pair of tracksuit bottoms. I could see all our lads glancing towards me. They knew what I was thinking and were wondering if it was one rule for them and another for a man who had played in a World Cup semi-final for his country.

I said, 'Paul, have you got any shorts?'

'Yeah, but it's snowing.'

'Can you see any of the other lads wearing them?

'Fergie used to let me wear tracksuit bottoms at Manchester United.'

'Listen son, I'm not fucking Fergie – go and change and put your shorts on.'

We didn't get off to the greatest of starts. However, he played against Darlington and was absolutely outstanding. I mean, you wouldn't believe how good he was. We then followed that with a trip to Colchester three days later, and he had a horror show. We went on a bad run after that, decided we weren't suited to one another and parted company. There wasn't any animosity; not on my part, anyway.

We then went on to win at Scunthorpe 4–1 and were soon back on track. One of the crucial matches, which was broadcast live on Sky, was a game against Cardiff City. I picked myself because we had problems at left-back. Unfortunately for me, however, I was no better than how I described Parker at Colchester. I had a nightmare and the boots were hung up – well, they were in my own mind, anyway.

The true turning point in the season came in February when we were due to face Swansea City. I looked at the lads' faces ahead of this fixture and they'd just gone. Football people will know what I'm saying when I describe looking at the players and thinking to myself, 'This lot are digging graves for themselves. Their confidence is shot.'

So I sent them home. I pulled them in after one session before the game and just said, 'Go home. I don't know what the problem is with all of you, but go home.' They'd not been on the training pitch more than thirty minutes. I thought it might gee them up for the game itself, but we were one-down early on and it looked like our season was going up in smoke.

I don't know if it was good management or a stroke of good luck, but I'll claim it as the former. I called Paul Brooker from the bench. He went on to make the equaliser for Darren Freeman and then scored the winner himself. After turning that one around, we went on an unbeaten eleven-match run, culminating in an away game at Carlisle.

We went all the way up there and it was pissing it down like you wouldn't believe. Normally, I'd take the team for a walk before the pre-match meal, but my attitude was one of, 'fuck it, let's get out there.' That didn't go down well. They were very reluctant. I remembered saying to them in the dressing room, 'Is that what we are all about, eh? It's a bit rainy, a bit windy. We don't much fancy it today? They'll be saying, "Those southern softies don't fancy it, do they?" Are we going to take this challenge on?'

And they did. Micky Conroy and Rodney McAree scored the goals in a 2–1 victory. That effectively got us promoted. They still sing a song about it at the Cottage now. 'Who put the ball in the Carlisle net? Rodney McAree…' The man's still a legend to this day with the Fulham faithfuls.

We had an away match at Mansfield about three days later. I remember it well, but it wasn't just for the obvious reason. After the euphoria of knowing we were promoted, Bill Muddyman cornered me at the end and gave me the first hint of what might be coming next. He pulled me to one side and said, 'Listen, there are big things happening at the club. A billionaire is going to take over. I can't give you his name but everything will come to light sooner rather than later. What I need you to do is to put your thinking cap on in terms of what you are going to do next season.'

But in the meantime, next we played Northampton at home – our big homecoming. Ian Atkins 'the Spoiler' and his Cobblers side were coming to the Cottage in front of a crowd of 11,000. It was our big day. The first thing Atkins did was to congratulate me and asked me whether I'd mind if his side recognised our achievement by clapping us out onto the pitch.

'Not a problem, Ian, that's very nice of you,' I said to my opposite number in the dug-out. We always warmed up at the Hammersmith End, which was the one furthest away from the Cottage where we ran out. Anyway, as we walked out to rapturous applause, all Northampton's players forgot the tunnel they were going to make for us, and ran up to our half of the pitch and took our end! My players looked confused and bewildered.

We couldn't get going after that. It knocked us off our stride and we'd had three days on the celebratory pop. Another reason I remember the game so vividly is because I substituted centre-half Terry Angus after eighteen minutes. I still regret the decision to this day. I was young, naive and frustrated because I expected us to be on the front foot. We weren't and my impetuosity got the better of me. If he's reading this, perhaps he will accept my apology. I think we had conceded and he wasn't at the races. I was making a point – not the nicest one after we had earned promotion. But, like I say, I was very naive and hot headed.

Our last game of the campaign was against Cambridge United away. We finished second that year and, gut-wrenchingly, we lost the league on goals scored. That's right, we were denied a title on goals scored. It was a new idea brought in that season … and guess who came up with it?

You've guessed it: Jimmy Hill. Our chairman.

Who had the best goal difference that season? We did.

For that year only, the title was decided on goals scored and Jimmy Hill will go down in history as costing his own team the league title.

CHAPTER 8

THERE'S ONLY ONE 'F' IN AL FAYED

After securing promotion, I was full of confidence. I'd put together a side, had belief in my methods and had even picked up the divisional 'Manager of the Year' award from Sir Alex Ferguson.

The start of the 1997 summer was, frankly, one long laugh. As a reward, the squad and management team went out to Spain. Just before getting on the plane, I'd signed a two-year extension on improved terms. Unfortunately, that cut no ice with the squad when I made the mistake of falling asleep by the pool and Morgan and his mob threw me and the sunbed I was lying on into it. However, that was nothing. Corky was attacked in his room by some masked raiders who proved that national boundaries were no defence to a 'ragging'. That was Morgan again.

As the season of fun and games wound down I was given an idea of what was going on by Bill Muddyman. In particular, I learnt the identity of the man taking over.

As you know, it was Mohamed Al Fayed, owner of world-famous department store Harrods. Despite having agreed a new two-year deal, it was decided – as a show of faith – that I should be tied down for longer; five years longer, in fact. And this was great news, obviously: a big vote of confidence.

Bill and Andy were staying on the board, so I had a couple of friendly faces to stand my corner. All seemed set to be fair. My first meeting with my new boss was the day he took over. As you would expect there was significant media interest, so a press conference was called at Craven Cottage.

We were told to line up and that he was going to speak to us as he progressed through the room. I was at the front of the line with Ian Branfoot – and Al Fayed walked straight past us. Even when someone tried to introduce us, all I can remember him saying is: 'Where are my people? Where's my team?' He wandered presidentially onwards with barely a glance of recognition.

The press conference itself, however, was funny.

Someone asked him: 'How long have you been a football fan?'

'Oh, I've always been a fan.'

'Did you play football as a young boy?'

'Yes, I played football all the time as a young boy.'

'What position, Mr Al Fayed?'

'Captain...'

He was asked to name his favourite Fulham player. He didn't seem to have a clue.

Before that summer, we had been arguing with players over £10–15-a-week pay rises. All of a sudden, he arrived on the scene and that approach went flying out of the window. We signed a new kit deal with Adidas. Al Fayed proudly announced he wanted to be in the Premier League within five years. That was his main message at the press conference. And to go with it, the owner announced he wanted to tie me up on a long-term deal.

People thought I was on thousands. I wasn't doing badly: I was on £45,000-a-year, plus bonuses and my pension. It was a good wage, even though it's nothing compared to what is being paid nowadays. So the contracts were signed.

Next thing, Al Fayed has comes in to see me and says: 'Who do you want?'

Up until that point, all of my work had been in the lower leagues, scouting the likes of Gillingham, Charlton, Millwall, Brentford, trying to pick up players at bargain prices. Then, all of a sudden, they wanted me to make a bid for Ian Rush. I hadn't seen Liverpool's legendary striker play for a few years. Why would I have done? There was never the money to buy him without eating up my entire budget for the season, for a start. It was indicative of the fact that the situation had changed overnight.

I knew the players; I'd been on a journey with these lads. A few did stay, such as Matty Lawrence, Morgs, Sean Davis and Paul Brooker, but that summer I signed players such as Neil Smith from Gillingham and I spent £200,000 on taking Paul Moody from Southampton as Fulham Football Club struggled to get a grip on what was happening.

The club was in a state of flux as it tried desperately to come to terms with its status as a billionaire's plaything. We changed our kit. New club sponsors arrived. We appointed a press officer. From having nothing, we had everything. We had new dressing rooms and showers. The training ground was all spruced up.

My job as manager was under permanent speculation and almost every out-of-work coach around was being openly considered on a weekly basis. Kevin Keegan sat in the stands watching us play, denying he had been tapped up for the job with Ray 'Butch' Wilkins perched alongside him. You name it, whoever was out of a job was seemingly in the running.

One day, the press officer walked into my office and asked, 'Why didn't you tell me we are signing Ian Rush?'

I replied, 'Because we're not signing him, that's why. And when I need to tell you something, I'll tell you.'

There were so many people around the place. Whenever Al Fayed came, security were everywhere. You could always tell when he was coming because the number of bodies around the place rose dramatically.

I was called to Harrods to meet the owner. So there's me – and you've read my story this far – from a council house in rough part of Sheffield in the private office of one of the world's richest men in.

It was a case of: what do I nick first? I'm joking, obviously; he was more than helpful. My first words to him went something like this: 'Chairman, I appreciate what you are doing, but I need a bit of time. I've been working at the lower end of the Football League. I've only known about players at that level. When I sign a player, I need be sure he is the right one for us. I don't like taking recommendations – never have, never will.'

He just replied: 'I've got a South African goalkeeper for you – Andre Arendse. We're signing him.'

'Chairman, with the greatest of respect, I need to see this guy in action first.'

Fortunately for me, he was playing at Old Trafford for his country against England that week, so I went up there. He did all right. He didn't pull up any trees. At this stage, my loyalty was still to the group of players who had got us promoted and I was determined not to be dictated to by anyone.

That didn't matter. We signed Arendse, but, determined to stick to my guns, when I picked the first team of the season, Mark Walton was in goal.

Of course, the word suddenly comes down the line.

'Micky, chairman's not happy – why aren't you playing his man?'

Me being me, I just dug my heels in. It felt like a point of principle. I felt with a few additions, we could have had a go at real success, but I also wanted to stay loyal to the players who had stuck by me. Maybe it was the wrong policy. Maybe I should have seen the writing on the wall and accepted that if I didn't do it sooner, then I would be the one losing my job, because one way or the other, the chairman was going to get his way.

It was getting to me. I either had to do it my way – or not at all. I confronted Al Fayed. Well, I tried to. After a game one Saturday afternoon, I arranged to see him at Harrods on the Monday morning. I was going to have it out with him along the lines of: 'Back me or sack me.' I had made up my mind. It couldn't have kept going on the way things were. Despite the fact that we were only a few weeks into the season, I felt there had to be a resolution. I had decided that enough was enough. I'd said to Ian that I couldn't keep reading newspapers with my job on the line all the time.

But on the Saturday night, his son, Dodi, was killed with Princess Diana. I thought I'd never get the chance to have it out with him. Two days after his son's death, however, he said the meeting was still on. I turned up at Harrods, not knowing what the future would hold.

Nothing was resolved, unsurprisingly, and it was business as usual for a couple of weeks afterwards. Then, one morning, the press officer who used to come and see me didn't show up.

When he eventually showed his face at lunchtime, I asked him where he'd been. He said, 'The word on the street is that you are going to be sacked.' And, sure enough, half an hour later, I get a call from Ian saying we needed to get to the Muddymans' offices as quickly as possible. I asked why and he said, 'I think you need to brace yourself. We're both out.'

A few weeks previously, when I'd signed that five-year contract, they had said to me: 'You will be Fulham's answer to Alex Ferguson. We're going to go on a journey with you in charge – you'll be here for ever.' One month later, they sacked me.

I didn't take it well. I was aggressive. There wasn't much finesse in my language.

Ian, having been through the process before, was more diplomatic than me. They paid up my money. They told me that the boss wanted Kevin Keegan in the building. I wasn't playing the goalkeeper that the chairman wanted me to. I hadn't given the players the new kit. I asked what they were going to do about my contract and they insisted they were going to honour it.

When I returned twenty-four hours later, they handed over two cheques. One was for my pension and the other was for my cash, minus all the usual tax deductions. I came out with about £140,000 – miles off the £1 million pay-off it was reported I'd got.

I rang Corky straight away. I told him, 'Go and get some of that Adidas clobber out of the storeroom, I've just been sacked.' Unfortunately for me, however, as part of the upgrade to Craven Cottage, they'd installed CCTV around the place.

Kevin Moore, who had stepped down from playing, became the stadium officer. He sat there and watched Corky swipe a load of sweatshirts, tracksuits, socks, shorts; the lot.

Minutes later, the phone goes and it's a none-too-pleased Kevin demanding to know 'What do you pair of pricks think you're playing at?'

Corky asked what he was on about.

'I've just watched you steal a load of Adidas gear.'

I went home upset, disappointed and, not knowing it at the time, with a lot less confidence.

The final nail in the coffin came after the weekend. I had arranged to meet the lads on the Wednesday for a drink and they were all keen to go. Keegan came in on the Tuesday, however, and must have heard about our plan.

He rang me up and asked me to cancel it.

'No', was my obvious answer.

'Well, I'm going to ban them from going out with you. We need to prepare for a game.'

'Kevin, you do what you want, mate.'

They still came out for a drink. They were good lads and we had been on a long journey together.

• • •

A few months later, when I was at Swansea, I had cause to talk to my successor again after I rang him up about some players.

I distinctly remember him saying to me, 'Micky, can I say something? I don't get it. Your lads are fantastic. Great lads. I don't know if they are going to be good enough for what I want – but they are great lads. They work hard in training and matches. They are conscientious. They have a go. But I've got to tell you – your infrastructure … you've got no kit man, no scouting system…'

I stopped him in his tracks before he went any further.

'Listen, Kevin, can I just stop you there? Three months before Mr Al Fayed took over, we had fuck all. I was tossing a coin with Danny Cullip to put an extra £10-a-week on his contract. Head or tails for another tenner. So don't patronise me about the fact there's no kit man or this or that. We didn't have any money. Corky packed the kit. I did all the scouting. That's what happens at the lower end. That's what it's all about. So don't talk to me about infrastructure and all that shite.'

I got hundreds of letters from Fulham fans when I left. It's only now, looking back, that I can appreciate all the good wishes. Looking back, those years were probably among my best times in management – possibly in the game altogether. I'd put a group of lads together. The staff were good. But at the time, it was hard to see. I suppose my domestic situation wasn't good at the time, either. I wasn't spending any time at home. I had three daughters by this stage with Mandy, but our marriage was reaching the point of no return and I'd met Claire, who became my second wife.

I always say that Mr Al Fayed had a five-year plan. He wanted to get from A to B as quickly as he could. I had been working at the lower end of the leagues and I thought you could make your way through steadily, and Eddie Howe at Bournemouth has since proved that theory.

But in his eyes, the fastest way to get to the top was to appoint Kevin and the likes of Jean Tigana because they could attract bigger players. I was uncomfortable with having a dressing room where some lads were on £600-a-week and others were on £6,000-a-week. It didn't sit right with me. I'd have felt I was shitting on the £600-a-week lads.

I did see Mr Al Fayed again. I got a medal for winning promotion when I returned with Brentford and I was told he wanted to present it to me on the pitch before kick-off. I wasn't very happy about that, but I went through the motions – mainly for the fans because I hadn't had a chance to thank them for their support. That medal is now in a pub in Ballygar. I gave it to Paul Kenny who helped us out when we were struggling, so it feels right that it sits behind a bar in my favourite Irish village.

CHAPTER 9

SWANS AT SEA AND NO GRIFFIN (S)PARK

I had a large cheque to bank but no job. I was nursing a deep sense of grievance. As I mentioned, within twenty-four hours letters began arriving at my house, forwarded to me by the club. It is no exaggeration to say that I received well in excess of 100 and, having left several clubs since then, I know how rare it is to get that many. I responded to them all, one way or another.

I'd never been out of a job before. My personal life was unravelling at this time, too. I was with Mandy and the kids were still young. As I had alluded to earlier, I'd received a two-week driving ban. Since my work was in London and I lived in Southampton, my solicitor said there was a possibility of me getting off with a warning. So I stupidly I took my car to court, expecting to be driving home, but I had to get someone to pick it up. The ban meant I stayed at Corky's for two weeks, which is when I met Claire – and my life took a different turn.

So, I had all of this going on in the background. I didn't have an agent, so no one was out there working on my behalf. For a couple of weeks, it was all quiet, and then I received a call from Lenny Walker, who had been Ian Branfoot's assistant, who said he had a club who were interested in recruiting me. I asked who it was, but he said he wouldn't tell me until I turned up.

When I arrived at his house near Aldershot, the newly appointed chairman of Swansea City, Steve Hamer, was also there. The Swans had been Fulham's main rivals last season but their manager, Jan Molby, was still in a job and they hadn't started this one particularly well.

I wasn't too comfortable meeting Hamer, if I'm being honest; I'd be a hypocrite to say otherwise. I'd been on the end of it when Keegan and Wilkins took my job at Fulham. I sat and listened to him and realised he was selling Swansea to me. They'd offloaded a couple of their players and, as I say, hadn't started particularly well. They weren't happy with Jan. They were going to sack him and wondered if I'd take over.

Was I interested? I was an unemployed football manager. I was open to all offers.

They had big plans. They wanted a new training facility and stadium and they wanted it in a place called Morfa, which is where the Liberty Stadium is now.

I told them that, because Jan was in charge, there was little point continuing any dialogue. If he had been sacked, then we could have held a serious discussion. That was my stance because of what had happened to me. However, they continued to discuss their plan. I was told my money would be doubled and I could choose my own assistant and chief scout. They were still haggling a couple of weeks later.

What really attracted me to the offer was the fact they were going to build a new stadium and training ground, and in the meantime they promised £500,000 to add to the current budget. This meant I could add more players to a depleted squad. That was a significant sum at that level; it meant I could revitalise the squad. Eventually, it reached a point where they said, 'Right, we are sacking

Jan today; so if you're interested in the role, you have to come down here now.'

I remained loyal to those who had stood by me. Corky would come down as my assistant and Ian was pencilled in for the job as chief scout. Once Swansea said they were showing Jan the door, then the wheels could be set in motion.

However, Corky still had a job at Fulham. To be fair, Keegan quite liked him; so Corky says anyway, and he wasn't under pressure to come with me. But he was having his own personal issues at the time, so he was happy to throw in his lot as we plotted out our future in south-west Wales.

The first thing that hit me was how far away it was. Even driving down I had doubts because they still hadn't dealt properly with Jan. I was looking at the situation and thinking: 'Well, if they are going to treat him like that, how are they going to handle me if I don't get results?' I had no such problems with Bill and Andy Muddyman at Fulham. I knew them and they knew me. If they said they were going to do something, they did it.

They weren't an unknown quantity, but these people were. I know that Jan got the hump with me –he doesn't speak to me anymore. I can understand why, but they were going to sack him anyway. I insisted that they did it in the right way. Maybe the alarm bells should have been ringing, but they didn't.

I agreed terms, but nothing really happened. There wasn't any contract to sign. In hindsight, I should have realised things weren't quite as they should have been. The more pressing issue, for me and Corky at least, was where we were meant to be staying. The hotels wouldn't accept Swansea City's line of credit. Within the first five days of us being down there, we had stayed in five different places. The plan was for me and Corky to get a flat, but that never materialised.

What was worse was the state of the team. They were rubbish. Swansea has fervent support both home and away. They get behind their team, but this was a poor side. I remember the first training session. Corky turned to me and asked, 'Have you seen this lot play?' I replied that I hadn't. He continued, 'They are absolutely shite, by the way.' Having had a look at the squad, I have to say I agreed with him.

The problem was the better players had been asset-stripped. They'd gone and hadn't been replaced. Jan's philosophy was to play, and this was ingrained in the players. They were taking chances, passing it around at the back – only they weren't good enough to do it.

The squad needed an overhaul, so I got on to the board.

'When will you release the funds to improve the squad?' I asked. No reply.

'You've promised me this money, when can I spend it?' All I was met with were excuses. Phrases such as 'We can talk about that another time', but Swansea City needed players.

I got on to Keegan. They were my players he was working with anyway, and he didn't want some of them. They would be more than good enough for me. The only problem was I couldn't get my hands on any money. I started getting suspicious, so I came up with an ingenious solution; or what I thought was ingenious.

The conversation went something like this: 'Kevin, I know you want some players out. If I took them, could I defer the payment on their wages?' Since I was under the assumption that the funds would be released in the near future, I asked Fulham to pay their wages. Then, in three months' time, when we had the money, we would pay them back in full. I put it to Steve Hamer and the board that I had negotiated a deal with Fulham for three players to come in. They kept telling me the money was there. But their answer was 'No.' I told them I was getting players for nothing and asked what the problem was if the money was coming.

The alarm bells were clanging by now. We had played Exeter in the first match and lost narrowly. Then we faced Sam Allardyce's Notts County side. This was the season that Sam's mob absolutely tore up League Two, winning it by a canter before the end of March. But we managed to give them a really good game. The atmosphere was first-class and we lost it right at the death. We then played Mansfield midweek and lost it again by a single goal.

But I'd had enough by this stage. The management were just bullshitting. It all came to a head when we met Neil McClure, the club owner, after the game at the Vetch. There were rumours circulating already that I wasn't happy and that I was going to resign. I went into the meeting with him with an open mind. We had a drink and talked about how we saw it going forward.

He told me I couldn't bring in the three players from Fulham. I told him he had brought me here under false pretences: there was no £500,000. I asked where my contract was; why there were problems with the accommodation.

He told me that it all hinged on getting planning permission for Morfa. We went around in circles, going over the same ground, getting nowhere. Eventually, I said to him, 'What happens if Morfa doesn't get the green light?'

And he said to me – and this is the God's honest truth – 'If that happens, we turn off the lights and there is no Swansea City.'

I replied, 'If that's your thinking and if you think I'm going to bring players down here on that basis, then you can shove your job up your arse.'

He told me, 'You can't talk like that.'

'I fucking can. It's all smoke and mirrors. This is bullshit.'

'Look, you're just upset because you're losing games.'

'Too right I'm fucking upset. I'm a football manager and we are losing games. You are stopping me from doing my job. You promised I could sign players. We haven't. I've lined them up for nothing and you still won't let me sign them.'

I turned to Corky, who was in the meeting with me. 'Come on, this is over.'

The conversation ended with McClure asking me to sleep on it and we would have a chat again at the Vetch in the morning.

And that's what happened. We met up. I just said: 'I'm resigning.'

He said: 'No you're not. I'll give you another £25,000-a-year.'

I replied, 'I don't want the money. I've just been given money by Mr Al Fayed. I don't need the money. It's not what drives me. What turns me on is coming down here and doing a job but you are stopping me from doing it. So, for the last time, is there any money available?'

'No.'

'Well in that case, I'm out.'

'What are you going to do?'

'Well, there's a big mob of press boys outside. I'm going to walk out of this office, down the stairs, tell them I've resigned and why I've resigned. Then I'm going home.'

'What are you going to say?'

'That you've brought me down here under false pretences. You told me there was money for signings. There is no money for signings.'

He looked me straight in the eye and said; 'If you do that, I will make sure you never get another job in football.'

I replied: 'Do what you want; I'm still going.'

Halfway down the stairs, I thought about it. I didn't know if he was serious. I had to think about what I was going to say.

As I walked out, they asked to speak to Corky. When I was asked what had happened, I told them that I had resigned and that the job wasn't for me. I got in my car, headed for home. I really wanted to blow them out of the water. But, as I was driving along the M4, it occurred to me how strange it was that they wanted to speak to Corky as I was leaving. As I got towards the Severn Bridge toll, the phone rang. Corky was on the other end. 'You're not going to believe this, but they have given me the job.'

'They've done what?'

'They've given me the job. Gaffer, I came down with you, I left my job at Fulham for you. I can't say no because you know what my circumstances are.'

He got the job. He got the flat. They allowed him to bring in two new faces, Nick Cusack and Adrian Newhouse: two Fulham boys. To discredit me, they said I'd been tapped up for another job. They did a real assassination job on me. They fucked me over good and proper.

Their next game was against Doncaster, and they won it. Then they picked up a win in the derby against Cardiff City. I was quickly forgotten.

I didn't take a single penny out of Swansea City. Not a bean. I couldn't believe I had gone from one of the top up-and-coming managers to the debacle at Swansea. Talk about a rollercoaster ride, and I had a front-row seat. After being told I was going to be the next Alex Ferguson, I now had a black mark on my CV. And I was out of work. Again.

The scary thing was that if I hadn't had the Al Fayed money supporting me, I'd have stayed down there and swallowed all the lies. That money had at least given me some security and made it possible to walk out when I decided I wasn't going to be bullshitted any longer.

• • •

One Saturday soon afterwards, I went down the pub to watch the football results come in. The phone rang; it was David Webb, the ex-Chelsea defender. As a player he was as hard as nails, and he was to become the owner of Brentford. He was certainly the decision maker at the time and he sounded me out. Could I go and meet him?

So I met him in a London hotel. They'd sacked their manager. Would I be interested? Rivals of Fulham, same division, struggling team… Dave made it quite clear they were looking to sell the club. There was no hidden agenda.

The job on offer was two-fold: to keep them in the league and reduce the wage bill to make the club more attractive to prospective buyers. With regard to the budget, it was a balancing act. David was great with figures as well as being a scary man. I could tell he was tough. We all remember the Leeds *v.* Chelsea FA Cup final. It was a classic match of its time; classic violence, anyway. He was at the heart of it. It wasn't an act, let me tell you.

I decided to accept the job on a six-month rolling contract, which basically meant I got six months' money if they sacked me and there was six months' compensation if someone wanted me. Obviously, I didn't have Corky to call upon as he was managing Swansea. So I turned to my old pal from Southampton, the Rod Stewart look-alike Glenn Cockerill, to be player-coach. I didn't know any of the staff, but there to greet me was Kevin Locke, the old Fulham legend, who was Dave 'Webby' Webb's mate, really. Initially, I had my reservations be-cause I didn't know if he would be reporting everything back.

Bobby Booker was looking after the Under-18s and there was also a lad there called Kevin Burke who was a groundsman and physio. It was a really friendly and down-to-earth club. At Fulham, I wasn't sure about some people or what their motivations were, but there were no such misgivings at Brentford. There was Bob Lampitt who had been in accounts for years, Lisa Hall who is now the club secretary and Peter Gilham who was the stadium announcer … they were all solid individ-uals who wanted me to do well.

I remember going around Griffin Park and taking a look. I went into the dressing room and there were two camp beds in there. I asked Bob what was going on. 'When there's a night game, we stay over', came the reply. Bob and Kevin used to kip at the ground because they would have to be back early doors. That was the level of loyalty and commitment they offered!

On my first day, Glenn turned up in leopard-skin winklepickers and had his shirt unbuttoned almost to his navel, looking more like Rod Stewart than Rod himself! That day was also when I met Bob Booker for the first time. He has since become one of my best mates. He is one of the most loyal and trustworthy friends I have ever known. He would do anything for you.

I remember taking my first session. I was doing possession work in a grid. Unfortunately, Ijah Anderson broke his leg, so I was a left-back down before we even got started.

The first game was against Northampton, who was managed by Ian Atkins. His teams were always big, strong and physical, and played to a pattern. It was a tough one; they were horrible to play against. If he could get eleven six-footers in his team, he would. They would hit the channels, work off set-pieces.

We were four-down at half-time. Our keeper was a lad called Kevin Dearden and he was 5 ft 10in. tall. Ian, being Ian, had surrounded Dearden with an arc of three or four players all over six foot. They swung the ball in and scored three times from the corner. That was the result settled.

I turned to Bob Booker and asked, 'Where's my goalkeeper? I can't see him!' However hard Kevin tried to jump up and down, he couldn't make himself seen. All I could see of him were his pair of gloves. I remember going in at half-time and asking, 'What do you want me to say to you? What words of wisdom do I have to produce to turn this one around?'

It was at this point that I decided, once and for all, to hang up my boots following a particularly forgettable match in the Johnstone's Paint Trophy. My game had always been based on fitness and hard work. I was a hod carrier, wasn't I? A grafter for the good players. I could get around the pitch.

When I wasn't able to do as well as I thought I should be able to, I decided to concentrate on football management. I played for Brentford but I just didn't have the legs anymore. There were days and games when, honestly, I didn't feel physically right. I think I was dehydrated. It was an easy decision to pack in. I think, looking back, I made the best of what I had.

With modern science and the way things are done now, I think I'd have been better. We didn't know about the real impact of alcohol back then. We lived from game to game. We won, we went out. We drew or lost – we still went out. If we didn't have a midweek game on a Tuesday, we would go out on Sunday lunchtime. It was just the culture. I didn't have enough fluids inside me. That's why I say with modern techniques, I would have been better. Nutrition, rehydration, ice-baths, technology – we had none of that.

Hard work never goes out of fashion. I would have always earned a living. Perhaps I'm being overly critical because when I was doing well – and I'm talking about when I was in the Premier League – I was a good player. There was talk of Manchester United being interested. Tottenham was following me when I was at Gillingham. Then Peter Taylor tore me to pieces and that was the end of that!

When the time came, I was happy enough with what I'd done. I'd contributed and played in the top-flight. If you'd said to me as a teenager coming from an estate in Sheffield that I would end up as a Premier League player I'd have said, 'Thanks very much, I'll take that.'

While I've criticised my dad for some aspects of my upbringing, he did give me that drive and determination to succeed. I was tough mentally, as a player; perhaps not so much as a manager. As you'll see as my managerial career unfolds, I didn't have enough confidence in my skills as I did when I was playing.

A lot of it was bluff, management. You can't bluff your way through games as a player. I think it was Keith Houchen at Coventry who criticised me in his book, saying I was a sulker. I'm going to disagree with that. I wasn't happy when I wasn't playing. Why should I have been? I wasn't sulking, though. When Monday morning came around, I'd be bang at it again. I was able to compartmentalise and say to myself, 'Right, last Saturday has gone. I need to get back in that side.' I would argue strongly that my own personal issues never impacted the group. There was no negativity from me to disrupt the spirit in the dressing room. But if you are growling and letting people know you're not happy on the training ground, surely that's just showing people you care.

I didn't want people patting me on the back and patronising me. If I wasn't good enough, then I was going to try and be better. If I had a problem, then I needed to sort it. I'm old-school in that regard. Sometimes that led to confrontations. I wasn't going to shy away from that. My game was built on pace, work-rate and, once you're over the age of thirty and you don't have a trick as a wide man, you've got a problem.

I can't apologise for being unhappy when I wasn't playing. Let me tell you, having been on the other side of the fence as a manager in the modern era, I would have loved to see more of that attitude from players who were sitting on million-pound-a-year contracts. I don't see it enough now. You have to tread on eggshells around the modern player.

I was more than happy with my career, despite the injuries. The shoulder injury I sustained when I booted Neil Smillie up in the air meant I lost a lot of confidence. I didn't want my shoulder to come out again and that, psychologically, stopped me in my tracks when I went to tackle people. It was bloody painful, let me tell you.

However, all of that is now in the past. At this point, I knew I was going to either stand or fall by my decisions as a manager. As far as that was concerned, I'd gone from being a manager the year who had won promotion to fighting a relegation battle while trying to balance the books.

Brentford had a big squad with players who weren't good enough. We needed to change. I signed Danny Cullip and Paul Watson who were a couple of the Fulham boys, who, let's just say, didn't hit the ground running. They took their time to settle in and there was added pressure on them to achieve considering they came from Brentford's closest rivals.

I also recruited former Manchester United centre-half Graeme Hogg which turned out to be one of the funniest signings ever. We didn't have any digs for him, so he stayed with a youth team player whose mum put him up. She had put other youth team players up before, but never fully fledged professionals like Graeme.

One day, not long after he arrived, we received a call. He had bought a new pair of boots and had worn them in the bath to mould them to his feet – only he'd scratched the new bath. So we apologised and agreed to foot the bill for a replacement. Days later, we get another call saying that he had been smoking in his room and had left a fag burn on one of the tables. We just about smoothed this over.

But the final straw came after he had arrived back to the house after having a few drinks with a big bar of Dairy Milk. Being a generous sort, Hoggy decided that the family dog would benefit from sharing some of his chocolate. Anyone who owns dogs will tell you that chocolate is the one food you cannot give them. Clearly, Brentford's new signing didn't know this, and their pet Doberman promptly collapsed!

So, as you can imagine, we had to get him out of there pretty sharpish. It was just after this episode when it started going wrong at Brentford. We went on a four-game unbeaten run, but they were all draws – and that was to prove to be the story of the season. I wanted players out. I was trying to get people in. The team wasn't that good.

By this stage, after taking a look at the squad, I had an idea of what work needed to be done. There was a big problem with the captain, Jamie Bates. He was a centre-half and was immaculately turned out. Bob Booker swore by this fella saying he could get 100 per cent out of him. He was tanned, smartly dressed; carried himself well. Looked a million dollars.

But, as soon as training was finished, he was off and away. No hanging around. We got to the end of the season and his form tailed off dramatically. I should have left him out, but I was clinging on to the fact he's an all-round good guy – a leader – and I needed people I could rely upon. The season finale at Bristol Rovers was a game that will live in my memory for ever. Our relegation fight was going to the wire. It was either us or them. We needed a draw, they needed a win.

It was a packed house at the Memorial Ground and Jamie Bates was having one of the biggest nightmares I had ever seen. To describe him as awful would be doing him a favour. At the interval I found myself saying to him, 'Jamie, if I didn't know any better I would swear you are trying to get me the sack.'

'Nah, gaffer,' he says. 'No way.'

Five minutes into the second half, nothing had changed. He was having a torrid time. I was fed up with him; I wanted him off the pitch. We lost the game 2–1. It was a massive disappointment and I was looking over my shoulder, afraid for my job. I had a meeting planned in London on the Sunday afternoon. I felt confident I could get the team back up the following season.

At 8 a.m., I was just about to leave for this summit and my phone rang.

'Gaffer, it's Jamie,' he said. 'Have you got a newspaper today?'

'No, I've not been out yet.'

'Well, I suggest you go and buy the *News of the World*. I need to see you when you get to London.'

I left and picked up a copy of the paper en route.

The headline read: 'Soccer club skipper sells missus for sex.'

Allegedly, three months previously, he was in a sauna with his missus and punters were coming in. She was apparently offering various sexual favours, while he was looking on.

When I met up with him, he insisted, 'It wasn't like it said in the papers.'

There wasn't much I could reply to that, apart from, 'Fuck off, Jamie.'

So, we were relegated. The problem was there were too many draws. We didn't win enough matches, we weren't competitive enough. In the last ten games for instance, we won four, drew three and lost three. That's mid-table form. I even won an award for manager of the month award.

When I took over, we had nineteen points from seventeen matches. If I'd had the whole season, over the last twenty-seven games we would have earned enough points to stay up. In the end, we drew seventeen matches which is a staggering amount. But that was our main issue: we couldn't get victories.

I was left in limbo at the end of the season. Webby was not happy. He wasn't happy with what we had done. The club was still up for sale. We couldn't sign anyone until we knew what was happening. We couldn't organise pre-season. It was frustrating. I remember ringing him up and asking how to go about things.

He said I'd got the club relegated and, until the club was sold, I was to do nothing in terms of recruitment. I was to sit on my hands. He also said that I was lucky he didn't come round and beat the shit out of me. It was at this point, on the advice of the chairman, I decided it was time to go on holiday.

While I was away, I read that Ron Noades had taken control of Brentford FC and he was going to be the manager with Ray Lewington as his coach. Bear in mind at this time I was still the manager of Brentford FC. Two days before I returned home, I received a call from the club informing me I had a meeting with Noades at 10 a.m. on Friday, a couple of days later.

I decided to get in early at 9 a.m. I knew he wasn't there because I had the keys to the manager's office. I thought to myself: 'What's the best way of pissing this bloke off?'

So I unlocked the door, went into his office and put my feet up on his desk. He walked in. He hadn't been tipped off I was there and he was very surprised to see me.

I stood up, offered my hand and said, 'Hello Mr Noades, very nice to meet you.'

But he didn't want a conversation with me – he was going to sack me. The last thing he wanted was a convivial chat about my holiday. 'You know why you're here, don't you?' he said.

'Sorry, no. I've been away. I've tried to relax and switch off.'

'Well, I've bought the football club and I'm going to be the manager.'

'What a great idea Mr Noades – two managers.'

'No, no, no. I'm going to be the manager, and you're out of here.'

'Oh, that's a surprise. You know what's in my contract. What are you going to do about that?'

'Well, we'll sort it out now.'

At Brentford, you were paid monthly. I was due to be paid that month's money the week I had returned from holiday. Unbeknown to me, he had told the accounts people not to pay me. I had no idea. I thought I'd been paid and I hadn't been. Ron knew full well he had done me over. I thought I was going in there to argue the toss over six months' money and that we'd eventually settle. He wasn't generous but he did it the right way – having done me for a month. When I realised, I rang him back but he wasn't having any of it. I learnt a lesson there. I should have let others take care of it.

It had been twelve months to forget about. I'd had a shocker. My stock went from so high to so low in such a short space of time. Apart from the obvious lesson about the contract, I also learnt that when clubs change managers halfway through any season and they get relegated, it's not the lad who kicked off the campaign who gets the end of it; the manager at the end is stuck with the blame. I left Brentford after nineteen games. Was it long enough to turn it around? I don't know, because it was obvious when I walked in that the team wasn't good enough. My Brentford team had a go.

If I said I was low when I walked away from Brentford, then I was lower than the proverbial snake's belly. I'd had three jobs and I'd been sacked from two of them. I was at Swansea for ten days and that was a tale of broken promises. I felt guilty about Jan Molby – and I still do. But Ray Lewington and Ron Noades didn't give a fuck about me, nor did Kevin Keegan or Ray Wilkins. To say I was disillusioned was an understatement. Everything was getting on top of me. My personal life wasn't in a much better state, either.

Claire had had enough of the situation with Mandy and she said, 'Enough's enough.' I decided to tell Mandy what was going on. So, all in all, the summer of '98 was one to forget.

At this stage, I was thinking to myself: 'What do I do now?'

And my salvation came from an unexpected place.

CHAPTER 10

THE FOREST'S AFIRE WITH HARRY AND BIG RON

I didn't know Dave Bassett; I'd never spoken to him before. I'd never come across him during a game, either. But, as luck would have it Bassett, in charge of newly promoted Nottingham Forest, rang Corky looking for an assistant. He liked the idea of taking someone young under his wing who could relate to the players better than he could. Of course, I hadn't long finished playing myself and I was still reasonably fit, so I went to the City Ground to speak to him and suddenly found myself in the Premier League with the top-flight's new boys.

From being out of work I was now looking forward to facing Arsenal at Highbury on the opening day of the Premier League season. Football's fickle finger of fate, eh?

When I turned up, Mick Kelly was Dave's assistant but in reality, he was the coach. He was a really strong character, Mick. Probably the best goalkeeping coach I've seen. However, this particular season his responsibilities included coaching the outfield players as well.

Nottingham Forest was not a happy football club, despite it being elevated to the top-flight just a month or so prior to my arrival. It was the summer in which Pierre van Hooijdonk refused to come back to the club, saying it lacked ambition. The striker did not complete any pre-season training, so there were issues when I walked in on my first day.

Since Mick was the coach, it was my job to warm up the players. We didn't have fitness coaches in those days, so that was down to me, too. I used to warm them up every morning. I was fit at the time, so it wasn't a problem. I never gave them anything to do that I couldn't do myself.

Mick had given me a possession game to get the lads working. My first passing drill was with the likes of Chris Bart-Williams, who was mucking about, Kevin Campbell and a few others. They weren't really listening to me on that opening day. Their idea was to see how far they could go, how far they could push me and what, if anything, I was going to do about it.

By this time, I had been a manager myself. I knew what was going on, and I wasn't standing for it – so I stopped the session.

'Listen, lads, you don't know me, but you are going to get to know me and but I don't care if I'm here all day. It's up to you. I know you've got kids to pick up from school and people you want to meet. You'll all want to go home at some stage. But – and listen to me carefully – I don't care if we are here all night. If you don't get this right, we will put the balls away and I'll run you. We either get this right – or you'll be staying all day. So, let's go again.'

They soon got the message that I was serious. I liked a laugh and a joke but there was a line, and they needed to know when it was crossed.

• • •

Forest's pre-season tour that year was taking place in Finland.

Dave Bassett, or 'Harry' as he was known, was making his own way home to Sheffield, so it was left to me and Mick to take the boys back.

We'd had a good trip. They were a boisterous set but there were some good lads in there as well. One of the more vocal characters was Alan 'Tank' Rogers, a stocky little left-back. A good lad, but as mad as a hatter. Anyway, we were both travelling back with the team but Mick wanted nothing to do with them. 'Come on,' he said. 'We're going up the back, away from that lot.'

So we took our seats. You could hear them at the front; they were a bit rowdy and noisy but nothing out of order. The plane was packed but no one had complained. We were an hour or so into the journey when all of a sudden, the intercom went off, followed by the words: [Bing bong]. 'Brace, brace. We're going to crash. Brace, brace.'

Everyone started screaming, kids were crying. It was bedlam. The plane was in uproar. But, when I looked up and saw Rogers nipping into the toilet, Mick caught my eye and said: 'That was Rogers.'

Everyone knew who it was. Rogers had been watching the steward-esses make their safety announcements and thought he'd have a bit of fun. You wouldn't have said it was fun if you had seen the reaction of all those on board. I saw the stewardess make a beeline for Rogers the minute he came out of the toilet.

Thirty seconds later, the intercom went again. [Bing bong] 'Whoev-er is in charge of the Nottingham Forest party would they please make themselves known to the nearest member of the cabin crew.'

Mick nudged me in the ribs. 'That's you, off you go.'

'Fuck off Mick. You're the real assistant manager. I'm only the assistant manager on paper. You organise everything, you're the senior man.'

'No, no, son, you are the assistant manager.'

The intercom went again.

[Bing bong]. 'Will whoever is in charge of the Nottingham Forest party please make themselves known to a member of the cabin crew as a matter of urgency.'

I pressed the button above my seat. The eyes of the entire plane were now staring at me. Kids were still crying. The stewardess came over. 'That was one of your party', she announced.

'Oh, was it?' came my reply.

'That one there, we're going to report him.'

'OK, well, listen, if it was one of our party, I can only apologise for what he has done.'

It's at this moment I realised we had Mr Korn, the club chairman, on the plane as well. I thought to myself, the balloon is going to go up after this one. When we eventually piled off the plane and made our way onto the transfer bus, the chairman made his way over to the players. He pulled Rogers aside and told him: 'I've been away with Nottingham Forest for thirty years. I have never felt as humiliated as I do right at this moment. You are an absolute disgrace.'

We were expecting the police to be greeting us at East Midlands Airport. For some reason, the airline didn't call security, but we were banned from travelling with that particular company for years.

That was a pleasant task, explaining that episode to Harry. Needless to say, Rogers was fined two weeks' wages for his moment of madness.

He was always in the thick of it. Later that season Mick and I took the team to Portugal for warm-weather training and there was another incident. But this time, we staff got our own back.

We were having dinner at the hotel and Mick and I were talking when, out of the corner of my eye, I saw Rogers steal my colleague's room key. I tapped his leg. 'Mick, I've just seen Rogers grab your key.'

As soon as Rogers was out of earshot he whispered, cool as you like: 'Just leave it a couple of minutes, son.'

Clearly, what Nottingham Forest's left-back was planning to do was head upstairs to Mick's room, trash it and then retire to the sanctuary of his own bedroom with his partners-in-crime, as if butter wouldn't melt.

A few moments later Mick said cheerfully, 'Come with me.' We headed upstairs.

There, caught in the act were Rogers, Ian Woan and a few others busy tying together the arms of Mick's tracksuits, pulling the curtains down, unplugging the television, throwing the bed against the wall. The usual stuff. Only this time, they were caught red-handed.

Mick, our resident Cockney, threw the door wide open. 'Oi, you little shits, what the fack do you think you're playing at? Get out of my facking room. I'll see you in the morning…'

They had trashed the room and Mick's clothes but hadn't caused any damage; he'd got to them just in time. The next morning, he called a team meeting. His speech went something like this: 'Right, last night, you, you, you and you were in my room. Do you know what you have done? Forget my gear – just forget my facking gear for a moment – you've only gone and broken the bed. And the hotel is not very happy about it.

'They want £1,500 for it, so I want the cash in my hand because I have to pay the hotel £1,500. Don't give me any bollocks about not having any money. Get me that money. You think it's funny do you? You can all take two weeks' wages as well. Get me that facking money in my hand by tonight.'

I stood quietly, watching and listening to his rant. Unbeknown to the players, there was actually nothing wrong with the bed.

We went out to training: a double session. At the end of the day Alan Rogers walked over, apologised and handed over £1,500. They all went to bed. Mick made sure the boys had all left before he then turned to me and the other members of staff on the trip and promptly started counting out the money into our hands, laughing.

'One for you, one for you, one for me … happy days!'

Rogers didn't know about it for years afterwards.

All jokes aside, that season didn't get off to a good start. Van Hooij-donk failed to return to the club as he was on strike and we had to sell Kevin Campbell to Trabzonspor in Turkey for £2.7 million. Their goals had been largely responsible for lifting the club out of the Champion-ship the previous season. Forest lost over forty goals at a stroke.

We brought in Nigel Quashie, Neil Shipperley, Andy Gray, Dougie Freedman and Jean-Claude Darcheville. They weren't proper replace-ments at that level, but it was difficult for the club because the situation with the stroppy Dutch striker could have gone either way.

Apart from warming up the starters and subs, I used to run the lads who hadn't played after games. I was the link between the dressing room and management. They just weren't winning games; they couldn't score enough goals.

Pierre's gripe was that the club wasn't showing any ambition, but it shouldn't have been his problem. That side of it has nothing to do with any player. It's for the board to decide who the club brings in. It's the job of the footballer to play to the best of his ability. You can't have players dictating to managers who they do and don't sign. However, van Hooijdonk had withdrawn his labour and gone on strike. When he eventually came back, he took part in sessions but it didn't take long to work him out. He was only happy when he was moaning, and he wasn't having Mick Kelly at all. As I've said, Mick, in my opinion, was the best goalkeeping coach I have ever seen.

Van Hooijdonk used to ask, 'What's he trying to teach me?' He felt Mick, being an ex-goal keeper, was not qualified to advise him on his position. However, it didn't matter who was taking the session; it seemed nothing was good enough for van Hooijdonk. He would com-plain about the size of the pitch. If it was too big, we would cut the sides down for the following day's training. He would then moan it was too small. There was no pleasing him.

It got to a stage where Harry and Mick pulled me aside regularly and said, 'Micky, take him away', because he was such a negative influence. My job then was to get a bag of balls and borrow a keeper and allow him to take his free-kicks from the edge of the box.

I used to wind him up saying things like: 'I scored a great goal at Stevenage once.'

He'd look at me and go, 'Stevenage? Where's that?'

I would bat it back and explain that 'a goal is a goal wherever it's scored'. I wanted to gee him up, but he was hard work. Eventually, it got to a stage where I became a confidante for him. I'd report what I could back to Harry and other parts I'd keep quiet about. It was difficult, no question about it.

Harry had the headache of the rest of the lads in his ear. They were pissed off because the club's leading light had left them in the lurch while they were the ones having to make good of it every week on the pitch. As soon as Pierre walked through the door, they would soon shut up. I don't think any of them had a pop at him. The only one who did was goalkeeper Mark 'Big Norm' Crossley. It wasn't in fact anything to do with the fact he'd gone on strike; apparently, Norm and his missus were in a restaurant when Pierre walked in with his wife. Anyway, Norm was blanked. He wasn't too happy and pulled his team-mate up about it. As for the rest of them, it might have been a lively dressing room but not one of them had the balls to stand up to Pierre and tell him his behaviour had been a disgrace.

Forest had a sprinkling of good players but not enough to keep them in the division. It didn't help that there were differences of opinion between Harry and Mick. They enjoyed a good relationship, but, occasionally, the manager would pull me to one side and urge me to get in early tomorrow and tell Mick we're doing such-and-such.

Funnily enough, it didn't matter how early I arrived at the City

Ground; Mick was always already there, writing down what we were going to do on the chalkboard. It would then be down to me to break the bad news to him.

'Er, Mick I've had a call from Harry. He wants to do such-and-such this morning.'

The response would be along the lines of 'Oh, for fack's sake. What's he facking want?'

'He wants to do some defensive shape.'

'Defensive shape? We can't score a facking goal. I've written it all up on the facking board, I've been here for facking hours...'

There used to be hell on. Harry knew full well what he was doing. I was just the fall guy.

'It's all right for facking Harry,' said Mick. 'He facking comes in at ten past ten. I've been here since seven sorting it all out.'

There wasn't any real animosity between them, but I was definitely piggy-in-the-middle at times.

For example, after we'd lost on the Saturday around Christmas, Mick wanted to do a session with wingers coming off the line, playing through the thirds or whatever. But Harry wanted them to go on a run around Holme Pierrepont, the country park where the national water sports centre now is.

Mick had gone off on one when he was told Harry wanted them to go for this run. Harry was nowhere to be seen. I took the squad up to the lake and I ran it with them. We had members of staff dotted around the place to make sure they couldn't cheat. I had a game getting Darcheville to run it.

'Micky, why are we always running after a game. It's running, running, running. Why do we always run?'

'Listen, Jean-Claude, I'm doing the run with you. It can't be that hard. So, get on and do it.'

Anyway, as I started to go round the lake, I looked across the water and saw the big striker running in the wrong direction. He was doing it on purpose.

'Oi, you fucker – you're going the wrong way.'

He eventually turned up about two hours after everyone else. Not a major surprise I guess, since he was going in the wrong direction.

We were struggling and rumours were doing the rounds that Harry was on borrowed time, despite the fact he'd got them promoted from the Championship. We were driving up to Blackburn Rovers on a scouting job when I received a call from Dave Kidd from *The Sun* tipping me the wink that Harry was going to be sacked and that I was going to be placed in temporary charge.

He asked me: 'Have you heard anything?' And Harry was sitting in the car next to me. Harry asked me what was going on, so I told him. He went quiet for a moment and said, 'Well, I'd better chase that up.' We still went to the game and went through the motions, but the rumour turned out to be true.

I was devastated. I'd built up a good relationship with Harry and I felt sorry for him. I don't think he was necessarily the best coach, but the situation was out of his control. He was more than competent and was a very good motivator, very good in the dressing room. That was where his real strength lay.

I think he was frustrated at Forest that year because of Mick's involvement. That's not to say he was intimidated, but perhaps he wanted to be more hands-on. As the relationship developed I think he found it more difficult to shove Mick aside, and the van Hooijdonk debacle was destabilising. It was a story every day.

My initial reaction was that I didn't want to be there. I was frustrated because I wanted to do more but my role was to try and take the pressure off Harry as best I could. If he said jump, I would.

I did the job I was told to do. That's the way it is when you are an assistant.

Harry's advice to me was, 'Sit tight, see what happens. Don't do anything daft.'

A call came through from Irving Scholar, who was the owner at the time. He asked me to take training and told me I'd be in charge for the next game at Coventry. Van Hooijdonk wasn't in the side at that time, Harry wasn't entertaining him at all.

I spoke to my former colleague about the situation and asked what I should do. He said: 'Get them organised and do what you think you need to.' I picked his brain, worked all week and gave Craig Doig, one of the youth team players, his debut. We started all right and I brought Pierre back, but we were hammered, losing 4–0.

Immediately afterwards I was told that Ron Atkinson was coming in with Peter Shreeves as his assistant, so within minutes of the final whistle the writing was on the wall for me. People like Steve Stone, Steve Chettle and Ian Woan had said some kind words in the media but I wasn't getting anywhere near the job. The powers that be had made up their minds.

I have to say, Ron was a different class; everything I thought he would be. He was funny, flamboyant and a great motivator. I remember his first morning vividly. All my time prior to this had been structured. Mick Kelly, Dave Bassett's assistant, had set everything up, whereas Ron was more off the cuff about things.

The first thing he did was to clear the staff out of the referees' room. There were about eight of us: me, Liam O'Kane, the physios, kit men etc. That's where we all showered and changed, but we suddenly found ourselves relegated to a small kit room around the corner. I asked why.

'Boys,' Mick said. 'Ron is a private person.'

'What do you mean, he's a private person?'

'Well, he doesn't want anyone in the changing room apart from me and him.'

We thought it was strange, but followed the new rules.

Training itself was all short, sharp stuff. Shreevesy himself was a decent coach. The pair of them, it seemed to me, had a successful career in the game by keeping the players happy by giving them what they wanted. They jollied them along and didn't really upset any of them. Mick Kelly was involved more with what had happened on the Saturday and structured the sessions around faults with a view to eradicating them.

It all went OK. Pete said there was going to be a meeting in one of the dressing rooms at the club at 1.30 p.m. and everyone was due to be there. Big Ron went into his room. Shreevesy went with him. However, someone had nicked Ron's hairdryer and he refused to come out of his room. He wouldn't come out until Carol, who was the manager's secretary and had looked after the late, great Brian Clough back in the day, made her way into Nottingham city centre to buy him a new one.

The other rumour doing the rounds was that he used to carry a man-bag around with him, years before they became fashionable. No one dared look in it because there were suspicions he was carrying around his wig in it. Now, I'm not saying he wears one. I wouldn't be that disrespectful, but that was the talk at the time...

Anyway, he called a meeting for 1.30 p.m. By 3 p.m., he was still nowhere to be seen. Eventually, he came out – looking immaculate – suit on, carrying his man-bag. He gave a speech that I'd heard before and probably most of the players had already heard, too. It began along the lines of, 'You start off with a clean slate, not interested in what's gone on before, work hard, get some results.' It was pretty much the standard fare. Once the meeting had finished, I went to speak with him. I was Dave Bassett's man and so I felt an enormous sense of loyalty to Dave. I told him I wanted to leave and I shouldn't still be there when he wasn't. But Ron didn't want me to go.

He said, 'Listen Micky, I've heard a lot about you and I want you to stay and work with me and Peter.'

Ron told me I had to get on with it. I spoke to Dave, and he told me to get my head down and see what happened. Steve Stone wrote an article in the *Nottingham Evening Post* saying I was the man for the job, although it didn't feel like that after we had four smashed past us at Coventry.

After that, we had a decent week, but one thing I learnt was that Ron wasn't a coach. He said after one game, 'Right, I'm doing a session on defending crosses.' He had been going on about fifteen minutes and not one cross had gone in. Ron just didn't know how to move it on from a coaching perspective. What was clearly needed was some sort of overload: a two versus one situation out wide to create a cross. Anyway, after thirty minutes he finished the session with all the players wondering what the hell was going on.

Then we had our first game: Arsenal at the City Ground. It's famous for one very specific incident. We dropped the cars off, had a pre-match meal at a hotel in Nottingham and then it was over to Ron for his pre-match team talk. He was absolutely brilliant. He made everyone feel ten foot tall. I actually fancied playing after listening to him. There wasn't much organisation during the week but on game day he was ready for it. Ron was similar to Harry in that respect. Anyway, we got on the bus to the ground and there was a bit of a fanfare. The fans were up for it; Arsenal were in town. I warmed up the lads.

Big Ron came down the tunnel, fifty cameras on him. He strolled down the tunnel, enjoying the moment, waving to all four stands… but then he started walking past our dug-out where and Shreevesy and I were standing.

I nudged Pete. 'Where the fuck is he going?'

I shouted after him. 'Ron! Gaffer! Gaffer, gaffer...'

Pete joined in with the shouting, but Ron carried on, totally oblivious. I thought he must have been going to shake hands with Arsene Wenger. Only he didn't approach Wenger at all. Instead, he stepped into the away team's dug-out and, all of a sudden, he turned to his right and was looking straight at Arsenal's substitutes.

The footage of this bizarre incident can be found on YouTube. He did a double-take before the realisation of what he had done slowly crept across his face. He then had to walk back to his own dug-out with all the fans laughing, and promptly sat down.

He turned to me and Pete and said, 'I looked at the substitutes and thought "how can we be bottom of the league with these substitutes...?"'

We fell about laughing. But the positive vibe of the occasion didn't translate to much on the pitch. We were a goal down early on and finished the game losing 1–0.

It didn't matter what Ron said and how well he motivated them, the simple fact was the team weren't good enough. He signed Carlton Palmer – not shy in the least, was Carlton – and even that wasn't straightforward. Ron called a meeting with the players for Carlton's introduction. Everyone was in the home dressing room, waiting for the manager.

Shreevesy had counted all the lads in and reported to the boss that they were all present and correct. Ron entered, followed by Shreevesy, Liam O'Kane and me. He shut the door.

The manager had control of the room and he started to address the lads. Meanwhile, I surveyed the room, and I noticed an unfamiliar face staring back at me. I thought to myself, 'Who's that? He's not one of ours.' I decided not to say anything, though, because drawing attention to it would have landed Shreevesy in trouble.

While I was mulling over my next move, Ron spotted him. 'Who the fuck are you?' he shouted in astonishment at the man in question.

This fella just sat there – only now he was dying of embarrassment. The rest of us, bar Ron, were dying to laugh.

'Er, sorry,' he stammered, 'I'm Carlton Palmer's driver ... aren't I, Carlton?'

The former England international nodded his head. He knew he was going to kop it from the rest of us – and his boss.

Ron pointed at the hapless driver and shouted: 'You – piss off.'

I guess Carlton had been banned from driving for whatever reason. Wherever this driver was supposed to be, the home dressing room most definitely wasn't it. Ron couldn't believe what he had witnessed – and Shreevesy received a bollocking for allowing him in there in the first place.

That was Forest; there was always something going on.

Another change Ron insisted upon was dressing in suits on match days. Looking back, I'm sure one of his mates must have had an outfitter's. We were all given a suit, but we found out later that we had been clobbered for it and got charged for receiving one on our P11Ds at the end of the season.

But Ron was clever, particularly with van Hooijdonk, for instance. There was no love lost between van Hooijdonk, Dave Bassett and Mike Kelly. In a nutshell, they hated each other. Ron, however, had a way of talking to him that belittled him but also had the effect of giving him confidence as well.

He immediately gave van Hooijdonk a nickname. He said the Dutch striker was 'the pinch-hitter'. I didn't know what he was referring to at first, but apparently, in baseball it refers to the man most likely to score a home run when all the bases are loaded. If he scored, everyone could run round and the pinch-hitter grabbed the glory, scoring four runs instead of just the one.

Pierre would ask, 'Why are you disrespectful to me like that?' And Ron would say, 'Well, anyone can score from set-pieces and free-kicks.'

It used to get Pierre's back up but that was Ron's way of dealing with it. He didn't blank him or fall out with him. He just brought him back down to earth with a serious bang.

Anyway, we lost that first match against Arsenal. Then we went away to Everton and returned with a victory. Our next match was against Manchester United at home, in what turned out to be one of the most extraordinary games I've ever been involved in.

Dwight Yorke and Andy Cole scored early on but we managed to pull a goal back. We were 2–1 down at half-time. Ron walked into the dressing room to give one of the most inspirational team-talks I've ever heard. 'Listen,' he explained. 'We can beat these. They aren't that special. They just think they are. Let's start the second half well. We can win this game. I'm telling you now.' Again, I left that changing room thinking anything was possible. I must be a soft touch for Ron's team talks.

Within twenty minutes, Cole and Yorke scored again.

And then Yorke was then substituted and Ole Gunnar Solskjær took his place. That change, believe it or not, was greeted with shouts of, 'That's a result, that is,' among us on the bench. A quarter of an hour later, however, the Norwegian had scored four. In the eightieth, eighty-seventh, the last minute and injury time. We lost 8–1.

How wrong can you be? 'Very', in our case. However good Ron was – and he was great at talking to players – the team just wasn't good enough. Changing the manager didn't have the desired effect.

On the morning of that game, Palmer was in the paper praising how Ron had changed the mentality of the team. He spoke about how the team was a lot stronger, particularly defensively since big Ron had joined the club. But eight goals later...

Thanks for that, Carlton.

By this time, I was feeling like a bit of a spare part around the training ground. Ron liked me doing passing drills and the warm-up. But while he was always pleasant to me, I felt I wasn't being utilised properly. I approached the manager and told him I wasn't enjoying my role. They came up with the idea that I should look after the reserves. I got on well with both of them and I liked Peter's humour – and, as gestures go, it was appreciated. It became my role to keep the reserve boys happy and make sure everything was all right in the dressing room on match days. I was still involved. Did I see the reserves as a demotion? Probably, but at the time there were a lot of first-team boys who were playing in that team.

I found it quite easy to wind them up and get them going. For instance, one of my favourite tricks was to bring in a sheet of paper before kick-off. On it, I'd written down the names of forty football clubs, totally at random. I would tell the players that this piece of paper had the clubs coming to watch the reserves that night. It was a total fabrication, of course. I'd just pin a list on the board and they'd all start asking: 'What's all this, then?'

Then I'd give variations on this speech:

'Look, lads. These are the clubs represented by scouts at today's game. I know some of you are unhappy and you don't want to be here. The question you need to ask yourselves is: "How am I going to get away from Nottingham Forest?" I'll tell you how you are going to do it. You are going to have to play for the reserves. You are going to have to play well. You are going to have to do an honest job. People will go away from here thinking good things about you. They will think it was a reserves' game, but he put a shift in. Don't forget lads, I've worked at this level. I know how it operates. Managers, assistant managers, first-team coaches – even chairmen – will watch these games. So, put a shift in and let's have a go.'

I couldn't use the tactic every week, but they seemed to enjoy playing games for me. We won five or six on the spin.

It was at this stage when Ron decided to bring in a little left-winger from Portugal called Hugo Porfirio. He was a left-footed player
with great ability on the ball. The manager wanted to give him some
game-time so he could get him into the first-team as quickly as he
could.

Ron said he was coming to the reserve game against Manchester
United at Mansfield Town with Shreevesy to see how Hugo shaped up.
I was under instruction to play him on the left wing. We had a strong
side out and we had five wins on the spin.

The game kicked off and within four minutes they scored because
their right-back played the ball down the line and followed his pass. He
got it back in return, reached the by-line and crossed where Manchester United score. Our left-winger was still on the halfway line.

I shouted, 'Hugo, when the full-back gets the ball, you run with him
and make sure he doesn't get a cross in.'

All I had back was, 'OK, coach.'

I wasn't happy but he had only just got here, and we all make
mistakes. We equalised on the quarter-hour. Five minutes later, the
full-back overlapped again, crossed the ball and we were 2–1 down.
Porfirio did not move a muscle to prevent it.

I stood on the side-lines thinking: 'Is he winding me up? I've told
him once and he's done it again. He didn't try a leg getting back.' I
turned to Frenchy, the physio, who was standing beside me. 'I'm taking
that little fucker off. If he does it again – that's it – he's off.'

I shouted onto the pitch again. 'Hugo – go with the runner. Make
sure you go with the runner.'

And I got a thumbs up in return.

We equalised, so now it's 2–2. The lads were playing a blinder to keep us in it. Within five minutes – you know the story by now – he's not moved with the runner, but they didn't score this time.

I said to Frenchy and Greavesy, the kit man: 'Make sure you stick like glue to me in the next ten minutes and watch what I do. When I make this substitution, follow me up the tunnel.'

They looked at me like I had lost my mind. So I repeated, 'When I make this substation, follow me up the tunnel.'

Then I pulled Hugo off.

He had his arms out-stretched. He was moaning, groaning and chuntering to himself.

I wasn't happy. At. All.

'You,' I said pointing to him. 'Fuck off up the tunnel.'

I followed him up. At the top, near the dressing room, I went right in his face. I wasn't going to do anything, but if he did something, then it would all kick off. That's why I wanted the other two there – as witnesses. I rounded on him.

'You are a lazy sod. These boys are working their nuts off for you. They don't know what lies around the corner. They're trying to get a move away and look after themselves and their families, and I've got you, you lazy little shit and you don't give a fuck.'

He saw how angry I was and he backed away. Of course, the game was still going on, so I told him to get changed and wait for me. I returned to the game.

The whistle went for half-time and I felt calmer as I headed back into the changing room. It was still 2–2. The pep-talk went like this:

'Boys, you've done great. But as for that little shit here, he has let you down. Forget about him.'

All of a sudden, a mobile phone went off.

'You know the rules. Whose mobile phone is that?'

You've guessed it: Porfirio's. That tipped me over the edge. Did he know the rules? Of course he did.

'Right, I'm going to fucking kill you...' and as I went to move towards him someone put their arm across and prevented me from doing something I shouldn't.

When we went out for the second half, I felt a tap on my shoulder. 'Micky, is there a problem?' asks Shreevesy in his unique way. 'Only, Big Ron wanted Hugo to play the full ninety minutes.'

'There was a problem, Pete, but I've sorted it.'

'Well, Ron did want Hugo to play the full ninety minutes.'

'I know he did Pete, but you saw the start of the game. He let the full-back run away from him twice, he didn't try a leg and they've scored twice. What do you want me to do?'

'Micky, Big Ron wants him to play.'

As if I hadn't heard him the first couple of times. 'Listen Peter, tell Ron from me that if he wants me to be in charge of the reserves, then I will do it as I see it fit. If he doesn't fucking like it, tell him to fuck me off because I'm not going to take that from anyone. I don't care who they are. If that's the way it's going to be, then I will go.'

The next morning I get the nod that Ron wanted to see me.

I entered his office. He started: 'Micky, I'm disappointed what you did last night with Hugo...'

'Ron, listen, you've put me in charge of the reserves. On my contract it reads "assistant manager". 'It doesn't say reserve team manager. I've tried my best to get them going. But I won't accept that from anybody.'

He thought it over and then said: 'Yeah, you're absolutely right. I wouldn't have accepted it either.'

At this stage, I knew I was coming to the end of my time at Forest. I felt my talents and experience, such as they are, weren't being used properly. One of the worst days I've ever had involved Ron towards deadline day, one Friday morning.

He came out and announced, 'We'll have a raz [Ron-speak for a small-sided game] and some shooting and crossing.'

The problem was he had a few deals on the go. He wandered onto the training pitch with his man-bag and his mobile phone. Someone had pulled out of training and so we only had thirteen for a seven-a-side. Since I was still reasonably fit, they shouted at me to put on a bib – which I did.

Ron interjected: 'No, no, no, I'll play.'

The lads were looking at him thinking, 'What the…'

But Ron just shouted, 'Micky, Micky, give me your bib, I'm playing…'

He then asked: 'Who was your team as a kid Micky?'

'Sheffield United, Ron.'

'That side with Tony Currie in it … who played on the right wing?'

'Alan Woodward.'

'That's who I'm going to be today. Alan Woodward. Hold these.'

He passed me his man-bag and his mobile phone. He kept his hat on, probably in case his syrup blew away.

His said, 'If that rings, let me know' before sauntering over to the other side of the pitch and beckoned me across. He actually wanted me to stand by him out on the wing in case his phone rang.

At this point the lads can see what was happening and they started taking the piss. By now, the fuse had gone.

The problem was Ron was the wrong side of fifty. He couldn't get anywhere near these lads but he kept shouting, 'Micky, look Alan Woodward…'

I was growling at him.

The half-time whistle blew. As he walked off the pitch, his phone rang. His ears half pricked up but I just put the phone down. He shouted, 'Was that my phone?'

'No, Ron.'

Of course by this time, following the change-round, he was on the other side of the pitch.

He called me over again. So there I stood, holding his mobile phone and his man-bag, freezing my nuts off watching him attempt to do his best Alan Woodward impression. Not very well, I might add.

After the game, Shreevesy sidled up to Ron to find out what the plan was.

'Crossing and shooting, Pete, crossing and shooting.'

So Ron went and stood out on the right again and he barked out his instructions.

'Right lads, what I want you to do is ping the ball out to me over here. I'll deliver it and you finish.'

He walked over to the right wing. Just before he got into position, he shouted over, 'Micky, Alan Woodward, again, look!'

Honestly, you couldn't make it up. The lads were spraying passes out to him but they were deliberately poor so that Ron had to run to get the ball under control. The session wasn't the greatest and I was *still* holding the man-bag and phone. Anyway, we were attacking the goal with conifers behind the goal rather than a fence. If you missed the target, you had to go in there and fetch the ball.

So I said to him, 'Before we start, why don't you go up the other end because when we start, you'll find that the balls will go into the trees and we'll lose them.'

'No Mick,' comes the reply. 'I want to do it here.'

'OK, but who's going to get the balls?'

He replied: 'You are.'

My head was close to going. All I could hear was 'Micky, go and fetch that for me, would you?' There I was with his man-bag, phone, balls and trees. I was seeing stars. I had to try and keep my calm but the lads were smashing the balls into the trees when we did the shooting session. Two or three were going in higher and higher. I climbed up these trees getting the balls back. Of course, it wasn't long before the giggles started.

Ron was continuing: 'Micky, there's one up there...'

I was up a tree and something went inside my head. I had been on all these coaching courses and had gained all my badges. I had both managed and coached players. I had got a promotion under my belt and I was building up my experience. This was the Premier League, and I was stuck up a tree fetching balls.

I got down and called over to Shreevesy.

'Here's Ron's man-bag and his phone. I'm off.'

'Micky?'

'No, fuck this for a game of toy soldiers. I'm off.'

I walked off the pitch. Training was still going on, but not for me. I went for a shower.

We were leaving that evening to go to a night match and the tradition was to go to the Italian restaurant on the bridge over the Trent. So I went for a plate of pasta. In walks Shreevesy who asked if there was a problem.

'Yes, there's a problem...' I gave him the speech about my coaching, courses badges and experience. And I finished by saying, 'And do you know what I've done today … I've held the manager's man-bag and his phone and I've been collecting balls out of trees. I think that's a piss-take. Do not ask me to do that again because you can fuck off. I'm not doing it.'

Pete was always one who gave Ron what he wanted. In fairness, he had to use his discretion. Certain things he told him, certain things he didn't. I'm sure to this day Ron was totally oblivious to it. He was just in the moment … he was Alan Woodward after all, wasn't he?!

• • •

And Ron, being Ron – oh, it could only happen to him.

When we used to travel to away matches under Dave Bassett, all the staff met in the bar and had a drink while the players ate. My job was to make sure the players were all fuelled properly, which didn't include alcohol. The lads would tuck in to their grub at around 6.30–7 p.m. We would have a couple of drinks and make sure they were packed off to their rooms. The staff would eat together about 8–8.30 p.m., have a few drinks, tell a few stories and go to bed. That was the norm. But it wasn't how it worked under Ron.

He only ate with the people he wanted to. When Ron and Peter Shreeves first arrived, they dined together. The rest of the staff ate on another table. Anyway, this particular time, we were playing Charlton Athletic at the Valley and we stayed in a hotel close to the Dartford Tunnel.

As they got to know me, I got an invite from Shreevesy and Ron to go and eat with them. I felt a bit uncomfortable about it. I did pull Pete up about it but he said Ron liked to eat with certain people. I couldn't turn it down – the request had come from the manager.

We had a nice meal and a bottle of wine, although the rest of the staff were doing a quiz and I still felt uncomfortable about not dining with them. I said to the pair of them, 'Thanks very much for the meal. I'm just going to see the staff, as they're having a quiz.'

Ron's ears pricked up. 'A quiz? I'm good at them,' he said. 'Yeah, I fancy that. I can have a drink and we can do the quiz.'

At this point, we walked into the bar area from the restaurant. There were about eight lads, sub-contractors and builders all having a few drinks and a laugh. There was a good atmosphere. The drink was flowing, the music was playing and everyone was in good spirits.

They noticed we were there – or, more specifically, they noticed Ron. One lad made his way over. 'Ron,' he said, 'I'm a big fan of yours. Lovely to meet you. Can I tell you a joke?'

Nottingham Forest's manager didn't even acknowledge him. He didn't even look at him. The bloke was at Ron's shoulder. 'Can I tell you a joke, please?'

Ron turned and said, 'Look, son, we're having a pleasant evening. We're doing a quiz. I'm enjoying the music and I'm with the staff. Tell your joke by all means and then if you'd go back to your friends, we'd be grateful.'

The chap told his joke. I can't remember it, but it wasn't bad. But Ron was stony-faced. He didn't move a muscle. The boss wasn't having it. At. All.

'OK, son, you've told your joke. It wasn't funny. Leave us be.'

The fella headed back to his mates. From where I was sitting I saw that they were all laughing at him. Ten minutes passed. Then the same bloke came towards us again.

'Look, Ron, I know you didn't find that last joke funny, but this one will kill you.'

Ron looked at him this time. 'Listen, son, I'm having a nice time here. We're in the middle of a quiz and enjoying the music and you are trying to spoil my evening.'

'No, I'm not, Ron, honestly. I know you didn't like the last one. But this one is a winner.'

'OK, son. Tell us your joke. And then leave us alone. Please.'

So the fella started up again. And it was a belter. We were trying not to laugh; it was good but we had to follow Ron's lead. And he didn't flinch, Ron. Not a flicker.

'Listen, son, thanks very much. Leave us alone please.'

At this point, the bloke was brassed off. He went back to his pals looking dejected, and they were laughing at him even more.

I thought to myself, 'That's it; he's been blown out twice. He won't come back again.' How wrong could I be? Fifteen minutes later, he was back.

Ron stopped him this time. 'Listen, I've told you. You've told me two jokes. Neither was funny. Fuck off back to your mates and leave us alone.'

I thought that was a bit harsh when the bloke started saying, 'No, Ron, look...'

But he interrupted: 'No, fuck off and leave us all alone.'

With that, the boss decided it was time he, too, hit the sack. He thanked us and said good night, but to reach the lift he had to walk past these lads. By now, they had been drinking all night and, as Ron approached them, I could see them all nudging each other.

In my mind's eye, I can still see it all playing out, even now. As Ron headed past the lads, it kicked off. It happened in slow motion. All of a sudden I thought to myself, 'Shit, the manager's in a fight...' In fairness, Ron gave as good as he got. He's a big bloke, and he wasn't about to take a step backwards for them. There were a few punches thrown by both sides. Eventually, it was split up.

Ron came back down to where we are all sat. 'I fucking sorted him out,' he said.

Only as I noticed that, as he spoke, his front tooth was missing.

I piped up. 'Er, gaffer, one of your teeth is missing...'

'You what?' he felt around his mouth. 'Oh, no. We've got to find it.'

'Eh, what do you mean?'

Consequently, every single one of Forest's backroom staff was on their hands and knees in between the feet of these lads looking for big Ron's tooth. After a minute or so, one of the builders shouted in triumph, 'Here it is!' Ron thanked him and disappeared to bed. The next morning we needed to find a dentist. Only Ron couldn't find one that he trusted to do the repair work to his mouth.

Anyway, we played the match and it ended in a goalless draw. One of the Sunday newspapers had a picture of Ron stood on the side-lines and the caption underneath it read: 'Big Ron in pensive mood'. But what he was actually doing was holding in his tooth with his index finger.

He was a legend, Big Ron. I loved being around him.

Shortly afterwards, a call came through for me. It was a bloke called Dick Knight, the chairman of Brighton & Hove Albion. Funnily enough, I'd met him at a game at Northampton when the Seagulls were playing there, but I didn't know who he was if I'm being honest. He came over to me at half-time and had a chat with me. He seemed pleasant enough but I didn't think any more of it at the time.

When he started talking on the phone, he reminded me of it. He asked if we could have a chat. He said that Brighton was changing manager and he asked whether I'd be interested.

I needed a change of scene and I wanted to get back into frontline management. I arranged with Dick to meet him at a hotel in London – and that's where my story with Brighton began.

CHAPTER 11

DICK KNIGHT, DAVID CAMERON AND THE SOAR-AWAY SEAGULLS

It's fair to say that Dick Knight is an impressive guy. One thing most people, most fellas anyway, will remember is the 'Hello Boys' advert used to sell Wonderbras in 1994. That brainchild was one of Dick's.

He was smoking heavily when I met him. After every meeting we had, I'd end up smelling like an ashtray, and it was no different after we first spoke at the Grafton Hotel on the Tottenham Court Road in London.

Obviously, I was still being paid by Forest at this point, but after Harry was sacked, I didn't feel truly comfortable at the club. I still felt a loyalty to him and I haven't got a huge amount of time for assistants who hang around at a club long after the manager, who brought them in, has left the place. It never sat well with me being there, even though I had some good times working under Ron and Peter at the City Ground, so it was probably right that I moved on.

I actually had another opening on the table: Wycombe also wanted to talk to me. I went down there for an interview for their managerial vacancy. While it was a good interview, I didn't really think it was for me at the time.

As I came out of that meeting, my phone rang. It was Claire; there were people banging on her front door. They were journalists from the *News of the World* and they wanted her side of the story about our domestic arrangements. No sooner had I put the phone down to her when my wife called; other reporters had been thumping on her front door at the same time and she was none too pleased, either.

I had been tipped off that something was afoot by Ron, who had great connections in the media. I had to tell Wycombe I was pulling out of the race for the job explaining that there were going to be some revelations about my private life in the papers this Sunday and didn't think it was right I put them in that position. It would have been embarrassing for everyone concerned. Obviously, by the time Sunday arrived, events had been overtaken by a big international story that had broken on the Saturday – and, fortunately, my love life was not what the readers wanted.

So I need not have bothered owning up, although the papers did run the story later in the season, but by this time I had been safely installed at Brighton. We were top of the league at the time and they clearly felt I needed bringing down a peg or two.

Not long after the initial story broke, Dick was on the phone. Forest were happy for me to go. They understood I wanted to manage again. So I went down to meet him and he offered me a four-year contract, which was a real vote of confidence. We had five games left and Dick offered me a bonus for staying in the league.

The Goldstone Ground had been sold by the then owner, Bill Archer, to property developers, so Brighton & Hove Albion played at Gillingham. Fans had to suffer a 150-mile round trip to the Priestfield Stadium to watch the Seagulls' 'home' matches. Even so, the Seagulls were averaging about just 2,800 fans, but they had excellent support all the same. I remember when I used to play at the Goldstone Ground, the club always had a rock-solid core of punters. Unfortunately, by the time I joined as manager, their patience had worn thin as the team dropped down the leagues.

In the past they had had some good players, although they were light years away from having the likes of Jimmy Case, Steve Foster, Michael Robinson and the rest. In the eleven matches prior to me taking over, however, they had lost all but two, which they drew. So with no ground, the team on a losing streak and players who were short of confidence, it wasn't a great start. In fact, to be frank, it was in pretty shit order, but at least I had a chairman and owner who cared and were prepared to have a go.

By the end of the campaign we finished seventeenth, but the final league table made it look far healthier than it actually was.

In the background was the campaign running to persuade everyone in the area of the need for a new ground. My mates and I nicknamed it 'Falmer – my arse', although I never said this to Dick's face. There was always so much talk and we never felt like it was going to get done. There were temporary buildings that doubled up as the club offices – my own office did double duty as the medical room. We were due to go back to the Withdean Stadium, which was built to host athletics rather than football, but at least we'd have a base to call our own.

But before the first game of the season, I was absolutely horrified at what I saw. Shot-putters had gouged out great lumps of turf from the playing surface and it was a mess. But I used to tell everyone, 'Look, it might be a shithole, but at least it's our shithole.' I was trying to send a message to the club that, while we could make excuses for everything and anything, we needed to make the best of a bad situation.

One thing was for certain, at least: the opposition wouldn't like playing us at the Withdean. It didn't help, either, that I took the mirrors off the walls in the away-team dressing room. You know how precious footballers can be about their appearances, particularly before games. The changing rooms were really poor, anyway. That's why we used to love night games: you couldn't see how bad it really was.

Anyway, Brighton had to make a big push to get the campaign going. When I was introduced to the supporters at the Town Hall, I stood up in front of the assembled throng and spoke about how proud and privileged I was to be manager of the club. It sounds shallow because a lot of managers say it, but I really was. Despite the problems it clearly had, it was a proper club; and potentially a big one, too.

The squad itself needed an overhaul, but the money was tight as we needed to spend £2.8 million to make sure the Withdean was fit to stage league football. After my first match, I realised that a clear-out was absolutely the first order of the day. Before the season started we bought Paul Watson and Danny Cullip from Fulham and we recruited Paul Rogers. We also brought in little Charlie Oatway, a tenacious, tough tackling, no-nonsense midfield player who was to play a major part in the rise of Brighton through the seasons.

There were a few who stayed; Kerry Mayo was one. Bizarrely, Alan Cork and I met his other half in a pub in Brighton. Yes, you heard right: I'd brought Corky back into the fold. I had no hesitation when it came to working with him again – we were mates and he was fantastic with the forwards, so I got him on board. Anyway, we were in this pub and the girl behind turned out to be Kerry Mayo's missus. The funny thing was that she was actually called Kerry as well – hence the chant 'There's only two Kerry Mayos' the Brighton fans used to sing.

Behind the scenes as I tried to resurrect Brighton's fortunes, my marriage had crumbled and Claire and I decided to move in together in a flat in town and, soon after, our son, Mitchel, came along. At the time it was really awkward, because I was travelling down to Southampton two or three times a week to see the kids. I say 'awkward' but perhaps 'worrying' is a more accurate term because, at the time, my youngest daughter, Lauren, starting having fits. There are lots of reasons for this happening to kids, but in my mind it was down to stress caused by my actions. I felt so guilty about that, but there was no going back as far as I was concerned. And thankfully, over time, Lauren's fits stopped.

It didn't help either that my dad was undergoing a second heart operation. I spoke to him the night before and it was just the standard chat you would expect to have. I knew it was serious, so I told him that I hoped it would go well and that I'd come up and see him when it was all over.

I got a call from my mum the next day. 'Look,' she said. 'I've just had a call from the hospital. You'd better come up here and say your goodbyes because they don't think he's going to pull through.'

I raced from the south coast to Sheffield Northern General hospital where he was in intensive care. They allowed me and my mum into his room, but they told us they didn't think he was going to make it. My mum went home. There wasn't anything she could do. I just sat there, talking to him. Just talking and talking.

It must have been the best pep talk I had ever given because, two days later, he came round. I normally finish a few teams off when I start talking so I like to think my chatter helped somehow. But I think it said something about him, too: he was a fighter, a scrapper.

Anyway, with all this going on in the background I had one team to assemble and another to dismantle. Obviously, there were players under contract who were on decent money that we couldn't get rid of, such as Rod Thomas, a winger, who was a cult figure at Brighton. He was a fan's favourite but as a player he was, shall we say, enigmatic. Having been a winger in my earlier days, I had a bit of a bee in my bonnet about those players in particular. I wanted them to produce crosses; if they were wingers who didn't produce crosses, what on earth were they? Rod used to do the odd dribble but I was forever onto him about getting the ball into the box – which he didn't do on too many occasions. I wanted him out because he wasn't doing what I asked of him – that's the way it has to be when you're the manager. After all, as I discovered at Fulham, it's your neck on the block.

Anyway, we couldn't really have had a much better start when we had Mansfield down at the Withdean for the first match of the season. They had a man sent off after ten minutes and we won 6–0. It would be nice to say that this game set the tone for the season but, sadly, it didn't. We were inconsistent, but I always had the support of Dick Knight and Ray Bloom, one of the other directors. The objective of the season was not to get relegated and the name of the game was progression. It took us a while to get going and I came under significant pressure at one stage. Around the turn of the year we went on a run where we didn't win for nine matches. We signed Bobby Zamora after that and that was the big turning point for us.

In his own book, Dick tells a story about how we went to a game and he saw Zamora playing. It's not quite how I remember it. The reality was that we were struggling for goals and needed a big centre-forward. There was nothing for it but to get on the phone and the one who came up trumps for me was Ian Holloway at Bristol Rovers. They had a reputation for bringing through strikers; Jason Roberts and Nathan Ellington were two other success stories and Rickie Lambert was another one a few years later.

Ian, otherwise known to everyone in the game as 'Olly', told me they had a lad, just nineteen years old, who was a bit of a beanpole: 6 ft 2in. tall, to be precise. He had just been on loan to Bath City and had scored goals but he wasn't considered by Olly to be good enough for his team

Micky, aged five

Micky (in the chair) with his brother Keith, Grandad Billy, Uncle Joe and Auntie Alice in Skegness

Micky celebrating
a Stuart Pearce goal
with Stuart Pearce
and Trevor Peake
at Coventry in 1985

© PRESS ASSOCIATION IMAGES

Micky celebrating after
scoring a goal at the
FA Cup quarter final
against Wigan in 1987

© GETTY IMAGES

Micky playing for Leeds United in 1988 © GETTY IMAGES

Micky playing at Fulham in 1995

© PRESS ASSOCIATION IMAGES

Micky, Bobby Zamora
and Dick Knight

© BRIGHTON ARGUS

Micky and Dick Knight

© BRIGHTON ARGUS

ABOVE Micky celebrating at
the Withdean, 16 April 2001
© BRIGHTON ARGUS

LEFT Micky with the cup after
securing promotion at Brighton
in 2001 © GETTY IMAGES

Micky with Dennis Wise
(photobombed by Harry Bassett)

Micky and Bobby Booker with the League Two Trophy in 2001

Micky presented with his promotion medal by Dick Knight on Micky's return to Brighton as Leicester manager in 2002

Micky saluting the Leicester City fans in 2003 © GETTY IMAGES

Micky with Les Ferdinand at Leicester City training ground in 2004 © GETTY IMAGES

La Manga press conference in 2004

© GETTY IMAGES

Micky, Keith (his dad), Keith (his brother), Harry Bassett and Alan Cork on Micky's wedding day in 2005
© THE STUDIO 17

Micky and Claire on their wedding day with Keith, Margaret (Micky's mum), Sandra and Mick (Claire's mum and dad) © THE STUDIO 17

Micky appointed as manager at Port Vale in 2009
© THE SENTINEL

Madison, Mitchel, Claire and
Micky outside one of the many
bars in Ballygar

Micky celebrating promotion at Wycombe in 2013 © THE SENTINEL

Celebrating Port Vale's promotion in 2014

Claire, Mitchel, Madison and
Micky in Portugal

Micky at Shrewsbury
© THE SENTINEL

Claire with Micky's daughters, Stacey, Steph and Lauren

The grandchildren, Jake, Elliot and Grace

Micky working in the vines at Villefranche-de-Lonchat, France

Claire and Micky at a friend's wedding

Micky applauds from the side-lines © THE SENTINEL

Micky working as a Premier League
delegate, shown here with Michael Oliver
in 2017

at that time. I asked how much money he was on and was told £120-a-week. I said, 'Send him over.'

I remember the first time I saw him he came onto the training ground; he looked like a kid. But he was tall and gangly with a useful left foot: there was potential there. We were going to Chester City and, at the time, the papers were saying that I could be under real pressure if we didn't get a result. But Dick had reassured me in the run up to that game that my position was not under threat. However, I believe it helped that we were out of sight within an hour with Zamora hitting three. We went on to win 7–1.

Dick had told me to change the formation to 4–4–2 at a meeting before the game. Obviously, at Fulham, we'd been promoted with three centre-halves and I was stubborn at the time thinking, 'It's worked before, so I'm persevering with this.' Dick let me know that we should change, but I refused to. Against Chester, however, when the pressure was on, I went 4–4–2 and had a go. And the rest, really, is history.

We went from then until the end of the season unbeaten. Eight wins and six draws was promotion form and we finished off the campaign with a real flourish. Perhaps Dick did know what he was talking about after all.

Would it be too much to say that the phone call to Olly saved my managerial career? No, I don't think it did, although I've got a lot to thank him for. Zamora was also a good player and a clever footballer. Aside from that cracking left foot, he had the uncanny ability to fall over and win free-kicks in really dangerous areas, and he developed a system with Paul Watson that saw us score loads of goals. Bobby would win a free-kick and walk away for Paul Watson to take it when his striker was in position. Then they would use what Bobby Gould would call 'eye telepathy' – Gouldy was big on stuff like that – and the ball would generally arrive where Zamora could claim himself a goal.

There was no hand gestures between the two, no pointing, nothing. We won a fair few points off the back of it.

As the season progressed, the defining characteristic of this mob turned out to be that they were a physically tough team; they were as hard as nails. They were mean, horrible, bastards. If there was a fight, they'd have a go.

But I had an ace up my sleeve as far as they were concerned. I knew that they hated running. They absolutely loathed it. Throughout my managerial career, as I've said, I wanted my teams to be fit. If I didn't feel they were working hard enough, they would be run. On numerous occasions at the Withdean, as we were making the trek towards the dressing rooms, I would hang back.

Inevitably, a combination of Danny Cullip, Charlie Oatway or Paul Rogers would be starting an argument. One of them would be saying, 'Fucking sort it out because you know what he wants. Make sure he gets it because if you think I'm running on Monday because of you wankers, then you can think again.' Players don't talk like that to one another anymore. They just don't. You might think it's a good thing but, personally, I'm not so sure. They would inevitably work it out between themselves because they were a smashing group.

I could wind Cullip up something rotten. Off the pitch, he was a lovely fella; not so much on a football pitch. He was very aggressive. When I used to come in at half-time, I would have my back towards him so that I wasn't addressing him. I would say something along the lines of, 'You forwards, you are going to have to score three goals today to win this match for us because the way they are defending – this lot here – the way they are defending that's what you are going to have to do, score three. They are rubbish.' I would hear Cullip growling behind me, obviously thinking, 'Is he talking about me?' I had him in the palm of my hand. I wish I could have done it with all of them.

After running up seven goals at Chester, we ended the 1999/2000 campaign by winning thirty points in the final fourteen matches, finishing mid-table but just five points from the play-offs. So, next season, we started as favourites. During the summer the first priority was to sign Bobby, but we couldn't offer Bristol Rovers the money they wanted. We ended up doing the deal the week before the season got underway. It was fraught and it was tense but we held our nerve. And it paid off spectacularly.

In Dick's book, he calls it 'the greatest signing I ever made'. Not too sure about that one, Dick, but there we go. Anyway, the deal was done at £100,000 and it was key. I wanted to sign Richard Carpenter who I had at Fulham as a midfield enforcer, and we got that done too. I also signed a lad the previous season called David Cameron, a centre-forward. My scout in Scotland had told me he was a good player. He had all the attributes, big, strong... but he was a strange boy. If the bus was leaving at 2 p.m., he would get on the bus at 1.55 p.m., having sat in the car with his missus for ten minutes.

I ended up getting the hump with him and, in one particular game when I was under a fair bit of pressure, I substituted him after nineteen minutes. I was an absolute swine for changing my mind about my line-ups. I could, and did on a rare occasion, go to bed with one team in my head and then have a brainwave and change my mind when I got up in the morning.

That's exactly what happened when we went to Hull. I came down to breakfast with Corky and said, 'David Cameron is the man for this game.' Alan's response? A very helpful, 'I'm washing my fucking hands of this one.'

I started him all the same. But we were struggling so I took him off after, as I say, just nineteen minutes. We lost to two second-half goals, but we weren't very good and Cameron hadn't made any sort of impression.

I normally faced the press after matches, but I allowed Corky to deputise. I don't know why, because Corky went to answer the media's questions the first time we had been beaten at home and, as a plea of mitigation, good old Corky dropped himself – and me – right in it because he said: 'Our problem is, we've got too many nice boys for Brighton.'

So, the gay campaigners were out in force and I was called into a meeting with the chairman. He said, 'What Alan said is bang out of order. I want you to reprimand him and make sure it doesn't happen again.'

So, I did as I was told. We had a couple of words. We moved on. Until Hull City, that is, where I asked Corky to deputise for the second time. He said, 'No problem, but they are going to ask me why you took off David Cameron after nineteen minutes.' To which I replied, flippantly, 'Well, just tell them he was fucking useless.'

First question from the floor: 'Alan, can you tell us why David Cameron was taken off after nineteen minutes.'

You've guessed it.

'He was fucking useless', comes the reply.

Another call to see the chairman. We had upset Brighton's gay community and now we were publicly berating our own players. Thanks Corky, way to go. The result was that the chairman basically blocked him from doing the press. Ever again.

• • •

We also signed a keeper called Michel Kuipers. He was a great keeper in terms of shot-stopping. He went on to have a fantastic career at Brighton. But could he kick? Not even if his life depended on it.

I remember taking him out one pre-season and practising his

goal-kicks with Mitre balls, since they were our sponsors at the time. We taught him to aim his kick at the company's name on the ball, and he did show a few signs of improvement. This was all well and good, until one pre-season game when we went away and they were using a different manufacturer. You've never seen panic like it. 'They are not using Mitre balls, what do I do?' he said to the pair of us.

'Just kick the fucking thing.' While it isn't in the coaching manual, that's pretty much what he needed to do. Honestly, footballers. You couldn't make it up.

The first day of what turned out to be our promotion campaign, we went to Southend. There were 3,500 Brighton fans serenading us with 'Bring on the champions!' No pressure there, then. But we only won one out of the first five games and rumours started again that I was going to be sacked.

After being beaten by Kidderminster Harriers, we were bottom of the league. The team was good enough but we were not getting results. It just wasn't happening. But then we had just one good result when we drew 1–1 against Millwall in the cup and it turned things around. And that was a particularly pivotal night for us because it was the first time that we played 4–3–3. It certainly boosted our confidence and Rogers played like a number ten, getting forward and scoring a few. The team spirit was fantastic.

However, I was dealt a blow when Corky left in the September. He had an offer from Sam Hammam, who he had been with at Wimbledon. He took up the offer to manage Cardiff City, although he said it was like leaving his brother and going to work with his dad. I was just happy that, out of the two, I was being referred to as his brother.

To replace him I turned to Bob Booker, who had been my youth coach at Brentford. It was one of the best decisions I ever made. If I needed someone, this was the man. He was superbly well organised and one of the funniest men you could ever wish to meet. Sometimes I thought I'd employed him just for purely selfish reasons, to keep me entertained. He was just brilliant to have around the place. I also brought in Dean White as chief scout, mainly because we wanted to tap into the non-league market and he had been a manager at Hastings. Dean was a straight talker, never afraid to open his mouth and tell us what he thought. Sometimes you get number twos who will just blow smoke up people's backsides, but Dean wasn't like that at all. If you asked for an opinion, you got one.

The only fly in the ointment came from Cardiff City, where Corky had just gone: Sam Hammam wanted to buy Bobby. I half got the hump with Corky at the time, as it seemed he'd left and now wanted to sign our best players. I didn't think it was on. That saga rumbled on for a while, but Dick and the board stood squarely behind me and refused to sell.

We suffered a particular blow when we lost at Scunthorpe with about a dozen games to go. I didn't think we had put a lot of effort into the game and I was pretty pissed off. We didn't get back to Brighton until 2 a.m., but I still had them back in training six hours later, where I ran them around a pond for ninety minutes. It's old school and I'm not really sure you could get away with it these days – bearing in mind we were second in the league – so it wasn't as if they were doing badly. You might say it was harsh on them and, perhaps now, with hindsight, I wouldn't do it this way. But at the time, I was a youngish manager and I felt that they hadn't put the effort into the game that they should, so I wanted to make a point.

Bob Brooker and I went down to the pond on bicycles and found that the boys were not in the best of moods and had decided that someone was going to pay and, you've guessed it: Bobby and his bike were dumped unceremoniously into the pond.

So my professional life was on the up – which is more than can be said for my personal life which was complicated, to say the least. Claire became pregnant and, being the bottler that I am, I couldn't bring myself to tell my three kids. It wasn't until I invited them to Mitchel's christening that they discovered they had a half-brother.

That was awkward, but it was typical of me. I was happy to face things head on when I was on the football pitch but privately, I would rather skirt a difficult issue and try to keep the peace as best I could. Anyway, the kids came and the day went as well as it possibly could.

Anyway, Claire was breast-feeding and she'd decided to start expressing milk and had built up a stock in ice cubes in the freezer. One night, after we had played Rochdale, Matt Hicks, the player liaison officer, Bob Booker and I decided to have a drink back at my house. Claire had gone to bed as she knew it was going to be a late night.

We were in the conservatory chewing the fat, working out what we were going to do etc. Anyhow, we ran out of beer and the only thing we had in the house was a five-pint keg. The only problem was it wasn't cold, so we came up with a plan. I rushed off to get the beer and Bob went to the kitchen in search of some ice.

We poured a drink and Bob dropped the ice in. We thought it was weird when the cubes hit the liquid: it half-fizzed. However, we were well pissed by this stage, so the obvious hadn't quite connected. We just kept drinking.

It must have been about 3 a.m. when, having finished the keg, we turned in. Hicksy went home and Bob was in the spare room.

The next morning, Claire went downstairs and, to her utter dismay, found all the finished bottles in the kitchen together with the empty ice-cube trays. As I shouted down, 'Claire, any chance of two coffees, please?', she raced upstairs with a puzzled look on her face. 'Where's my breast milk gone? It was in the ice trays…'

At which point, Bob and I realised what had happened: we'd been so pissed that we drank breast milk. Claire just retorted: 'Well, at least you will both grow up to be big, strong boys one day.'

Anyway, on the pitch we were flying again. We rattled off a succession of victories and we just needed to beat Chesterfield at the Withdean to win the championship. And so we did. That was a fantastic night. Danny Cullip scored with a header from a corner twelve minutes from time and so, from being bottom of the league in the September, we were champions. It was a fantastic achievement and a proud day for us all.

I remember the final day at Shrewsbury. We'd won the league and I'd been awarded manager of the year. As a reward for the promotion, the chairman allowed the players to go to Puerto Banus in Spain. It was, as you might expect, carnage.

I had it in my mind that I would make Warren Aspinall, who was nearing the end of his career, chief scout. He had a reputation for walking on the wrong side of the line, so I'd told him what was going on and advised him to keep his nose clean while we were out enjoying our title triumph. The plan was that I'd tell Dick what I wanted to do when we returned home. All Warren had to do was enjoy himself and steer clear of trouble; that way, he'd get himself a job on his return. Sounds simple, doesn't it? Apparently not.

He blew it in spectacular fashion. Dick and his wife were having a late drink together in a nightclub at 2 a.m. Dick went to the toilet and at this point, Warren sidled over to Mrs Knight and whispered some sweet nothings in her ear. To this day I don't know exactly what was said, but Dick made it quite clear on my return to work that I was to dump Warren, smartish.

Aside from that minor setback, I was looking back on the season with more than just quiet satisfaction. The side I'd produced at Fulham were pretty big units. They were strong and physical. But this team at Brighton was different. They had more in their locker than the Fulham vintage. If teams wanted to have a game of football with them, they'd have a game. I'd assembled a group who were better footballers than they were given credit for. Brighton were making progress and I was fairly confident that, with not too much tinkering, we could be a force in League One, too.

Dick says in his own book that the players were slightly fearful of me. I'm not too sure about that but if that's what he thought then I'm not going to argue. As for me, I respected Dick because he stood by me, although there were a couple of periods when it didn't go according to plan. There was one game, after Kidderminster, I think, when I asked him if it was time for a change. But he took me and Claire out – I think he wanted her to hear it as well – and he said: 'No, you're the manager, you get on with it.'

And the lads must have heard about it, too, because all of a sudden they raised their game. What happens now is that if a manager is under pressure, the players crumble. They can use the situation to their advantage, and it's horrible for managers when the players start using the fact that their manager is under pressure as an excuse for not putting the effort in. But that lot didn't. They stuck out their chests, worked harder and turned it around.

The real fun and games started at Brighton the summer after we won promotion. We went on a pre-season tour to Ballygar, that haunt of mine from the Fulham days. The trip was all going according to plan until we played a friendly that was dubbed afterwards in the papers as 'The Battle of Longford'.

Stephen Kenny, who is now manager of Dundalk, was in the home dug-out. At this point, he was just starting out on his managerial career. They had a lad up front, kicking everything that moved. We were getting irate on the bench and two of our lads ended up falling out with each other.

There was a pass which went astray and they were both blaming each other. They nearly came to blows with one another before the real stuff started. Anyway, the referee pulled them towards him and read them the riot act.

I then decided to take Richard Carpenter off – we had only played fifteen minutes at this time – I put Steve Melton on. I gave our substitute specific instructions to give the lad who was booting our players up in the air a taste of his own medicine.

'Make sure he knows you are around,' was the actual order. As you might have expected, within five minutes the instigator of this trouble has been given a whack. Longford's bench was in uproar.

The game became feisty. Charlie Oatway got sent off together with their centre-forward. The referee had just lost the plot. We then had another man sent off. It was two minutes before half-time and we were down to nine men.

This was the cue for all hell to break loose. Charlie, who had been sent off, remember, began running after their player who had been dismissed before he was. The opposition's player was walking towards the dressing room with Charlie in hot pursuit.

Only our lads had seen it. They charged after Charlie. At which stage, their lads saw what was going on. They also charged after Charlie. It was chaos and the half-time whistle hadn't even been blown. Obviously, I should explain at this stage for those who aren't familiar with Mr Oatway that he could start a fight in an empty phone-box.

I was playing catch-up by this stage. All I could see was bodies and fists flying. As I raced over, looking to sort it out, Kenny is in my ear, saying: 'You're a disgrace' to which I replied in my best vernacular:

'You can fuck off. You caused this with your lad smashing everything that moved. We're here for pre-season.'

As I headed towards the changing rooms, Bobby was behind me. Never one for a fight was Bob, and he was taking every precaution necessary to ensure he had no chance of being involved in the confrontation.

I got them into the dressing room, eventually. There was a combination of black eyes, bruises, ripped shirts and the adrenaline was flowing.

Twenty pairs of eyes were on me, waiting to hear how I'm going to handle it.

I just said, 'Well done, lads. Get your gear on, we're out of here.'

The locals weren't happy. They were outside, kicking our coach to bits. But I wasn't prepared to carry on with nine men. It was a joke. In the end, they had to call the Garda to come and escort our coach out of Longford. Back to Ballygar we scuttled.

I can honestly say I've never seen anything like it on a football pitch – it was a proper brawl. And the next morning Brighton and Hove Albion made the front page of the *Irish Sun*.

Back in Blighty, the new season was almost upon us. I decided that while the squad didn't need a major overhaul, it would benefit from freshening up. The quality of the characters coming into the dressing room was as important as their ability on the pitch; and on that score, I had no worries. Certainly not with Simon Morgan, who had already been on one journey with me at Fulham. After we signed him up, he played over forty matches for the Seagulls during what turned out to be another promotion campaign.

I also brought in a German centre-forward who had been at Fulham, Dirk Lehmann, and a full-back from Portsmouth, Bobby Pethick. The main question, I suppose, surrounded Bobby Zamora who had smashed thirty-odd goals during our promotion campaign. Could he do it at a higher level? The answer turned out to be a resounding yes.

It wasn't long after the start of the season that I took a call from Dave 'Harry' Bassett, offering me the position of assistant manager at Leicester City. It was a tempting offer, particularly as it was made clear to me that I would be groomed to be manager of the East Midlands club.

Harry hit me at a good time. We were still playing at the Withdean with no new stadium on the horizon and we suffered a 2–1 loss to Brentford that Friday. But even though he says in the foreword to this very book that I was in a hurry to move, I'm not sure that's entirely how it was from my perspective. I was a young manager with two promotions already to my name. And while I thought that we had a shot at another promotion, it wasn't a certainty. I knew I had put together a team of winners and I knew I had a goal-scorer in Bobby Zamora, but football's fickle finger of fate could have disrupted that at any time.

As I've said before, hindsight is a wonderful thing and, had I been in charge at the age of fifty-five rather than forty, then I perhaps would have taken a different decision. I would have stayed put. As it turned out, my successor Peter Taylor was the lucky beneficiary who was there when Brighton shot up into the Championship. He did tinker, slightly, did Peter. But there wasn't a single bad thought in my head when they were promoted for a second time. I'd been on a journey with everyone there, from chairman Dick Knight downwards.

The only issue for me was that I was watching from afar. I'd accepted Harry's offer and I was off to Leicester City.

CHAPTER 12

DOWN AND UP WITH THE FOXES

People still ask, 'Why did you go?'

As I say, the role at Leicester City had been sold to me with the promise that I would eventually take over from Harry. The call from Leicester came out of the blue and it hit me at the right time. Our problem with facilities at Brighton is not to be underestimated and I was a young-ish man in a hurry to get things done. I'd worked with Harry at Forest and he knew his brief was to prepare me to take over his role. The problem was, however, that there was no timescale set.

Should I have stayed at Brighton? Possibly. I had everything going for me there. The board backed me as best they could. I had no problems with the players. It was my squad. The fans were onside and we were near the top of the table.

Why leave to be a number two? That was the question I was asking myself four days later after our first match at Stamford Bridge ended in a 2–0 defeat.

At first I wondered why Dick hadn't tried very hard to keep me. I waited for them to make the effort, but the moment never came. When I realised the fee for keeping me on was £250,000 – for a club that was struggling for cash – I could at least understand why.

While it was nice to hear Harry calling me the 'young, sexy one' at an early press conference it wasn't the best of starts. It was made worse for me and Harry when we found out what was going on when Leicester City played away from home. The first game I attended as Harry's number two was that defeat at Chelsea, and what we saw horrified the pair of us. It was basically a free for all among the staff. The club was struggling financially but the staff were just having a right jolly-up and the club was paying for it.

Listen, there's nothing wrong with having a glass or two of wine and Leicester City footing the bill. But everyone was acting as if they were on a stag do. One of the first things Harry did was to stop that. He didn't mind a glass or two being taken by the staff at mealtimes, but for anything else the staff had to meet the cost themselves. That move didn't go down well with certain people, as you can imagine. It hardly endeared Harry to them.

I was trying to get to grips with a new role too. My job essentially was to get to know the players. And the first thing I learnt about Leicester City's players was not only how well they could play, but also how well they could drink. For instance, I was introduced to Sambuca by Frank Sinclair. I was out with the lads and Frank lined up the shots, produced his lighter and set them alight. He warned me not to drink the liquid for a few moments, but I didn't listen and ended up hardly being able to speak properly for a few days afterwards. That hiccup apart, I did get close to them and I got to know the types of personalities they were.

I remember early on we were going to train at Filbert Street and we needed the floodlights on. I was out on the pitch setting out the cones when Ade Akinbiyi and Trevor Benjamin came out. They looked at the lights and were clearly having trouble adjusting.

I shouted over, 'What are you doing?'

'Oh, we're just getting used to the light', came the reply.

It did not look right to me. I went and found Harry. I said, 'We are in big trouble here. We've got two centre-forwards who can't see properly.'

Later, when I became manager myself, I discovered the extent of Benji's problems. His corneas weren't round; they were shaped more like squares. So when he put his contact lenses in, he couldn't get them to fit properly so he was always losing them. It got so bad that Corky said to him, 'Benji, just head the second ball you can see, not the first one.' I'm not joking.

As for Ade, he'd been bought for big numbers by Peter Taylor. He was a real beast of a man. He got into great positions but he could never finish. Back in the day, we used to let the supporters in to watch training at our training complex at Belvoir Drive, and it got so bad with Ade that, whenever we had shooting practice on the training field, he used to go inside. It would be embarrassing. Not only was he missing the target on match days, but he couldn't even do it when there was no pressure. Everyone remembers the goal he got against Sunderland where he whipped his top off, but it wasn't enough.

More worryingly, we couldn't shake off this tag of being drinkers. Mainly, I suspect, because it was true. I could feed a certain amount of information back to Harry but it was up to him to decide if he listened or not. For instance, Sinclair used to drive up from London a lot and, on occasions, slightly worse for wear. At the time, Frank was probably on two written warnings, so one more and he would have been out of the building.

One morning, his wife actually phoned Harry and told him that Frank had just returned home at 7 a.m. and he was now on his way up to Leicester. The word went out from Harry: when Sinclair gets here, he's to go straight to Harry's office.

As Frank pulled into the car park, I clocked him. I pulled him aside as he made his way into the dressing room. 'Gaffer wants to see you, Frank.'

'What about?'

'No idea. But he said to get you the minute you turned up.'

Anyway, half an hour later, the manager's door opened and Harry comes out.

'Everything all right, Harry?' I ask.

'Yeah, yeah, no problems,' comes the reply.

Shortly afterwards, I was on the training ground and we were doing some running drills. You know what it's like when you stand next to someone and they are sweating so much that the drink is coming out of their pores? Well, that was Sinclair.

'Frank, how on earth did you get away with that?'

'I dunno,' he said. 'I thought I was a goner.'

You'll have to make your own mind up about whether he deserved to be sacked or not. Getting rid of him, in my opinion, wouldn't have been the smartest move. Frank was a lovable rogue and worked hard for the cause, when he was sober.

I was just enjoying being on the training ground again, getting to know the lads without the pressures of management. Harry has since highlighted the fact that the team was a bit soft. Maybe so, but we were always competitive in games.

Not least the game against Bolton when both Harry's and Trotters's boss Sam Allardyce agreed to take part in an experiment that required them to wear heart monitors throughout the game. It was something the League Managers' Association had dreamed up to show the stress their members worked under.

Whoever selected the game for this trial couldn't have picked a better one if they had tried. The match itself was full of drama. In fact, it probably gave false readings because the majority of matches aren't as full of incident as this one was. Bolton were down to nine men midway through the first half. Paul Warhurst had been dismissed and then Dean Holdsworth followed suit within the opening twenty-three minutes. In the twenty-fourth came the moment which most Leicester fans – and, I'm sure, even most neutrals will recall – when Robbie Savage was substituted by us for his own protection. He had already received one yellow and it was quite clear the Bolton players were targeting our shy and retiring centre midfielder.

Harry had read the script – correctly in my view – and dragged him off. The fiery Welshman wasn't happy about it at all. We had a different view and I still, to this day, think it was the correct decision. The only problem for us was that Sav's replacement, Muzzy Izzet, was given a red card with half an hour left to play. From being two-up against nine men for sixty-seven minutes, we ended up hanging on to a point for dear life.

But if there was one game that summed up our campaign that year, it was the one at Middlesbrough. It will be remembered because Frank Sinclair scored one of the most spectacular own goals you will ever see. The match was only a few minutes old when Frank tried to pass the ball back to Ian Walker, some forty yards from his own goal. It caught the wind and sailed over the goalkeeper's head.

As the campaign wore on it was obvious our fate was sealed. I was becoming increasingly frustrated around March 2002. Not with Harry, but more so with the job I was doing. I felt I had made a mistake in leaving Brighton.

I did a press conference ahead of a game against Southampton when I was asked about management. I said something along the lines of 'Well, I'm going to be a manager at Leicester City – if not, I'm going to be a manager somewhere else.' The thing is, I had been tapped up by a couple of clubs. Hull City was one of them. They wanted me to take over at the end of the season.

Even so, the press conference isn't a moment I look back on now with much fondness. Obviously, it didn't go down well with Harry and I regret saying it. I was just in one of those moods. It's not the first time my mouth has got me into trouble. The situation on the pitch was bad enough, without me contributing to it, and now the focus was even more on Harry's performance as the manager.

We always had a great relationship, but he wasn't talking to me before the Southampton game so it was up to me to apologise. I had put him in this position, after all. He wasn't happy because all I was doing was holding a gun to the club's head. And he didn't deserve that. He'd been really good with me.

Despite my apology, Harry still wasn't happy and I was told in no uncertain terms about it. I was called to the boardroom to see John Elsom, the chairman, for a chat. I was expecting the worst. I had some input but Harry picked the team for the Southampton match. When they go out onto the pitch, when they cross that white line, it's on your head – no one else's. You're the one who has to justify what went on to the supporters and the board of directors afterwards. You're the one who gets the plaudits if you win and the criticism if the team loses. That's the way it is. What happened at Southampton pretty much summed it up; we were winning two-nil and then they equalised with three minutes to go through Marian Pahars.

That Monday when I went to meet Elsom, I was given a bollocking. I was also told that I would get my opportunity as manager but that it was to be their decision when that would be.

Anyway, we were relegated shortly after that following a game against Manchester United. It was mutually agreed that I would become manager and Harry would stay at the club as director of football, organising the scouting, dealing with agents and negotiating the deals, and I would be allowed to get on the training ground to get the players going.

My first game was a friendly against Celtic at home. I gathered the players together in the home dressing room before the start and said I wasn't prepared to tolerate what had gone on before. I thought there was a drinking culture at the club and added, for good measure, that if I smelled alcohol on them or they turned up clearly the worse for wear, I'd fine them. It was going to be that simple. Muzzy Izzet said to me afterwards that it was like I'd changed overnight. But I had to. I had to take a stand.

We lost against Celtic and, the next day, Gerry Taggart didn't show. When he eventually did, after a night out with the Celtic boys, he was fined. Apparently, he wasn't at the pre-match meeting because he was injured and had missed my spiel about the new regime. Matt Elliott swears he wasn't there, but I could have sworn that he was.

The standard fine was about one week's wages. Leicester's boys were all on very good money back then – it was one of the reasons why the club later ended up in so much trouble. That night out cost Taggart a five-figure sum. But, clearly, some players don't learn.

Elliott was the skipper. On the Thursday before my first game against Everton a week or so later, there was the normal pre-match press conference. Before we went training at 10.30 a.m., I was in the office when my secretary put a call through from Matt saying that he couldn't get out of his house because the electric gates at his house weren't working. Since, it was a real issue and not some imaginative bollocks dreamed up to try and excuse the fact he'd been out on the sauce, his explanation was met with all of the good humour and sympathy I could muster.

'Well, just jump over the gates and get a taxi', I said.

'I can't gaffer,' came the reply. 'I've called someone out and they'll be here in a few minutes, I'm ringing to say I'll be late.'

Well, I wasn't going to cancel training but I had an additional problem, because the first fifteen minutes were open for the cameramen and women to get footage. It's called an 'open session' for the rights holders and local crews to come out to film running or players knocking a ball around. Only on this day, my club captain was turning up fifteen minutes later than everyone else. I took the boys out for their session even so. I wasn't holding it back for Elliott.

Anyway, he parked up and went straight into the changing rooms. I expected him out in a few minutes. It took a while but when he eventually appeared and was walking towards me, I could see that he had been drinking. As he got up close, I could smell it on him. I put my hand over my mouth to disguise what I was saying from the cameramen. 'Matty, have you been drinking?'

'Gaffer, I didn't go out,' he said. 'Me and the wife had a bottle of wine and a few beers indoors.'

'OK, son. Well, do yourself a favour and get off the training ground. You're no use now to anyone. Come back in tomorrow.'

The press boys saw and so there was obviously a few questions at lunchtime when the session ended. 'Yes, he came out to see me,' I said. 'He's got a slight niggle so we're going to give him twenty-four hours' rest and see if he is OK tomorrow.'

That small hurdle was negotiated safely. The fact was, however, I needed Matty because Duncan Ferguson was fit and flying and we needed Elliott to combat him in the air. When Elliott came in the next day, he'd been asked to come in and see me. Before I said anything, he said, 'Boss, thanks for yesterday. It won't happen again. I apologise. Thanks for what you did.'

'Thanks for what I did? Matt, fuck off home. And, by the way, you're fined a week's wages.'

That night in (if it was a night in) also cost Elliott a five-figure sum. Within a week, I'd saved the club well over £50,000. But, more importantly for me, I'd put down a marker. The captain had tested me. It was important I took that stance.

We went up to Goodison Park and drew 2–2. We double-marked Ferguson, with Frank Sinclair in front and young Matt Heath behind. We did well, too, until the eighty-sixth minute when the big man equalised. That was a blow. It would have been sweet obviously if we'd come away with a victory given the stunt that Elliott pulled.

But if I thought that was the end of the test as far as that lot were concerned, I was sadly wrong. One week later, my secretary Clare pulled me after training.

'Micky, there's a lady here that wants a word with you.'

'About what?'

'She won't tell me. She says it's something to do with Robbie Savage. She's in the reception area and wants to speak with you directly.'

The woman was ushered into my office. She was the typical older lady. Silver hair, quite small, neatly turned out.

'Hello,' I said. 'I'm Micky Adams, the manager. What can I do for you?'

'It's Robbie Savage,' she said. 'He's nearly killed me.'

I'm trying to keep a straight face. 'What do you mean Robbie Savage has nearly killed you?'

'Well, I was walking down by the training ground entrance and when I crossed the road, this car came racing out of the training ground and... and, I don't know how it didn't hit me. Robbie Savage was driving it.'

I said, 'Right, OK. Well, let me get Robbie in and I'll get him to apologise to you. Is that OK?'

'Well, yes. But he's nearly killed me...'

So I went outside, found Corky and asked him to get Sav for me. I was thinking to myself, all he's got to do is apologise and look contrite and that will be that.

Sav walked into my office and I explained the situation to him.

'Robbie, a lady has come to see me. She says she was walking down by the training ground and you almost hit her with your car.'

'She's lying,' he said.

'No, no, Rob. Look, all you've got to do is apologise and say you'll be more careful next time.'

'No, she's lying.'

The woman was taken aback. To be fair, so was I.

'I'm not lying,' she said.

Sav carried on, 'How does she know what car I drive? How can she tell it was me? Can she be 100 per cent sure it was me?'

I jump in. 'Sav, you drive a yellow Ferrari. It's got the number plate 'Sav 8' written on it. It's a bit of a giveaway, wouldn't you say?'

With that, he started to calm down. Eventually, he apologised and the lady left giving Sav a flea in his ear about the speed he was driving at.

Anyway, as the season was winding down, just when you think it can't throw any more shit at you, it does. The episode that became known as 'Jobbiegate' was a new one to all of us. I know former referee Graham Poll has had his say about it in his book, so here is my story.

The scene was a Midlands derby at Filbert Street against Aston Villa. It was about 2.50 p.m., ten minutes before kick-off. I got a call to go to the officials' room immediately where a very irate Poll hits me with 'Robbie Savage is a disgrace. He's used our toilet, come out of it and wiped his hands on the assessor's coat.'

I wasn't expecting this. 'Sorry Graham, what do you mean "he's used your toilet"?'

'What I mean, Micky, is he came to our toilet area while we were out for a warm-up. He's used it. He's not flushed it. And then he's washed his hands and wiped them on the assessor's coat. And now he's laughing at us.'

As a manager, what am I supposed to do about this? Obviously, I tell Graham I'll be getting to the bottom of it; I didn't actually use that phrase – I wish I had. But I needed to get Sav's side of the story first. He said he had a dodgy tummy, needed to go and all the cubicles in the home dressing room were occupied. Clearly, the Football Association weren't buying it because he was fined £10,000 after Poll made a complaint about it.

As the season drew to a close, the one highlight for me personally was a trip to Craven Cottage. Going back as a Premier League manager felt like a huge achievement. I got a great reception from the punters there, which was hugely appreciated.

The season was rounded off with the last-ever game at Filbert Street, ahead of the move to the Walkers Stadium. We came back from a goal behind to win 2–1 against Spurs. Paul Dickov equalised and Matt Piper, on his last appearance for the club prior to a £3-million move to Sunderland, scored the final goal at Leicester's famous old home.

After games there was nothing better than going up and seeing John and Janet Elsom at Filbert Street to have a drink. John and Janet were a great partnership, and Janet was a great hostess and represented the club in a professional manner. She certainly had her work cut out keeping John in check. John was good company, but he could be dreadfully indiscreet. For instance, I once went upstairs to the boardroom with Claire to be greeted by John, who'd clearly had a couple. This particular day, he'd made it perfectly obvious where he was looking and instead of saying, 'How are you?' he said, 'How are they?' while looking down Claire's cleavage before hastily correcting himself.

By the end of the season, we had severe financial problems and we had to have a clear out. Like I said, Leicester City paid good money but, like most clubs in those days, they struggled to make the transition once they'd dropped down into the Championship.

After a few years with Martin O'Neill, who never left the club in any real danger, I don't know if complacency set in but there were some very tasty contracts being handed out. Matt Jones is one example of this. He was a lovely, young lad who we signed from Leeds United, and was featured in a series called 'Players and their Pads' or something along those lines in the match-day programme. He was pictured outside his big mansion, which boasted a private pond with its own swans. I pulled him aside soon afterwards and said, 'How do you think that looks? We are down near the bottom of the table and you're in full view of the punters showing off what you've got. How would you feel if you were looking at that?'

But that was the mentality at the time. There were players on great contracts and I just had to get rid of them. Gary Rowett was offloaded to Charlton for £2.5 million with a bad knee. I've rarely been so relieved to hear a player had passed a medical. I'm not sure how he managed it. Matt Piper went to Sunderland for £3 million. He was heartbroken because he wanted to stay, but our money situation dictated meant that he had to be sold, too. We lost Sav to newly promoted Birmingham City for £2.5 million; Lee Marshall went to West Brom for £700,000; and Ade Akinbiyi was sold to Crystal Palace for £2.2 million. They were the main ones. Obviously, it would have been useful to have a couple of them stay to help in the Championship, but it wasn't to be.

Even though we raised over £10 million, it wasn't enough. We needed to reduce the wages of the remaining players as well. I just had to deal with it as best as I could.

Muzzy had the chance to go to Middlesbrough for £6 million. I wasn't desperate to see him go as he was too good a player to lose, but we needed the cash. As it turned out we ended up keeping him, as he really didn't want to go. We had a £15 million wage bill in the

Championship which was still one of the highest. This was the time before anyone had thought of the bright idea about reducing the salaries if clubs were relegated.

All these money troubles were hanging over the club when we went on a pre-season tour of Finland. I got them all together before we got off the bus at the hotel. 'Listen, if there are any problems here, I will send you home.'

I told them they'd be allowed a quiet drink at certain times. Don't forget, they'd already taken me on over drinking. And I was concerned by the presence of the senior professionals, such as Dennis Wise and Matt Elliott, who were on the trip. It's the senior professionals who want to test you out.

Inevitably, it all kicked off, this time over a card game. I remember the morning afterward when Corky knocked on my door and said there had been an incident. 'Wisey has punched Callum over a game of cards. We think Callum has broken his jaw and he's gone to hospital to have it checked out.'

It's the last thing you need. The trip was meant to be a team-bonding exercise. It wasn't helped by the fact that the local daily paper, the *Leicester Mercury*, had sent its club reporter, Bill Anderson, to accompany us on the trip.

I couldn't hide my disappointment in Dennis, but for me, he was vital to play a major part in getting us out of the league. I asked him in and enquired as to what happened. They'd been playing cards, they'd had a row and he'd ended up punching him.

I said, 'Dennis, you know the rules. If you step out of line, you're going to be punished. You might be a senior professional but I can't have it. You're going to be fined. Get your bags packed and get yourself to the airport and back home.'

He understood that. In the meantime, Callum went to hospital. He'd fractured his jaw and needed an operation, and it was all over the press back home. It couldn't have fallen any better for Bill.

I needed to speak to Martin George, who had taken over as chairman. I phoned him up and said, 'Sorry to have to report, chairman, that there has been an incident during the pre-season tour. Dennis Wise has punched Callum Davidson after a row over a game of cards. I'm fining him the maximum I can which is two weeks' wages.'

There was silence on the other end of the line for a moment. 'No, Micky, you're not fining him,' said the chairman. 'I'm sacking him.'

I replied, 'Whoa, chairman. I've dealt with him. I've sent him home. And I'm fining him the maximum.'

But he wouldn't have any of it. 'We are disciplining him,' said George. 'And we are going to sack him.'

So then I had to get hold of Dennis. I phoned him up and said, 'Look Dennis, the club are taking a hard line on this. They want to sack you. There's not a lot I can do about it. But, as your line manager, I will back you. I will say I was going to give you a two-week fine and that was to be the end of the matter.'

I've got to be honest; I nearly lost my job over it. The club wanted me to back their stance and I refused to. I was asked to sign a piece of paper which effectively meant I'd be siding with the club with a threat that if I didn't, I'd have to pay for the trouble myself. I said that if that was the way they wanted it, fine. But I also that I'd seen hundreds of fights on training pitches and, if we sacked someone every time there was a fight, there would have been countless ex-professionals – some of them very high profile – who wouldn't have half the careers they had.

Not every fan will agree with that, but I don't really care. It didn't help the situation either that I had a soft spot for Dennis. He was a good player and I genuinely thought he could help us.

It became farcical when it turned into a disciplinary matter. An inquiry was held and there was a hearing. Andrew Neville, the secretary, Martin George, Harry and I all had to attend. Dennis had hired a Queen's Counsel who pulled the club to pieces over their failure to follow the correct protocol when sacking him. He ripped us to bits. It was embarrassing.

I then had to deal with the players. A lot of them didn't like him and didn't want him back. They weren't prepared to have him back, either, regardless of how the hearing had gone. They didn't want a show of hands about it because they didn't want it to get back to Dennis who had backed him and who hadn't. So they decided to have a ballot, via me. They all came into my office saying yea or nay and the majority vote was that they didn't want him back.

Dennis thought I had something to do with it. I didn't. I wanted him back, but the club wanted to make some savings from the termination of his £1 million-plus annual wage. Eventually it went to an industrial tribunal, and the original decision of the club's was upheld: he was sacked.

That sorry episode happened right at the very start of the season. But, despite the sell-offs, there was still a nucleus of good players. Ian Walker was there and we still had Muzzy. From a playing perspective, we still had a chance.

When we got back to Blighty, the season began to draw upon us.

I remember saying to the players, 'You've all had your chance to go – and you're still here, which means either people don't fancy you or they cannot afford you. We're in the Championship now. You can't be happy about it. I'm not. So what are you going to do about it? Are you going to accept it? Or are you going to get back to the promised land?'

I couldn't see too many of them nodding their heads, but I had clearly struck a nerve with some of them who felt they were better than they were. I challenged them to do something about it.

We also had two trialists in that year: Nicky Summerbee and Billy

McKinlay. Those two added value to the squad. I don't know how we got permission to sign Summerbee in particular. It was before there were any transfer embargos for clubs in administration.

He made me laugh because he always referred to himself as 'the Option'. 'Give me the ball, I'm the option', he would say. He always wanted the ball wide right. He was a good winger. He had featured in the Sunderland side which ran away with the Championship under Peter Reid and knew his position well.

McKinlay was a ready-made replacement for Dennis. His passing wasn't as good, but he could play. He was an eight or nine out of ten every game and always worked hard, even when he was doing so for no wages to start with. When Billy was asked by a reporter whether it was true he was playing for free, he said, 'I'm not playing for nothing. I'm playing for everything. My future and that of my missus and kids.' That's the kind of character he was.

To plug the other gaps, we needed to promote the youth. Matty Heath, a centre-half, was brought into the first-team, as was left-back Jordan Stewart. Jon Stevenson, Stefan Oakes and the striker Tommy Wright also came through from the youth team.

We were in a new stadium. There was a buzz about the place. But these were still boys on Premier League wages and it was costing the club £15 million a year. I spelled it out to them: we needed to get promotion. So while there was the obvious excitement with the new stadium, I had to get on with mounting a promotion challenge.

We got off to a good start. We shipped six goals at Ipswich but that was the only defeat in the first eleven matches. Our next game against Sheffield Wednesday at Hillsborough in the League Cup was eventful – and not because we won 2–1.

They knew I'm a United fan, so I was getting dog's abuse from behind the bench. For a bit of background, Wednesday's fans refer to

Blades' supporters as 'pigs'. So, I'm getting 'You pig bastard, Adams' every few seconds.

I turned around to see them growling at me when we equalised later on so I put my finger up to my nostrils and shoved it skywards. For want of a better phrase, I gave them a piggy salute. Then I turned back towards the pitch and started organising the team for extra time.

I was at this moment that Corky pulled me to one side and said, 'Have you seen what's happening behind you?'

I said, 'No, and I'm not looking.'

'Have a look.'

There were about twenty stewards struggling to keep punters from jumping over the barrier to get at yours truly. Some lads from the Kop started running around trying to join in. It was like a mini-riot. Police reinforcements were called for.

The head steward came up to me and said, 'Micky, would you mind going and sitting in the stands?'

'Yes, I would. I'm just here doing my job.'

It had developed into a proper stand-off now. There was a battle going on which the police and stewards were only just about winning.

I looked at it and said, 'Well, if I've got to go, I've got to go...'

I walked up the tunnel and up to the directors' box, but there was but one seat available, right next to Harry Bassett and his missus. The fans saw me go up into the stands. I was still getting loads of flack. Then they saw Harry and they started on him, 'Look at 'em – pair of pig bastards...'

Under his breath, Harry turned to me and said, 'Cheers for that, Micky, I was having a quiet night until you turned up.'

A copper came into the dressing room afterwards and took me outside to hear what had gone on. Two days later I got a call from the police, asking me to go to the police station. It started off pleasantly enough. 'I'm here to tell you, you are here for caution,' said one.

'Anything you say blah blah...' I had no legal representation; I didn't think I needed any.

Then the old good cop, bad cop routine started. The bad cop said, 'You did it on purpose – to incite a riot.'

'No, I didn't. I was getting verbally abused.'

Then the good cop said, 'I can see why you would do it, Micky...'

The bad cop: 'No, he did it on purpose.'

Obviously, as I had done little wrong, nothing came of it. But it was one of the more eventful evenings I've spent at Hillsborough.

In the meantime, a bigger problem was looming at the club. The rumours about financial issues refused to go away and in the days leading up to administration, Elsom was adamant that we would not be heading into it. That appeased me and Harry.

I had to give the players credit for not letting the rumours affect them. To be fair, unless the club folded, they would get their money. The last words Elsom said to us were 'Administration won't happen. They'll do it over my dead body.' Later that night, I got a call from Greg Clarke – now the chairman of the Football Association – who, at the time, was a board member, asking me to meet him at a hotel. He dropped the bombshell. He told me that the club was going to be put into administration, and I was to try my best to keep things going in terms of results.

The news broke. We had enough cash to keep the club going for three months, but we had debts of £30 million and were looking for a new buyer.

The administrator arrived for a meeting with me, Harry and Andrew Neville. The conclusion was we had to make cuts to staff members. Any savings we could make in the meantime would be appreciated. He said to me, 'Look, you keep getting results and it strengthens the selling case. The money associated with the Premier League will make it a tasty carrot for someone.'

So there was no immediate threat to my job. I've seen other clubs go into administration at the lower end and they've cleaned out the manager because, nine times out of ten, he's earning the most money. The administrator saw me as an asset and I appreciated that – but he said we needed to make cuts. We couldn't sign players anyway, so all the scouts were laid off. When you go into administration, it is the local suppliers who suffer most, so one of the kit women had to go, but the lads came into their own and said they would pay her wages. Matt Elliott was responsible for that.

Gary, our chef, was fabulous and nothing short of a miracle worker. Before administration, steak, chicken, fish was all on the menu but, after administration, all we got was mince. How many dishes made up of that can you think of? Well, he came up with dozens of them.

It was decided that I should go down and talk to people at the stadium. I just told them I'd keep them informed as best I could. The important thing is to keep going and stick together. They were very worried, as you would expect. Harry did his usual, chummy, cheery routine, which he is good at.

We went to Old Trafford for a League Cup tie as a reward for beating Wednesday. It was an 8 p.m. kick-off and we lost to two late goals. The PFA, because they are based in Manchester, asked if they could come and see us after the tie. We sat down with them at 11 p.m. in the dressing room and discussed wage deferrals and how it would affect them. We all took a 50 per cent hit. It was way after midnight when we departed Old Trafford for home.

This was all adding to the maelstrom that was swirling around me as I tried to juggle my football life and private life. I had Claire and the baby in Leicester, my three daughters in Southampton, the club in administration and a football team to manage. I used to do two journeys a week down to Southampton to see my kids. I was still feeling guilty

I had left them and moved on. It was a horrible balancing act and I failed, on occasions, to keep everyone happy. It was about this time that I became hooked on a type of sleeping tablet, a drug called Sominex, because I was struggling to sleep. A lack of sleep is one of the pitfalls of football management. You can buy Sominex over the counter. I would break them into a quarter and then I would drop off into a really deep sleep. I started taking a quarter, then it moved up to a half before I ended up taking the full tablet. So I had all these balls in the air. My head was all over the place. One time I was driving back from Southampton, I was listening to Adrian Durham's programme on Talksport. 'I'm calling on all Leicester City fans to boycott Saturday's game. What a disgrace.'

It had been in the press that the players were considering a plan to reduce their wages through the administration period. Somehow he had the idea that Leicester's first-team squad wasn't going to help their club and he was making a song and dance about it. I thought to myself, 'I'm ringing him.'

I dialled the number. 'I need to speak to Adrian Durham, please.'

'What about?'

'The Leicester City situation.'

'OK, what's your name?'

'Micky Adams, the manager. Get me on air'.

So they put me on.

'Adrian, what are you talking about? We need Leicester's supporters more than ever because of the administration.'

'Really, well your players are a disgrace...'

'You've got the wrong end of the stick, Adrian. At their request they are in talks now with the PFA about taking a wage cut or deferral on their salary. We are just talking about how it is going to be paid back to them once the club comes out of administration. It all needs to be sorted. But please stop telling our fans that the players are greedy. They do care. Look at the results. We need them more than ever.'

He climbed down because he had to. I understand how it works; he needs a reaction, that's how they get callers on. But I wasn't going to let him trash the players. They had taken it on the chin, worked out a way to defer their wages and clubbed together to keep one of the kit ladies in a job. It wasn't on.

We all took a 50 per cent hit on the wages. Don't feel sorry for us; we were still earning decent dough. But, in general, people live to their means. If someone is earning £10,000 a week, then they will be spending it. I don't want to sound blasé about it, but the players had to make up the money from somewhere. That's the way it is.

After that, fortunately, we went on a good run. Everyone will talk about our Grimsby away game. We were battered and Muzzy managed to score an overhead kick. That was one of the best goals I ever saw – but that was Muzzy. He could do that.

When we played Sheffield United, Neil Warnock got dog's abuse because he wanted us to get a point's deduction. He was just playing the game – as Neil does. It meant the group were more determined. That siege mentality came in again. There wasn't going to be a white charger coming over the hill. We had to do it ourselves.

They were a decent set of lads. Financially, the picture had changed, the players' expectations were changing and they needed to be treated differently.

Some people don't understand what an achievement it was. We couldn't sign any players, so we had to make do with those we had. We really were on our own. Fortunately, we had strong characters, like Elliott, Taggart, the likes of them. They brought the whole group with them.

It was about this time, incidentally, that I went back to Brighton where Dick Knight and the board presented me with a promotion medal from their season on account of the fact that I had managed fifteen games with them the previous season. That was really nice of them and much appreciated.

The real thrust of the season happened the first three months of that year. We didn't lose again until Sheffield United, of all teams, on Easter Monday. At the time, there was plenty of talk about my moving on. My stock had never been higher and Doug Ellis at Aston Villa had just asked Leicester's permission to speak to me about the vacant Aston Villa job. Leicester's response was 'Yes, you can speak to him, but you've got to deposit £1 million in our bank account beforehand. If you take him, that's the compensation.' Doug wouldn't pay it, so I stayed put. I know Aston Villa is a very big football club, but I was happy to remain at Leicester City.

Anyway, we went to Rotherham needing three points to be promoted. We managed to scramble a draw thanks to Trevor Benjamin's goal but it was more than we deserved. The party had to wait a few days until we played Brighton at the Walkers Stadium. I'd rather not have played them, but we were two up fairly early on against a side which contained almost all of my players. After the final whistle, we did a lap of honour. My son Mitchel even came down with me. It was a real weight off my shoulders.

I remember sitting in the bath afterwards: I was absolutely drained. I didn't particularly want to see anyone or speak to anyone. I was just shattered thinking to myself, 'thank the good lord for that.' That night, however, we were having a shindig for Claire's birthday at our house and, not only had we just been promoted, but we had also just found out that we were expecting our second child. My mum, dad, auntie and uncle were keen on having a drink with me to celebrate the promotion. My dad couldn't having been prouder and was in good spirits, whereas my mother just drank the spirits. She wasn't a drinker – she only went out once a week – so she ended up a little worse for wear, to say the least. But she definitely enjoyed herself.

The next day we had to travel to Sheffield for a game against Sheffield United. Personally, I wanted to win the league. I couldn't tell the players not to celebrate promotion; imagine telling the likes of Elliott and Taggart that they couldn't go out for a drink after they had just been promoted and got all their money back. Quite a few players had been celebrating our promotion and so, not to put too fine a point on it, we had to select the eleven we deemed the most sober. But, unfortunately, the game at Bramall Lane didn't go to plan. We took the lead early but conceded a late goal and lost 2–1. Portsmouth won the league and we ended the season as runners-up .There was a bonus payable as well. Those boys picked up a right few quid, and they deserved it for their efforts, too. So for all the trials and tribulations, it was another promotion on my CV – my third. I was flying.

By this time, Jon Holmes – who had made his money in the football agency business – was in charge after the club came out of administration. He was a good chairman – he didn't interfere too much – but he was yet another chairman. Unfortunately, they could not afford to bring the budget back up. There was no extra money. No additional budget. The players were earning Premier League money in the Championship, don't forget. It was a case of seeing what we could get away with. We started recruiting players on free transfers who I called 'the misfits' because that's what they were. I brought in John Curtis from Manchester United, Ricky Scimeca, Keith Gillespie, Les Ferdinand, Danny Coyne, Craig Hignet, Lilian Nalis – and didn't hand over a penny for any of them.

There was a pecking order in the Premier League; pretty similar to what it is today. Those that can pay the transfer fees and wages are somewhere near the top, and that brought it home just what a difficult job it was going to be. Harry was telling me how hard the road was going to be – that you can go six, seven, eight matches without a win. The key, then, was to stay focused and believe in what we were doing.

I had become used to winning by that stage. If you think about my career, I started off ninety-first in the Football League and here I was getting a club promoted into the Premier League. I had come off the back of two and a half seasons of success. I'd agreed a new, lucrative contract. I'm not going to lie, I earned a lot of money when I managed in the Premier League.

I still maintain looking back now that the season that followed could have been very different. It started off with us going two-up in the first quarter-hour against Southampton. We were going along nicely when Kevin Phillips smashes one in from thirty yards. Then we conceded late on. It was a pattern throughout the season. We lost to a last-minute goal against Spurs. We also lost to Wolves, having been three-up at half-time.

As I've said, it was about this time I started taking the sleeping tablets and it was probably this game that started me off on them. That game at Molineux. We were cruising. Wolves were struggling. We went in at half-time, three-up. I pulled Muzzy and gave him a warning that I was going to single him out in front of the rest of them. It wasn't so much a set-up, but it pretty much amounted to the same thing.

'Muzzy, come on,' I say, 'I need you to keep this going. Whatever you do, make sure the first thing you do in the second half is a positive one. Look forward, move forward, pass forward. Don't look for the easy option. This lot are on their knees. Let's go and get another goal. They will leave gaps for you. They have to. Can we break forward quickly? Can we exploit the spaces with Les [Ferdinand] and Dicko [Paul Dickov]?'

The over-riding message then was to be positive.

We kicked off the second half and they were throwing bodies forward. Denis Irwin and Lee Naylor were charging on from full-back. We did have chances to score, but then, all of a sudden, this momentum built up and we could not disrupt it. I think Irwin got in something like nineteen crosses as Wolves just went for broke, winning 4–3. The place went wild.

Obviously, it was a cruel blow. It was interesting when, twenty-four hours later, I had the players in and showed them the DVD of the match. Or, more pertinently, the start of the second half. I had given them instructions to be positive. Not to play sideways balls. To be on the front foot. To keep going at Wolves. But when we replayed the second forty-five minutes to them, it was as if I'd never opened my mouth. They did all the things I asked them not to. Managers sometimes get lucky, and we all take that good fortune. But this had nothing to do with luck. It had everything to do with players not listening to specific instructions.

As the campaign wore on, late goals kept going in against us. And, again, I'm going to highlight something which I believe gets overlooked. You couldn't ever accuse us of being unfit. But it was that old chestnut about me being 'tactically naive'. People were looking at my substitutions and thinking that it was my fault we were shipping all these goals. If you had stopped matches after eighty minutes, we would have been in the top six. As it was, the game lasted for ninety and we were struggling to keep ourselves out of the bottom three.

But I'm not tactically naive. The thing is, a lot of teams had big squads and they were able to bring on quality replacements. With respect to the players on our books, that wasn't the case. For example, at Middlesbrough away, we were winning 3–1 and the fourth official had actually put four minutes extra up on his board. I took off Marcus Bent and Dickov and put on Ferdinand and Gillespie. Les, bless him, wasn't much younger than me. I wasn't in the position where I needed to keep him happy – but I did want to keep him involved. And so I took the decision to put him on. We couldn't lose a 3–1 lead, could we? It turned out that yes, we could.

Somehow James Scowcroft managed to clear the ball from inside his own area, back over his head to make it 3–2. Then they scrambled another goal and in the end we drew; another two points that we had just thrown away.

But at least we had a trip to look forward to. Some warm-weather training, a few beers and a chance to rejuvenate ourselves before the final matches that would define the success or otherwise of our season.

Oh yes: I was certainly looking forward to going to La Manga.

CHAPTER 13

LA MANGA

If you Google my name – and there's no reason why you should – one of the first options in the drop-down menu will be these two words: La Manga. While they have become synonymous with me, they do not define me, nor are they a fair representation of my work as a manager.

Unfortunately, since those few days in March 2004, I've become painted with a broad brush. Before Leicester City travelled out to Spain, I was regarded as a disciplinarian. When we returned, however, all that changed. Although nothing was proven and no charges were ever brought against the players, the mud stuck.

But I want you to judge for yourselves. Here is the story behind the lurid tabloid headlines. Big news? What do you think?

Premier League footballers were caught up in sex scandal. Actually, it was far more serious than that. There were allegations of rape and sexual assault.

The players and I were Public Enemy Number One. They'd crossed the line and I was in charge, so I had to carry the can. We were the villains. And everyone in the news media queued up to twist the knife.

This sorry episode all started back in February, about a month before the circus unfolded, when I had a conversation with my director of football, Dave 'Harry' Bassett, about taking the lads away for a few days. Now, of course, I wish I could turn back the clock.

At the time, though, I had solid reasons for my decision. I'd recently brought in Steve Cotterill to help with the coaching and I wanted to integrate him into the squad. I felt the lads could do with a change of scenery; in fact, we all needed one. And our place of choice to unwind was La Manga, a sports complex in mainland Spain.

However, there was a slight issue with that, since the club had been there before and Stan Collymore had let off a fire-extinguisher on a team bonding exercise at 4 a.m. Of course, that story had made its way back to Blighty and there was plenty of fall-out and none of it reflected well on the club. The chances of a repeat were slim, but a few people at the club made comments when La Manga was mentioned again. Harry and I assured everyone it would all be OK.

Now, for those of you who don't know, La Manga is a five-star training base. Complete with golf courses, eight pristine football pitches that all meet FIFA standards, hotels, restaurants and villas. It is located on an exclusive resort in Cartagena, near Murcia. A lot of clubs go there mid-season for warm-weather training. The theory is that it provides a break for everyone from the training ground and it enables you to actually get some work done without any distractions.

In our case, I wanted to lighten the mood because it was fairly clear by that stage that our fight to stay in the Premier League would go to the wire. We needed everyone pulling in the right direction after our goalless draw with Dave Jones's Wolves' side the day before. The lads were in reasonable spirits as we turned up at Luton Airport on the Sunday. It was a travelling day, so there wasn't going to be any training as such. That could wait until Monday.

The players wanted a drink. As footballers do, they wouldn't dare arrive at the airport and just start ordering. Muzzy Izzet and Matt

Elliott came to see me and asked for permission. I replied, 'Yes, no problem. But you are representing the club. Nothing silly.' Even though they were club employees, we didn't travel in tracksuits. I didn't want this to be seen as an official trip.

Nothing happened on the plane, apart from the noise and laughter you'd normally associate with thirty blokes. It wasn't until the coach stopped outside the resort that I laid down what I thought were reasonably relaxed rules, with an obvious sting in the tail for anyone who stepped out of line.

When we pulled up, the three women who turned out to be at the centre of all the controversy were milling around the reception area. They were the first thing I saw. It was the first thing everybody else saw as well. So I grabbed hold of the microphone and said, 'First thing's first: do not fall for that one. We can see there are young ladies here. I do not want any nonsense. You know the rules. If you misbehave and cause any problems for guests, I will send you home. Simple as that. I don't mind you having a few drinks. But if you turn up for training at 10.30 a.m. tomorrow morning clearly the worse for wear, then I will discipline you.' There wasn't a curfew set for that night. The only guideline was that they all had to be in a fit state to train.

At this stage, I need to give you some background information, because it explains why I wasn't awake and when there were problems later on. A couple of weeks before, I'd had a medical; it was something the League Managers' Association did every year. When the results came back, my liver was suffering for alcohol, so I had decided that I was going to have a month off the booze. This explains why, as we checked in to the hotel, I turned to the rest of the coaching staff and said, 'I'm going to bed.' I knew that if I'd sat down and the staff wanted a bevvy, I'd have had one, so I took myself off to my room at about 7.30 p.m. and slept pretty well.

I was drained after the game against Wolves the day before; that was the first thing. The second was that I didn't want to put myself in a position where I could have had a drink. So I said to my assistant Alan Cork, 'Right, you're in charge.' And left him to it.

That was my first mistake.

The next morning I went down for breakfast and, in the lobby, I spotted an old friend of mine I used to play with at Gillingham called Pat Walker, who was now an assistant manager at one of the Danish clubs. We had a laugh about the old days and he asked me if I fancied a drink. I didn't have the heart to tell him I was temporarily on the wagon. So I agreed to meet him that night, but later decided to swerve it. Sorry Pat.

Anyway, on our way out to training, I pulled Corky aside.

'Any problems?'

'No, gaffer.'

'Are you sure?'

'No problems.'

I took his word for it. We had a decent session and Steve Cotterill put on a crossing and finishing drill. I always gave them a bit of running at the end to put a sweat on them.

I allowed them to play golf in the afternoon. I had a knock too, and even bumped into Ron Noades, which was great because he'd sacked me at Brentford and there I was as a Premier League manager. This was the first time I'd seen him since then. That was sweet; bitter-sweet, as later events transpired.

When Monday evening came around, the staff were having a few beers and I was going to bed early again. The lads, however, decided they were going to go out, so Corky wanted to take them off the complex to an Italian restaurant. It was compulsory for everyone, except for me. I was trying to swerve anything to do with alcohol, remember.

I just wanted to use it as a time to relax. Clearly, I was in a minority although, in fairness, a few of the lads, such as James Scowcroft and Lilian Nalis, also didn't drink.

I thought, 'Great, I'll go up to my room and watch the Monday night game on Sky.' It must have been about 8 p.m., just before the match kicked off on television. Then it kicked off in my room. People were banging on the door and I thought it was Pat Walker, so I just blanked it. Then my mobile started ringing with a load of numbers I didn't recognise – so I blanked them as well. Is this starting to sound familiar?

Anyway, there was more banging on the door and the phone in the room went off. Honestly, it went on for about an hour, on and off. I was getting pissed off by this stage. I thought to myself, 'Blimey, Pat, I know I said I'd come for a drink but surely you can't be that desperate...'

The next thing I know, someone's trying to get in. It's the hotel manager, our fixer – the guy who was looking after us during the trip – and a copper.

The copper looked at me and said, 'We need you to come downstairs.'

His expression and the tone of his voice told me something serious was afoot. I went down to the hotel manager's room, where there were two more of his colleagues. I looked at them and asked, 'Is there a problem?' One of them, in broken English, said, 'Yes, there's been a problem. But no one has died.'

My initial reaction?

'Oh, great,' I said. 'You had me worried there.'

He looked at me and said, 'Mr Adams, there has been an allegation of rape.'

'Involving whom?'

'Your players', came the reply. 'There's also been allegations of sexual assault and physical violence as well on Sunday night. We need to see all the passports.'

I said, 'Do you mean to tell me my players have been involved in this? Because, according to my assistant manager this morning, nothing happened. He's said nothing to me.'

The copper said, 'We can't give you the details now. But we need to see the passports.'

At this stage, I should explain that it's common practice among football clubs not to allow footballers to have their own passports on trips such as these; they'll either lose them or forget them. One week before a trip, the relevant documents are gathered in by clubs and upon landing, a club official will hand them back to their owners again. When that country's immigration demands have been satisfied, they are returned to the club for safe-keeping throughout the duration of the trip. I know what you are thinking. But that's the way it is.

Anyway, the hotel had all the passports in the safe for us. Before I gave the players' passports to the police, I took all the staff passports out because he'd mentioned nothing about the coaching staff.

He took them from me. 'Right, what's going to happen is that tomorrow morning we are going to come back to the hotel. We will tell you which players we want to see. They will need to report to Cartagena police station at 11 a.m.'

That was it. They left and I was left standing there on my own in silence. I kept thinking to myself, 'Is this an elaborate wind-up? Corky said nothing happened.' I got my mobile phone out and call him.

'Corky, where are you?' I can hear the noise of the restaurant in the background. They were clearly having a good time.

'We're having some food...'

'Have you eaten yet?'

'Yes, we're just waiting for some pudding...'

'Fuck that. Get all the lads back to the hotel. I need a chat with them all. Now.'

Silence.

'Are you all right?'

'Am I all right? No, not really. Get them back here. Pronto. And you had better tell every single one of them to get back here, now. No one is to slope off. No one is to go out. Get them back here. All of them. If they don't come back, I'll send them home immediately.'

I put the phone down and asked the manager if he could make a meeting room available to us.

As soon as they returned to the hotel, I pulled Corky aside. 'You told me when I asked you this morning that nothing happened last night', I said.

'Well, it didn't', he replies.

'Are you sure?' I said.

'There was a bit of noise in the corridor and I told them all to quieten themselves down because if the manager finds out they've been disturbing other guests, he'll send you home. And that was it.'

When the lads got back, I gathered them all in the room the hotel had set aside. I said, 'Look, I'm sorry to mess your night up boys but I've just had the Spanish police in here. They are alleging that someone has been raped and it involves you lot.'

The reaction was instant. 'No way,' came one voice from the floor, interspersed with others saying, 'Nah, you must be joking.'

I said, 'Listen, this is serious. They've taken your passports. In the morning, they're coming back and they are going to want to interview certain players. So you had better have a little think to yourselves now about what you are going to say.'

Then someone piped up. 'Ah gaffer, you know those three girls...'

Yep, despite being told specifically not to go anywhere near them, they had ignored the advice.

'We were just messing about. There was banter and that's about it.'

'Look, if there's anyone here that has done something that they shouldn't, they had better wait behind and see me, because we need to start thinking about what might happen tomorrow. If we need lawyers, then we need to get them organised, because this is a serious matter.'

At this stage, the mood is still fairly bullish among them. I'm not sure they realised what might be about to hit them. To be fair, I didn't have much of an idea, either. And, by this stage, I was starting to lose my temper because they were looking at me and not owning up to anything.

So I said it again. 'Look, something's gone on that the police are not happy about. I do not want you on the phone to your wives, girlfriends or agents tonight. We need to keep this in-house for as long as possible.'

Then they filed out, one by one, and went to their respective rooms. But Ian Walker and Keith Gillespie wanted to go to the casino. By now, I was in a foul mood and told them, in fairly straightforward language, that I wanted them in the hotel. It wasn't until Keith wrote his own autobiography that I realised they'd sneaked out and ignored me. It's a good job I didn't find out at the time, because it would have cost the pair of them much more than what they lost gambling.

Anyway, they all went upstairs – as far as I knew, at least – but Steffen Freund, our German midfielder, was hanging around. Nice lad, Steffen. The rest of the boys liked him a lot. Clearly, something was troubling him.

'Steffen, have you got a problem? Anything I can help you with?'

Although he speaks good English, he does so with a strong accent.

'Gaffer,' he says. 'Vot is rape?'

'Well, Steffen, rape is when you have sexual intercourse with a woman who doesn't want intercourse with you.'

'No, no, no,' he says shaking his head and wagging his finger at me. 'She vanted it…'

Bloody hell. 'Are you telling me, Steffen, that you've had sex with one of these girls?'

'She was German and she fucking vanted it, gaffer.'

I turn to Corky and said, 'I think we've narrowed this one right down Alan…'

I told Steffen to go to his room. We had nothing to do then but wait.

It won't surprise you to learn that I couldn't sleep.

We were about to have serious charges laid at our door, and I didn't have a clue what was going on, apart from the admission from our German midfielder who insisted the sex he'd had was consensual.

At about 8 a.m. there was a knock on my door. The police had turned up. I thought to myself, 'Steffen is the only person they'll want to see.'

How wrong can you be?

One by one, the surnames were read out: Dabizas, Sinclair, Scowcroft, Dickov, Freund… nine of them. I was struggling to come to terms with it. I didn't know if it was a set-up or what. To be frank, I was pissed off. I wanted to go out training and this had messed up the whole point of the trip. I had thought that it was just Steffen who was in the frame and, OK, it wasn't great, but if what he was telling me was true, he could go and sort it out and we'd be back on track.

As it was, I had to knock on nine doors and tell the players that they had to report to a police station. I go to see Frank Sinclair. I knock on his door.

'Frank, you're with me. Half an hour, downstairs.'

'OK gaffer, no problem.'

I head up the corridor to get James Scowcroft. I knock on his door. I do the same with Lillian Nalis and Nikos Dabizas.

'Scowy, half an hour, downstairs.'

'Gaffer, what are you on about? I didn't even go out.'

'I don't care, Scowy. They want to see you.'

'Gaffer, please, I was in bed. I've done nothing wrong.'

'Scowy, they want to speak to you. If I don't come and get you, then they'll just come up.'

Clearly, he's worried. By this stage, I'd spoken to our media guru Paul Mace and told him what had gone on. He was trying to keep it under wraps. I had to ring up Harry and the chairman, Jim McCahill, and we found a lawyer in Cartagena. We had an hour in his office before we went to see the police. The lads, amazingly, were in great spirits. I told Corky to take the lads that remained to put on a session. At that stage, I still harboured hopes that we would be able to get back on track that afternoon. But it wasn't to be.

The lads were still protesting their innocence. Chief executive Tim Davies, reading the script correctly, had jumped on a plane and had arrived in time for us to head to the lawyer's office. The lads still all thought it was a joke. They were laughing among themselves.

The lawyer turned to me and said, 'You'd better calm them down; these are serious accusations.'

I replied, 'Would you mind telling them?'

So, I gathered them round, and the lawyer said, 'In Spain, these are serious allegations and if you are guilty of anything, the court's going to come down hard on you.'

In an instant, the mood was flattened.

The lawyer then took me and Tim to one side. She spelled out what was going to happen. The prosecutors wanted to see all of the players individually, and then they would take it from there. So, off we went to the police station.

At the front desk, an associate of the lawyer explained who we were and what we were there for. We are ushered upstairs into quite a large room in the police station. There were two doors. As soon as we all sat down, two armed guards came and stood in front of the doors. It was clear it was no longer a laughing matter. For a start, no one was now allowed to leave the building.

I ask the players again.

'Gaffer, we had a bit of fun. It was game-on with the girls. There was a bit of silly dancing. But honestly, that's about it.'

Everyone was then interviewed individually. The first person they want to see? Steffen Freund.

The lads are chuckling because they know he's had sex with one of them. I thought, 'This is it.' Out he goes and into a room down the corridor, but five minutes later he returns walking casually down the corridor with the lawyer.

He opens the door and enters the room where we are. 'Gaffer,' he said. 'I will see you later.'

'What do you mean, you'll see me later?'

'I am free to go. I told you she vanted it...'

It's turning into a dark comedy sketch.

I'm now thinking to myself, 'That's it. It's all a mistake. Brilliant, finished, done.'

Next one up: Paul Dickov.

He's a bit longer than Freund. But, after ten minutes, he comes back into the room. Only there's no sauntering back into the room for Paul. He's bent forward, with both of his arms behind his back in handcuffs, with two mean coppers pushing him around. They're shoving him through the room and towards the other door. The lads are genuinely gobsmacked.

Dicko shouted, 'Gaffer, can you ring my wife? They've taken my phone off me. I've got nothing.'

I grab a pen and a piece of paper off the female lawyer. 'Right, give me your phones and your missus' telephone number before you go in there.'

We're stunned.

Then, one by one, they all go in – and they all come out hand-cuffed. Apart from Steffen Freund, who went back to the hotel.

When the last one has been processed, the lads are in cells and I'm left with Tim Davies in that room. I've got all the players' phones, barring Dickov's. The lawyer comes back into the room. I ask what the next stage is. Her reply did not fill me with a great deal of hope. 'They've been arrested and they need to appear to answer the charges before a judge tomorrow' is the basic gist of it. She said that one of us could go down and see them in an hour's time.

So, I thought, what can I do in an hour? I'll phone the WAGs. So, one by one, I go through them all. Mrs Matt Elliott takes the biscuit for her attitude. The conversation went something like this.

'Hello, Mrs Elliott, it's Micky Adams.'

'Oh. Yeah.'

'Er, I'm ringing about Matty. There's been an incident at the hotel and, er...'

'Let me stop you there. Does it involve women?'

'Well, er, sort of, but I'm not really sure he's been involved. But I'm just ringing you to let you know that he won't be in touch for a day or so because he's, er, been arrested.'

'Good. They can fucking keep him. They can lock him up.'

And, with that, the phone went down.

In fairness, Mrs Elliott was a one-off; generally, there were tears down the phone. I told all the WAGs that I would ring them that night to update them on what was going on. Obviously, I didn't bother with Mrs Elliott. She'd made it pretty clear where she stood on the whole affair.

It was lunchtime by now and we had still managed to keep it quiet. The public, amazingly, knew nothing about it.

The lawyer then appeared and said either Tim or I had to go down to the holding cells to make sure they were OK. I exchanged glances with Tim and we agreed that I should be the one to go. I went down the stairs and the first one I saw was Scowy. He was standing up, hanging on to the bars in one of the two cells for dear life. I remember it to this day. I tried to lighten the mood a little bit. Wrong move.

He's looking at me, shall we say, emotionally. 'Gaffer, gaffer, have you rung my missus?'

'Yes, Scowy, I have.'

'What did she say?'

'That she's going to kill you when you get home…'

That finished him off. Despite the gravity of the situation, his colleagues just gave him a load of abuse.

I gave a little speech. 'Listen, lads, I've spoken to all of your wives and girlfriends, and there's been a mixed reaction, I have to say. Matty, your missus is a diamond.'

'Why, gaffer, what did she say?'

'That they can lock you up for all she cares…'

All Elliott did was give a little laugh.

I ask if they need anything. There's a collective call for blankets because it's so cold down there.

I ask if there's anything else. Someone mentions food.

I turn to go and I give them a little pep talk on the way out.

'Look, lads, providing you lot are all telling me the truth, I'm sure it will get sorted, sooner rather than later, and we can all get on with our lives.'

I go back up to see the lawyer. 'Can we get them some food and blankets?'

'Yes, yes, of course…'

We arranged for the hotel to put together a load of grub and blankets and send it to the police station where we were assured that the lads would be fed.

Yeah, right. To this day, I don't know what happened but not one of the players saw so much as an apple, and they certainly didn't have anything other than their own clothes to keep warm. Well, I say I don't know what happened, but I've got a pretty good idea. It doesn't take a genius to work out that the Spanish police had a great feed at Leicester City's expense.

The only thing for it was to go back to the hotel. The rest of the squad were waiting there, don't forget and we – the club's management – had a decision to make about them. The only thing for it was to send them home. We couldn't do meaningful sessions without nine players.

We arranged to get them home and I got the staff together. First words out of my mouth ? 'Please, someone, get me a pint...'

Incredibly, it still hadn't become public knowledge. But all of that was about to change.

But first, I had an issue to sort out of my own. If we were going to spend time in that freezing cold courtroom, I needed extra clothing. I hadn't taken anything with me apart from T-shirts. The forecast was good. I had no coat. So, I asked Alan to pick me up a jumper from the golf shop at the hotel. What's funny now is that he came back with this light blue number which is in every single picture of me throughout the rest of my stay.

On Wednesday, Tim, the lawyer and I had to go to the courthouse in Cartagena. When we turned up, there was no one there apart from a few people going about their normal everyday business. There wasn't even any press to be seen. Within ten minutes of our arrival, however, the world descended on the place.

There were guards everywhere trying to prevent photographers from taking pictures of us all. Television cameras everywhere. There were dozens of guards. People breaking through the cordon to take pictures of us all. Cameras going off left, right and centre. The story had broken in Spain that these footballers were appearing in court. My phone was ringing non-stop. And it was bedlam.

By this time, I'd had a word with our media guy and knew what was coming. Even though I'm experienced in dealing with the press, it's normally on football matters. This was proper news as far as they were concerned. The stakes had been raised. And I needed to know from Paul Mace exactly where I stood. The advice went something like this: 'Look, Micky, the eyes of the world are upon you now. Even if you are having a private conversation with someone next to you, somebody else might be listening. Don't smile. Basically, don't trust anyone. If you are asked a question, don't answer. Just bat it back with the standard "No comment." Fend everything off. Speak to me, the chairman, Harry, but after that – blank everyone.'

We then went to see the lads. They were all kept in custody. The day after, some of them were bailed. The three who weren't were Keith Gillespie, Paul Dickov and Frank Sinclair.

Even at that stage, no one was admitting to anything. It was embarrassing for the authorities. They were looking at passports that were almost ten years old. How the girls could have identified anyone, I really don't have a clue. Luckily, James Scowcroft has a mole on his face. I'm sure he would have been teased about it at school, but he was certainly grateful for it when it came to the crunch in that Spanish courthouse because it was the key to him getting off. The judge said to one of the girls, 'You have alleged this man attacked you. You've mentioned his blond hair but not once have you mentioned the mole on the side of his face, and it's there for everyone to see.'

Lilian Nalis had blond hair. So did Ian Walker. Walker was in the room with the girls while Lilian Nalis was tucked up in bed. But because he had long blond hair in his passport photo, they picked him out.

It took all day. In and out. When it finally finished, there was the media scrum outside that we had to combat. And that's the right word for it – it was a bun fight.

Tim pulled me to one side and said, 'Look, it's all right, I've ordered us a taxi. What I'm going to do is read out a short statement and then not speak to anyone from here to the car. We're going to get out of here "No commenting" and, by the time get down the steps, away we go. The taxi will be waiting for us.'

Tim stopped to do a short press statement on the steps. He finished and emerged from the media scrum, but it was soon clear there was no waiting car. We got to the bottom of the steps. We walked left. Then we walked right. The press are following us with cameras. It was like something out of Benny Hill. I'm now looking at Tim and shouting, 'Where's the taxi?' Suddenly, one pulls up out of absolutely nowhere and we jump in, smartish. It was not a co-ordinated exit, let me tell you.

Anyway, it was a case of going out of the frying pan and into the fire. When we first arrived, the hotel was deserted. Not any longer. If we thought this was going to be a haven of peace and calm, we were mistaken. When we returned, it was absolutely packed. You could not get a seat in the place. All the hotel rooms were full. We had no chance of walking around the hotel unmolested.

To be fair to the staff, they squared off an area so we could have a bit of space to ourselves. But what really upset me – and I'm still upset about it even now – was the reaction of the Professional Footballers' Association. Or should I say their 'non-reaction'.

One of the lads phoned up the PFA for help, and the response was that they were unable to help, because the players were abroad. I thought that was plain wrong. What's the union for if not to help members in need? After it all died down, I wrote an article in which I said I was disgusted with the attitude of both unions, the League Managers' Association and PFA. And I stand by it.

Gordon Taylor, the PFA's chief executive, hammered me later, saying they had done plenty to help and insinuating that I was lying. But it was two whole weeks after I got back until John Barnwell, the union's head, was on the phone. Two weeks after I returned home from one of the biggest scandals to hit English football in a generation.

The conversation went something like this:

'Micky, it's John Barnwell. I'm just ringing about La Manga. Are you all right?'

'John, you're the head of my union and it's taken you two weeks to see if I'm all right. If I was Alex Ferguson you'd have been on the phone straight away. I'd have access to the best lawyers. The lot.'

'Yes, but Micky you had Dave Bassett to call on.'

'You're right; but he's not the head of my union – you are.'

Anyway, the next day, all the players appeared in court. We managed to get some of the charges dropped. Scowy was released on ball for the sum of 20,000 euros. But three were getting locked up again: Dickov, Sinclair and Gillespie. I had the opportunity to go and see them, and I went straight down there. I have to say, there were a lot of tears. I've never seen three lads so distraught. They didn't have a clue what lay ahead. To be honest, I couldn't help them either.

The court sessions were all closed and all I still had to go on was what the players were telling me.

'Yes, gaffer, we had a few drinks,' was the line. 'Yes, gaffer, it got boisterous – but we didn't do anything to them.'

Even when they were in bits, they had not deviated from the story. I re-read the charges the other day. Keith Gillespie is supposed to have held one of the girls down while Paul Dickov penetrated her. It was all absolute rubbish. I believed them at the start. I knew they'd done nothing wrong.

It was Thursday night and we, as a management team, had to make a decision. Tim and I decided that we were going to have to go home without them as we had to focus on trying to get a win against Birmingham City in our next game. So we took the decision to go home on the Friday. Six of the players, along with me and Tim, flew back to Luton Airport.

Again, it was going to be the same drill with the media: saying nothing and just getting through it as best as we could. A few seats around us were closed off by the airline so that no one could approach us when we were on the plane.

It was horrendous again when we emerged from the airport, however. I'd taken the blue jumper off and it was around my shoulders. And, not forgetting the orders from my family, I managed to get my mum some cigarettes from duty free. So, there I am, looking like a tourist coming home with his plastic duty-free bag, rather than a Premier League football manager who's just had the biggest nightmare of his professional career.

When we got in a minibus and set off, we realised we were being followed by the press. The plan was to drive up the M1, lose the cameras and then travel back down the motorway to retrieve our vehicles from the car park. But I ended falling out with our second-choice keeper Danny Coyne over it. In the minibus, he said, 'My car's in that car park over there' as we drove past it. And I just lost my temper. 'So's mine,' I said. 'But we have been told by the police that we need to do all of this.'

'What a load of bollocks that is', he said.

'Just like the load of bollocks I've been through with you lot. If you'd listened to me last Sunday when we turned up at the hotel, none of this would have happened.'

When something like this happens, everyone all of a sudden is an expert. Turn on the telly and it was our faces you saw. 'Typical footballers' was the attitude. 'Pissed-up, out-of-control, more money than sense...'

There were some funny things came out of it, mind you. On Saturday morning, when we were back, I could hear banging on my front door.

This fella was at the front door. 'Micky, I'm from *The Times*,' he said. 'You've not spoken and we'd like your side of the story.'

I told him to get off my property as fast as he could. As he started coming back with something, I spotted a photographer in the bushes.

I opened the door further and said, 'Listen, I'm doing a press conference on Monday and you can ask whatever you want... anyway, how did you know where I lived?'

My next door neighbour Jeremy, who was clearing leaves from his garden, looked up and said, 'Micky, I'm really sorry. They just asked where you lived and I told them. I'm really sorry.'

'Have you not heard what's happened to me over the past week?'

'Well, I did hear a rumour...'

A rumour? He knew what I did for a living, and Leicester City were the second biggest story on the *News at Ten* that week! He still feels bad to this day.

As planned, we had a press conference on the Monday. I had ninety minutes with Leicester's press guy Paul Mace beforehand, which was helpful. It wasn't so much the local sports reporters I had the problem with; I knew most of them. It was the news hounds. There were going to be questions from anti-rape groups and all sorts. I was being guided through the various scenarios. And they were all basically coming from the same angle: that this lot are the scum of the earth.

I couldn't say too much because of the legal processes. But, as far as I was concerned, all they were guilty of was drinking to excess thirteen days before our next Premier League fixture. And even then, some of them hadn't even been guilty of that.

We had a few issues when the players returned to the training ground ahead of the Birmingham game. I had to stop training because the media world had converged on the Walkers Stadium. I called a halt to a training session and sent them home.

Besides, the players' minds weren't on it. There was a lot of resentment in the squad because they wanted Ian Walker to put his hand up instead of Lilian Nalis. Walker refused to do it, so they were growling at him. There were a lot of underlying resentments. I decided to give them the Wednesday off. But the stories kept coming piling up at our door.

When Frank, Keith and Dicko eventually came home there was a follow-up in the *Daily Star*, and there was a picture of Frank with one of the girls. He had his leg wrapped around her.

Apparently, she was teaching him an 'African folk dance...'

The story asked the readers to make their own minds up.

I called Frank into my office. 'Frank, have you seen this morning's newspaper?'

'Yes, gaffer.'

'Well, will you get into any trouble with your missus or is it all OK?'

'No, it will be OK, gaffer, she doesn't read the *Daily Star*...'

Frank did not give a toss.

So, there was some banter and fun, but not much. As time wore on, the truth inevitably came out. Nothing illegal had taken place and all charges were dropped. I still don't know to this day what actually happened. There was a theory that the girls were paid, possibly by a newspaper. I'm going to offer up my own ideas. The hotel itself was for sale. They were having difficulty filling the rooms. They heard we were coming out and they decided to put three girls of certain morals, shall we say, in there. The girls said that they had been paid by another tourist to go to the hotel and spend time with the players, but they never divulged who he was. After it all happened, they then got paid a lot of money by the *News of the World*. They did not admit to their line of work.

It's interesting that it happened on the Sunday night and nothing was reported to the police until Monday evening – almost twenty-four hours later. Afterwards, the hotel went from empty to full with publicity like you wouldn't believe. Was it helpful to have a sex scandal involving Premier League footballers at a hotel complex struggling to find a buyer?

We were front-page news on a global scale. When the charges were dropped, it was still a ten-paragraph story on page six in papers such as the *Daily Mail*.

In the aftermath, I offered to resign. It wasn't just a gesture. I felt that it happened on my watch, so I offered it to Tim Davies and the board. I could understand if they felt that it was an episode in the life of the football club that had shown them up in a poor light. But it was declined, and I was grateful.

It may surprise a few people that there wasn't one fine dished out on the trip. The players were absolutely adamant they had done nothing wrong. It was put to me that I should have hit the lot of them in the pocket for bringing the club into disrepute. But how could you enforce that? How could you bring that to bear when Lilian Nalis had stayed in his room? Or Nikos Dabizas and Danny Coyne, who had been having a couple of beers away from the hotel?

The whole episode left a nasty taste and had a damaging effect on my career. From being someone who was classed as a firm disciplinarian, suddenly I wasn't trusted. And I don't really think I recovered from it.

I had three draining seasons at the club. At the end of it all, I was tired. I ended fighting a relegation battle that ultimately failed. It had been tough, but I'm not seeking sympathy. That's just the way it was.

Of course, my story could have taken a different path had those events in La Manga not taken place. It remains the one episode of my professional life that will haunt me for ever. And that's the right word: it really does haunt me. I'd like to be remembered as a decent manager/coach, but when you look up 'Micky Adams Leicester City', what comes up? It's not saving a club from administration. It's not getting promotion. It's not playing in the Premier League. It's La Manga.

The one aspect where I felt like I had succeeded was with the players. I would like to think I earned their respect for the way I handled the La Manga episode.

At the time, I was what many would consider to be a young manager. I had just turned forty years old. That said, nothing can prepare you for an event like that. Nothing. It happens and you battle through it the best you can, even though, at times, the easier option would be to have chucked in the job and walked away.

In the years since then, it seems like everyone has a different view on it – and most people have stopped and told me about it, too.

So, would I have changed anything? In one way, yes: I wouldn't have gone. But we were thirteen days away from the next game of football and you have got to be able to trust your players to have a few drinks. And do you know what? It seemed a good idea at the time…

CHAPTER 14

THE END GAME AT LEICESTER

After La Manga, we managed to pick up two draws against Everton and Liverpool, but we were down before the final game of the season.

Honestly, it could have been so different had we not conceded so many late goals. As it was, however, a relegated Leicester City stood between Arsenal going through a whole season undefeated. I will always remember that game.

Now, Frank Sinclair loved a bevvy. It was his thing. And as a footballer, if you are dehydrated, you make mistakes. I always felt with him that he made his errors late on because of that.

Anyway, we were winning one-nil at Highbury. In all fairness to us, we were comfortable going in at half-time. We had already been relegated, so we were there to spoil a party. So we weren't too stressed. A few minutes after half-time, Frank had a rush of blood and hauled over Thierry Henry. They scored the resulting penalty and went on to win the game 2–1.

After the game, the Premier League were doing the presentations on the pitch and so our coach had got no chance of leaving Highbury. Not a prayer. So, we decided to go and have a drink. We piled into Arsene's room – I actually can't say with any honesty that we had been invited in – and we helped ourselves to all the booze that we could find in there.

When he eventually came in, he was really surprised to see us. But not as surprised as I was at what he did next. After saying 'Hello' – he was obviously relaxed because Arsenal had just won the league – he did something that I'll remember for a long time. He took the medal from around his neck and flung it into his bag in the corner of the room. It was as if he had already closed the chapter on the 'Invincibles' season and was already turning his attention to the following campaign.

Two days later, I got a call from Glenn Cockerill.

He said, 'I saw one of your players out the night before. I presume he wasn't playing.'

I asked who it was.

'Frank Sinclair', came the reply.

'No, you're wrong. He was in the hotel with me.'

'Sorry, Micky, he wasn't. He was in a restaurant with me…'

I had got the club promoted from the Championship before. The plan was to get them up again…

It was an awful summer. We wanted to rebuild, but what we really needed to do was give the squad an overhaul as a lot of players were out of contract. We also lost Paul Dickov to Blackburn Rovers. He was our leading scorer and he left for £50,000 due to a clause in his contract that allowed him to quit for that much if we were relegated. His agent, Phil Smith, actually got us £100,000 and acted like he was doing us a favour. Perhaps he was, but losing one of your top players for that amount wasn't much recompense.

Frank Sinclair went. Ditto Callum Davidson. My summer was spent trying to recruit – it wasn't enjoyable.

I ended up having a row with Danny Coyne, our reserve keeper, because he had been tapped up by Burnley. I said I'd deal with it when I returned. I could understand why he wanted to go but I was on holiday and the whole issue started getting to me.

We ended up signing David Connolly from West Ham. He was a complex character, one of those who wanted to know how I was going to make him a better player, as I'd done with Zamora and Dickov. I felt he was a good fit, but it was clear the squad was going to take time to gel.

Then I signed Martin Keown, who will have to go down as one of the worst signings of my career. I thought I was getting a good character; a leader. Considering he was someone who had won the Premier League with Arsenal, he should have been both those things. There was nothing wrong with the way he trained. He was getting older and there were times when he couldn't keep up with all the drills. I had no problem with that, but he was a constant moaner.

I always remember one of his first matches, away at Millwall. As we always did for away games in London, we travelled on the afternoon before the match. We got stuck in traffic and Keown started whining. 'This didn't happen at Arsenal. The coach driver used to ring up the AA and make sure the route was clear.' I told him, 'Martin, there's been an accident. The driver's not a psychic.'

He was difficult when it came to his pre-match meals as well. He wanted Dover sole that evening which, in itself, is not an issue, but when his fish wasn't ready, he ordered chicken as well. So the fish came out and he didn't want it. It was just thrown away. At those kinds of hotels, you are talking about a meal that cost £40. That irritated me.

Another gripe was when we did set-pieces. I have a set way of defending corners, for instance. I had one at the near post, one on the six-yard box, five markers, two on the edge of the box and one up the pitch. It was fairly bog-standard. The reaction?

'This isn't how we do it at Arsenal', said our new centre-half.

I remember having to pull all the lads in together and say, 'Let's just buy into what I'm doing. If it doesn't work, then we will change it.'

But there was always this irritating voice at the back saying, 'This is how we do things at Arsenal.'

Another example of what a pain in the rear end he could be occurred when We went to Derby County early in the season. We were one-up at half-time but I still had a pop at our two central midfielders, Gareth Williams and Lilian Nalis. I didn't feel there was any rotation in midfield, so I had a go at the pair of them. I used a few expletives, but we ended up winning 2–1.

The next day, we're in for a warm-down and there's a knock at my door. It was him.

'I've got to tell you, gaffer, the way you spoke to those lads at half-time, Arsene Wenger wouldn't have done that', he said.

By now, the fuse was ready to come out.

I replied, 'Listen Martin, with the greatest of respect, Gareth Williams is not Manu Petit and Lilian Nalis isn't Patrick Vieira. So fuck off and leave me alone.'

But the straw that broke the camel's back came when we travelled to play Gillingham. A board member told me that Keown had let it be known that, if anything happened to me, then he was available. I got wind of this. On the morning of the game, I said to Alan Cork, 'When you see Martin Keown, tell him to come over and I want you to stay and listen in.'

I had allowed Martin to travel to Priestfield in his car. When he got there, I asked, 'Good journey down?

'Yes, thanks, gaffer.'

'Have you got your car?'

'Yes, gaffer.'

'Well, get in it and fuck off. I can't deal with you. You're not my type of character, person or player.'

That's the way he was. When I listen to him now on television, he sounds sensible, but, I've got to be honest, I've got no time for him. He should have been better. He won't like me for saying this, but I don't care. He has attacked me from time to time in certain newspapers, but I can live with that.

So, it's fair to say this was a tough transition period and one I never got to grips with. But the fans were excellent. There were a few grumblings, but nothing major. But, still, little things were just going against me when they weren't before.

For instance, we played Preston at the Walkers Stadium. We were winning one-nil when Andy Lonergan, North End's keeper, lumped a ball forward. It missed everyone and bounced. Our keeper, Kevin Pressman, came charging from his goal. What happened next was Pressman shouting for the ball, he then slipped and it ended up going into our net. I remember some fans running down the stand behind the dug-out and shouting, 'Adams, sort it out.' Like it was my fault! All the coaching in the world could not have prevented the keeper falling over.

It was at this stage that my issues with sleep affected my judgement. I was restless and not enjoying myself. For me, that's a poor combination. And I've always made bad decisions when I've been tired.

I didn't really get a proper holiday in the summer. I was straight back into it. The team was taking time to gel and people like Keown were flicking my switch. So I pulled Harry aside one day and told him, 'I need a break.'

A lot of the time, it's not the people in the team who take up your time; it's the ones who aren't. Like I've said, there was a bit of disquiet in the stands – but it was by no means universal and the board were behind me.

But after three days away with Claire, I didn't feel any better. I just felt tired. When I got back, I pulled Harry aside and said, 'I think I'm going to step down, Harry. It's taken its toll on me. I need a break.'

It was the most stupid thing I have ever done. I was earning good money. I had eighteen months to run on my deal. Harry and Tim Davies, the chief executive, tried to talk me out of it. Claire was distraught. She thought I was stupid, that a win would turn everything around. She was probably right. I don't regret many things, but that's was one of my biggest.

I went into a press conference to announce it – and then I was gone. Simple as that. After I resigned, I slept well. But I couldn't help waking up the next day and thinking, 'What have I done?' I'd left a top football club. What was I going to do now?

We took a break to see Claire's sister Sasha and her husband Robin. They own a vineyard called Domaine de Beauregard in Villefranche-de-Lonchat, right in the middle of the beautiful Dordogne area of France. It was a fabulous place to chill out and get away from the hustle and bustle of life, where no one except immediate family knew who I was. The scenery is stunning and the nearest neighbour is miles away. It was perfect. I was able to take stock of my life while helping Robin out in the vines.

It was hard work but I was never one to shy away from a challenge. Of course, there were rewards of hearty conversation, good food and excellent wine every evening. In the short term, at least, it went some way towards making up for one of the worst decisions of my professional career, and it gave me some energy for what was round the corner.

CHAPTER 15

FRIENDS AND ENEMIES WITH GEOFFREY AND CHI CHI

After leaving a football club, the phone rings for the first three or four days. Friends, colleagues, confidantes, scouts and people from the game want to commiserate. And they are all well-meaning. But after that, total silence.

My immediate reaction was to take Claire and Mitchel away on holiday to Cyprus. As we were in the taxi leaving the airport, my mobile rang. An unfamiliar voice was on the other end. It was Ken Bates, who had just left Chelsea. He said he had a club that wanted to talk to me. He wouldn't tell me who, but he said he would ring me back on my return home. He made contact again and it turned out he was acting as a go-between for Firoz Kassam, the owner of Oxford United.

Ken advised me to carry out my homework before meeting Kassam, so I did. It was a pity the owner of Oxford United didn't. One of his first questions was 'Have you ever managed at this level before, Micky?' I found the question disrespectful, and the meeting went nowhere.

I also had a call from agent Gino Culbertson who put me in touch with Pete Winkelman at MK Dons. What a lovely fella. If passion for your football club won trophies, Pete would need a new sideboard every single season. He was so enthusiastic, and he offered me good money. He showed me the plans for a new ground, but I just couldn't buy into the dream while playing at a hockey stadium. Don't forget, I'd been waiting on a new ground for a few seasons at Brighton. I went to watch MK Dons play, but it just wasn't doing it for me – which was a shame, as I would have loved to have worked for Pete.

In the meantime, Peter Reid had just been sacked by Coventry City. He was a former teammate of mine at Southampton, and so I rang him up. He didn't speak badly of the club, but he felt it wasn't going anywhere. The results weren't good and the club was in freefall towards the first division.

I let the people know at Highfield Road – namely secretary Graham Hover and chairman Mike McGinnity – know that I would be interested. I went over for an interview and John Sillett, my old manager, was on the panel along with the other two.

I thought it went reasonably well. I didn't make any major slip-ups and thought to myself, 'I've got this.' Only Sills phoned me up afterwards and said, 'Everyone would like you to come, but you didn't give us the impression you really wanted to.'

I replied, 'I don't really understand that John because I've answered all your questions.'

'But you didn't actually say you wanted the job.'

'Well, look I turned up for the interview; I thought it was self-explanatory.'

So I had to go back for a second interview. And this time, I categorically said: 'I want this job.' And I got it.

They wanted to keep on Adrian 'Inchy' Heath as Reidy's assistant. I thought that was strange, because any new manager should be able to bring his own men in. He was, at least, a fun-loving character who kept

FRIENDS AND ENEMIES WITH GEOFFREY AND CHI CHI

the troops entertained. Despite him staying, I insisted on keeping Alan Cork with me and the board agreed to that.

One person they didn't want to keep was a fitness coach called Darren Robinson. He was facing the sack, but they failed to deal with the situation. I told them it was their job to release him and they didn't. They bottled it.

When I spoke to Hover about it, he told me to deal with it. I refused. It was their issue, not mine. He wasn't a problem to me at first, so he stayed put.

As far as the squad went, there was a lot of experience – Steve Staunton, Stern John, Tim Sherwood and a few others knew what Championship football was about. But the club had a problem with Sherwood. He was travelling in for two and a half hours every day, and then he would report to the physio, do a few laps of the training pitch and go home. The club was in dispute with him.

One of the first things I did was to have a chat with him and say that, as far as I was concerned, it was nonsense – he could do a few laps nearer his house. But he then went to the PFA who, in turn, phoned me up and asked me to put my offer to him in writing. It was a mess.

Funnily enough, before my first game, I got another interesting phone call from the board at West Ham United. The manager's job had just come up, but I declined the invitation to speak to them because I'd just agreed with Coventry to take their job, although I hadn't signed a contract at that point.

But it didn't take me long to realise what I had walked into. During my first match in charge at home, Stern John gave a foul away. It wasn't a bad challenge. It didn't even warrant a booking. Referee Mark Clattenburg went to have a word with him while our own support- ers were chanting 'Off, off, off...' They wanted Clattenburg to dismiss their own centre-forward. I immediately thought 'Wow, what have I joined here?'

Stern was an interesting character. One person I wasn't so keen on, however, was the skipper, Stephen Hughes. I was keen on him because he was such a good finisher. Unfortunately, however, he was a moaner. I'm sure he hated me. He hated running, so therefore he hated my training. I respected his ability, but he would not put in the hard yards. He thought he could play the way he wanted and at his pace. It just wasn't good enough for me. We ended up falling out. You can't have a club captain who slaughters the manager.

After mid-February we were managing to keep our heads above water. In the penultimate game of the season we had a trip to Plymouth Argyle. We were winning 1–0, but referee Lee Probert seemed to be playing on for no other reason than to allow them time to equalise. Eventually, in about the sixth minute of extra time, Tony Capaldi did exactly that.

I could see trouble brewing at the final whistle. Our boys were not happy, and a few of them had gathered around the referee. As I walked onto the pitch, the match official turned to me and said, 'One of your players has threatened to punch me.'

'Who?'

'Claus Jørgensen.'

He was about 5 ft 8in. tall and couldn't have knocked the skin off a rice pudding. I told Probert he was being ridiculous.

Anyway, theoretically the relegation issue went to the last game. And it was to be held at Highfield Road, against Derby County. It was also the final match to be played at a stadium which had witnessed more than its fair share of tears over the years; most of them shed in relief, if you were a Coventry supporter. But, if you had to sign-off, for once, the Sky Blues did not let themselves down.

The sun was shining, the stadium was packed to the rafters and we played magnificently. We were four-up by half-time and eventually won 6–2, with the last goal at Highfield Road being scored by full-back Andy Whing.

Corky was always funny about final-day walk-arounds. The tradition is for the manager, his staff and players to do a lap of honour at the final whistle. But Corky made the point – and it does have merit – that it's wrong that the supporters can call you all the names under the sun for weeks on end and then you are supposed to look happy and wave at them and all the rest of it. He point-blank refused to go out.

That aside, it was a fantastic afternoon. Meanwhile, it had been announced that Geoffrey Robinson, the MP who had started to bankroll the club, was taking over from McGinnity as club chairman. I had never met the bloke, but at the end of season bash Tony 'Banger' Walsh – the old wrestler who was a big Coventry fan – came over and asked me what I thought about Robinson. I'd never met him, so he offered to introduce me. So, despite my misgivings, 'Banger' introduced me to my new boss. Only at Coventry City could the manager be introduced to his new boss by a wrestler.

While I was intrigued as to what Robinson might do for the club, I was sorry to see Mike McGinnity go. He was good fun in the boardroom at the end of matches and it turned out that the man who came next was, without question, the worst chairman I have ever worked for. Our first meeting was awkward to say the least, and the relationship never improved after that.

But at that point, with the season ended, Coventry had organised a pre-season tour, and Ibiza was on the cards. Bearing in mind the controversy in La Manga with Leicester, the sunshine isle of Ibiza wasn't an ideal venue. I needed that like I needed swift bullet to the brain. But, anyway, we went and ended up playing QPR and a local team in a round-robin tournament on a plastic pitch. It was at the height of the season and the temperature in early July was punishing. The surface was bone-hard. Us Brits beat the team from Ibiza and faced each other in the final.

QPR had brought over 2,000 supporters, whereas we only had about 300. The two sets of fans were sharing one stand and, of course, everyone had been on the sauce all day and it kicked off. The game was stopped for twenty minutes while order was restored. Ian Holloway and I had to go on loudspeakers and appeal for calm. We grabbed hold of the microphones, told everyone it was a pre-season friendly and that, if the trouble continued, we would have to abandon the match.

It calmed down but, unfortunately, QPR came back and beat us 3–2. At the end of the game, there was a presentation and our opponents were celebrating like it was the FA Cup. They were all jumping up and down. Bearing in mind this was a pre-season tournament, it was ridiculously over-the-top. Back in Blighty, guess who we were pitted against in the first game at the Ricoh Arena? It was our very first game, and it all kicked off in the tunnel … but, this time, between the players. We won 3–0 – not a bad way to christen the new stadium! That campaign was a story of two halves, for want of a better phrase. Before Christmas our form was patchy but, after Dennis Wise arrived in January, it picked up considerably. One player who did have a good campaign – other than Dennis – was Márton Fülöp, the Hungarian keeper who we had on loan from Spurs who was tragically to die of cancer in 2015 at the age of thirty-two. He did fantastically well for me. Thanks to Dennis's arrival, we managed to turn the situation around, and any thoughts of being involved in a struggle were lost to the wind. In fact, had the season gone on another half-dozen games, we might well have sneaked into the play-offs.

I have to say that Dennis was a credit to himself He was everything for me that Martin Keown wasn't: he was a winner, a leader. He didn't question anything and just got on with his job.

Stern John was as good a striker as you would find at that level. Don Hutchison also came in and was doing really well until he picked up an injury that (all but for a few matches at Luton Town) ended his career.

Gary McSheffrey was pretty much a manager's dream at Championship level. He could come in off the left or right, link up with the forwards and score goals. He eventually reached the Premier League but, unfortunately for a Coventry lad, he had to do it with Birmingham City.

All in all, it was a good season and we finished eighth. As I write in 2017, it is still the highest position Coventry City have reached since they were relegated from the Premier League. And this was achieved despite my relationship with the chairman. He came to the training ground the first day I met him at the club. We sat down, and the first thing I noticed was that he had a pen and a piece of paper. Every time I said something about the team or strength of the squad, he would scribble away.

I looked at him and I thought, 'He's writing down everything I say.' So I got a pen and a piece of paper and wrote down what he was saying, too. Why would I do that? Well, sooner or later, I knew it would be brought up in conversation – most probably when results weren't going our way. It would be a case of him bringing out this handwritten script and saying, 'On 24 November, you said…' So I thought, 'Two can play at that game.' After we finished our meetings, I'd go in to see Jenny Poole, the manager's secretary, and ask her to transcribe it.

It's hardly a foundation for the most trustworthy of relationships, is it? We just weren't compatible as people. I used to dread his phone calls every Sunday morning. Depending on who he had spoken to, it was either full of praise or completely negative. He knew absolutely nothing about football. Nothing.

I remember he was very keen to go and wish the players luck when we played at Cardiff City. To be fair, he did ask me if he could approach them and my response was along the lines of 'It's your train set, Mr Chairman, you do as you want.'

I was sitting in the dug-out when he strode out onto the pitch. Our boys were warming up on the right and Cardiff were on the left, but, that day, Cardiff City were warming up in sky-blue T-shirts. He went left instead of right and was walking around their team, shaking their hands one by one. It would have been quite easy for me to have put him right, but I thought he could stew in a mess that was entirely of his own making. Eventually, someone pointed out the error of his ways and he sheepishly walked across to the other half of the pitch to begin handing out his best wishes to his own team.

And he used to be forever quoting disgraced Sky presenter Richard Keys. Our conversations would be peppered with phrases such as 'Richard says this' or 'Richard thought that'. Keys was a keen supporter, but he had way too much importance for someone who never paid for his ticket. But more of him later.

• • •

Ahead of what turned out to be my last season, they brought in Paul Fletcher as chief executive, Ken Sharpe to help on the commercial front and Mal Brannigan on the financial side.

They cooked up the initiative 'Operation Premiership', which was supposed to galvanise us into competing at the top of the Championship. The chairman had talked about giving me £3 million to spend early in the summer but, before the season had even started, he denied any knowledge of such a proposition.

We had an offer on the table from Birmingham City for McSheffrey.

They promised to treble his money but I was adamant he wasn't going. We also had a bid on the table from Crystal Palace for James Scowcroft, who we had signed for nothing from Leicester City.

Robinson said, 'We're selling James Scowcroft for £250,000 to Crystal Palace.'

I replied, 'You aren't selling him for £250,000.'

'I'm telling you we are selling him for £250,000.'

'Oh no, you're not. If you do, you will be looking for a new manager. First, he's worth more than that; and secondly, he's worth more to us than that.'

In the end he went to Crystal Palace and we doubled our money on him.

I ended up signing Chris Burchill and Elliott Ward from West Ham, but the biggest loss was Dennis Wise who had taken the manager's job at Leeds. He could have played for another season, no problem.

But we were competitive again. We won more than we lost. But when we went to West Brom in the mid-December, we were on the fringes of the play-offs after a five-match unbeaten run. And that is where it all unravelled.

Six weeks earlier, Tony Mowbray had been installed as the Baggies' new boss. I had been contacted by one of their directors to see if I was interested in taking over. I was due to go to a meeting but I bottled it, because we were doing well at Coventry. So, I could have been standing in the home dug-out and, at the end of ninety minutes, I wish I had been. We were smashed 5–0. We really did take a beating and we had thousands of fans there, too.

I decided to do to my lads what Chris Nicholl used to do to us back in the day. After I'd completed my press duties, I went to see the players in the dressing room, who had been ordered not to leave until I returned. I made my speech: 'As far as I was concerned, none of you showed up today. You all bottled it. I had an old manager who used to tell his players how they had done after the match before they left. I don't want anyone leaving here not knowing how he has played.'

I went around them one by one. 'Shit, shit, not bad, tried, rubbish...'

They weren't happy – firstly with the fact they had to wait around, and secondly because they had to listen to that. It was not one of my better decisions, and that's putting it mildly. I don't know how much of a difference it made, but between then and the end of January we didn't win another game. And then I was sacked. At the time, however, I thought there were enough characters in the side to cope with what I had just said. Clearly not.

I had also fallen out with Hughes. I'd had enough of him; he wasn't interested and wouldn't entertain what I was doing, but I couldn't touch him because he had a long contract.

So what I said to him was 'Stephen, you can stay. It's not a problem. I'm not going to make you come to games. If you want to come, come. If you don't, don't.'

I thought that was fair. But Robinson disagreed and phoned me to ask why I was victimising Stephen Hughes by banning him from coming to games. 'Richard has told me you are picking on him...' Hughes was obviously in his mate's ear.

Anyway, we went on a horrific run. Were they trying? I think we were, but we just didn't do enough to win them. Shortly afterwards, I was summoned to meet the chairman at the Houses of Parliament. I rang Harry and asked for his opinion. 'Son, he's either going to sack you or tell you things have to improve.'

I went in there with an open mind, but Robinson was very blunt. There was no verbal foreplay.

'I've been told I should sack you', he said.

'Well, sack me,' I replied. 'You know what's in my contract. Pay me. I'll go. But who's told you to sack me, Geoffrey?'

'Er, Richard Keys.'

'Who's Richard Keys?' I asked.

'He's the man off the TV...'

'I know who he is. But who is he? You're telling me you've been told to sack me by a fan who doesn't put one penny into the club?'

'Well, results have got to improve.'

'I understand that. But don't tell me Richard Keys is sacking me.

One week later, I was sat at home and my mobile rings. It's Andy Gray. Not Andy Gray, Keys's mate; it's the agent Andy Gray, the lad who used to play for Crystal Palace back in the '90s.

'Er, hello, Micky,' he said. 'I want to tell you this because I don't think it's right. I've just had one of the most bizarre calls from your chairman. I've picked up my phone and this fella says, "Hello, is that Andy Gray?" I said that it was and he told me it was Geoffrey Robinson, chairman of Coventry City. He said he'd been given my number by Richard Keys because he wanted to get rid of his manager and perhaps I could help find him another one.'

Andy Gray told him that he had got the wrong fella. Robinson apologised and put the phone down. Gray then gave me Robinson's home phone number. I didn't have that telephone number. He had never called me from it. So I wrote it down and phoned him up.

'Hello, chairman,' I said. 'How are you?'

'Er, fine, Micky, thanks.'

'You've just had an interesting conversation with Andy Gray, haven't you?'

'No.'

'You have, Geoffrey, Because he's just phoned me up and told me.'

'No, I haven't.'

'You have. Is this your phone number.'

'Yes, that's my number.'

'You rang him from your home number. Geoffrey, don't take me for a mug.'

And with that I put the phone down. I suppose, looking back, it was a question of who was going to have the final say. Sadly for me, results meant that it wasn't going to be yours truly.

After playing Leeds United away on 1 January and coming away with a 2–1 defeat, I overheard one of the directors on the phone after the match, telling the chairman that I had to go. He's exact words were: 'He's gone. He's lost the dressing room. We need to get rid.'

What he didn't realise was that I was standing right behind him. I knew the writing was on the wall, and I had even more of an inkling as the month went on. I wanted to bring in a couple of players but, as it happens when people have lost faith in you and the axe is being sharpened, suddenly no one was taking my calls. I remember phoning Fletcher and getting his answerphone. I left a brief message: 'Operation Premiership, my arse.'

It all came to a head when we played Bristol City, then of League One in the FA Cup. The late Mike McGinnity was around the place, but Geoffrey Robinson wasn't. Before the game, Adrian Heath, Corky, Mike and I were having a chat. The two assistants left the room, and so did I. At that moment, Adrian came back and, when I returned a couple of minutes later, Mike and Adrian were having a chat. Whatever they were talking about, I don't know. But it looked serious and, if I'm being honest, secretive.

I was paranoid about this. We lost the game 2–0. My one saving grace was that I had given Ben Turner, who has gone on to have a decent career, his debut. Straight after the game, I went to my office, where Fletch was waiting for me. He told me that the board wanted to see me at 10 a.m. at the stadium the next morning. I knew what was coming.

At the meeting, I was offered a three-month severance package, which I declined. My last words to them were: 'See you in court.'

I got the staff together, broke the news and suggested having a drink afterwards. We all agreed to meet up at TGI's on the outskirts of Coventry. When I got there, two people were missing: Adrian Heath, my assistant manager, and Darren Robinson. I didn't think too much of it. We were in the restaurant having a few drinks and Sky Sports was on the TV screen. Then, all of a sudden, the screen flashed up with breaking news: 'Adrian Heath appointed manager of Coventry City.'

Paul Fletcher was being interviewed saying that they might have uncovered the new José Mourinho. Heath, who hasn't had the decency to phone me up and tell me what was happening, was photographed waving a sky blue scarf above his head and talking about how long he had waited for the chance.

With friends like that, eh, who needs enemies?

That night, after a few drinks, I decided to ring up Richard Keys. I had sunk a right few and was worse for wear.

'I bet you're happy today', I said.

'I am, to be fair', he replies.

'That's OK, Richard. Every dog has his day. But let me tell you, if ever I meet you again, you will end up presenting your programme looking like Chi Chi the fucking panda.'

'Is that right?'

'It's a promise.'

And to this day, it won't surprise you to learn, our paths have never crossed.

But it won't surprise to you learn, either, that my offer still stands.

CHAPTER 16

BY GEORGE AT COLCHESTER AND NOT SO CLEVER WITH DICK

What had happened at Coventry was just one bad month in a two-year tenure. That was the fact of the matter. But it was also true that I was out of work. Every time you get the sack, your confidence takes a bit of a knock. You just don't realise it at the time. You have a look around and think, 'What am I going to do next?' By this stage, you are praying the phone rings.

There was nothing more for it but to go away on holiday. And it was there I received a call from Geraint 'George' Williams, the manager of Colchester United. They had just been promoted to the Championship. We met on the Pro-Licence course in Wales.

Up until this point I had been taken my badges with the English FA, but all their courses were run in June and that, as far as I was concerned, was holiday time with the family. So I looked at the Welsh route instead. The course was run by Kevin Thelwell who is now head of recruitment at Wolves. I was in the first intake, along with George, Oasian Roberts, Mark Aizlewood and Ian Rush. Rushie basically decided when he was going to turn up which, when you are a bona fide legend for your country, is fair enough.

So, as I say, I met George on the course. Mick Harford had just left Colchester to take over Luton, so he asked if I would consider being his number two. It was going to be a big ask keeping little old Colchester in the Championship. From their perspective, it had been a great achievement just getting there. Colchester's Layer Road was an old ground. It didn't have any facilities and the players trained at a college. They had to make every pound a prisoner, so Colchester's biggest problem was attracting players as their budget was one of the lowest in the league.

The chairman was a fella called Robbie Cowling and Robbie was a chairman who used to back his managers. There were some decent lads; the most well-known of them was Teddy Sheringham, by now in the twilight of his illustrious career. He had this habit, Teddy, of parking his immaculate big blue convertible Bentley next to my club Ford Mondeo. One day I got out of my car the same time as Teddy and I joked, 'Teddy, do us a favour, would you? Stop putting your car next to mine. It's embarrassing. Seriously, don't keep running up all these miles travelling in from London in your Bentley every day. Why don't you buy yourself a little run-around instead?'

He pointed at the Bentley and said, 'Yeah, I already have...'

Anyway, George was obsessive. He wanted to do everything right. For example, if he left anyone out he always wanted to explain why – which is not, in itself, a bad thing. But he wouldn't give me the reins at all. It was his job, but he was manic with it and he started to become very tired.

I remember we played QPR away and we were awful. We were one-down at half-time, but he would not let me have a say – not at all. I wanted to rip into a few because that's what they deserved. They weren't at it, and they needed a kick up the backside. But, just as I began to open my mouth, he put his arm across me and said, 'One singer, one song.'

He did bring me down in front of the lads, so I learnt then it was a waste of time. If he didn't want me to help in any way, what was the point of me being there?

He started to get more and more depressed as the season went on. It was getting on top of him. Around the turn of the year we had a decent result against Charlton away, but leading up to the game he was talking about resigning. I begged him not to. I said, 'Think about what you're doing. Think about your family, think about your career, think about the implications on the rest of your staff...' I remember saying, 'You've got to keep going.' But he wanted to resign, even though I knew by now that any season could change on one game.

The chairman understood that it was a tough ask staying in the league. In George's defence, no one could have done any more work on the training ground with the players than we had. Individually, they just weren't good enough. You can be as well prepared as you like, but if they aren't good enough, all the motivation and organisation in the world is never going to be enough.

There was one game against Watford where I was standing on the side-lines. We had been winning two-nil, but the Hornets came back into it by scoring twice in quick succession. I suggested putting in an extra midfielder, but I think he ended up taking off a forward instead. George never wanted me to contribute to team selection or give an opinion. That day against Watford was perhaps the only time I ever did, but it fell on deaf ears.

But little did I know was that there was going to be a fall guy, and that person was going to be me.

George came to the hotel before an FA Cup third round tie and told me: 'It's not working. I want to make a change.' The implication being that I was the one being changed.

I said, 'George, we both know I have no input on team selection, formation or tactics. And you want to replace me? What you are doing is using me as your scapegoat, implying all the bad results are my fault. That's what it's going to look like… and we both know I've had no influence on anything.'

But there was no point arguing with him. His mind was made up. I did the FA Cup game, but I should have walked beforehand. I felt let down because the two of us knew I'd had no influence. I was trying to guide him through because he needed help.

We've spoken since, but we aren't mates anymore. He threw me under the bus because of the results. It was a kick in the balls and no one was interested in my opinion. It was strange being there. What made it worse was that I had turned down a couple of jobs while being at Colchester, so I went back to the ranks of the unemployed, waiting and hoping the phone would ring and someone would give me another chance.

When my phone did ring again, it was my former boss at Brighton, Dick Knight. He asked me to meet him at the Grafton Hotel on Tottenham Court Road. I only took the call because it was him, but going back turned out to be one of the biggest mistakes of my life.

Dick was still chairman, but it was quite clear that a fella called Tony Bloom was now the main man behind the scenes – and there was a power struggle going on. I didn't know that at the time, and it led to me falling out with one of my best mates, Dean Wilkins, who was then the manager.

Dick wasn't getting on with Dean. I have to say I felt uncomfortable about it, because he had been the youth team coach during my first spell at Brighton. But Dick assured me they were going to make the change anyway, so it was a case of me or someone else getting the job. I told him that I wanted to speak to Dean about it and I ended up arranging to meet my mate at a service station on the M40 to explain what had gone on. The plan was for him to stick to what Dick thought he did best, and that was coaching with the first-team. I was due to come in above him and manage the situation.

It was frosty. He thought I had stitched him up. Dick told me he was going to make the change and the pressure of the job was affecting him.

I told him that I wanted him to stay. We talked it through and, at the end of the meeting, we seemed to have agreed on the way forward. I thought I'd reassured him enough for him to believe he should stay on. But he declined the invitation. He obviously wasn't happy and attacked me verbally. I did have to remind him about the hypocrisy of a member of the Wilkins family having a dig at me, particularly when his older brother had taken my first job at Fulham. I was happy for him to stay on board and, in an ideal world, I would have wanted to work with him.

We don't speak now, which is a regret because he was a good mate and one of the few people I felt I could talk to and confide in. But that's life. In hindsight, I shouldn't have gone back. I did do it for Dick, but it turned out his power was on the wane.

The team had performed reasonably well the year before. It felt good initially to go back. I did have people around me that I knew and trusted. Paul Rogers, my old captain, was in the Commercial Department. Matt Hicks, who'd had a brief spell as the kit man during my first tenure, was the player-liaison officer. I wanted Corky back but, for some reason, Dick wouldn't entertain that. The pair had had a disagreement when Corky left the first time, so I went back to Bob Booker. Dean White was still around as the chief scout.

It seemed as though the old gang was getting back together. The squad remained pretty much unchanged from the previous season. I also made a scattering of signings, including Kevin McLeod from Colchester and Dave Livermore from Millwall. Glenn Murray led the line alongside Nicky Forster, a veteran striker who most definitely knew where the back of the net was. Tommy Elphick, a young centre-half, was coming through. He went on to have a successful spell at Bournemouth where he captained them in the Premier League. There was also little Dean Cox who, though he stood at just 5 ft 3in. tall, was a combative wide player and became the subject of one of Brighton's best chants: 'We've got Tiny Cox, we've got Tiny Cox, we've got, we've got, we've got, we've got, we've got Tiny Cox.'

The season started very well. We won the first game at Crewe, but the one game I remember best was Walsall at home. They had two men sent off yet managed to win the game after scoring from a free-kick. We camped in their half and got crosses in, but their keeper had a good day. We were booed off.

However, just to show what a bizarre sport this can be, a few weeks later we faced Manchester City and all their stars, including Vincent Kompany and Pablo Zabaleta to name but two. I remember it because I gave Steve Cook, who is now playing centre-half for Bournemouth in the Premier League, his debut. I remember the Manchester City boss Mark Hughes going absolutely mad at his players during the change around in extra time. The game eventually went to penalties, which we won 5–3.

Shortly afterwards I came up with the idea of getting Robbie Savage down to give us a boost. He was earning a fortune at the time – something like £23,000 a week at Derby County – but he wasn't playing under Paul Jewell, and there was little chance of that changing. Incredibly, Dick managed to do a deal for something like one-tenth of his weekly wage and he came down to join us.

Once the loan was agreed, Sav came down in with his white Lamborghini. He refused our offers to find him some temporary accommodation and, instead, he managed to find somewhere in the middle of Brighton's gay quarter without realising what he had actually done. The chairman and I went to visit him at his digs. His room was complete with an illuminated floor and a glitter ball. We raised an eyebrow, but it didn't bother Sav in the slightest. He thought it was fantastic.

When he turned up to training the next day, my assistant Bob Booker dipped into his stockpile of costumes and managed to out-do himself. Sav parked up his car, only to find at the end of training that it had been clamped and had parking tickets plastered all over it. Bob had found a traffic warden's outfit from somewhere and had gone to town with stickers.

Of course, Sav went mental, swearing this and that until he realised (with all the other players laughing at him) that he had been tucked up. Sav is, well, Sav. What you see is what you get. He just wanted to play. He was perhaps not as fit as I would have liked; maybe that affected his performances.

I remember one game against Leicester (we won 3–2), I subbed him at half-time when we were two-down. I've always had an open dialogue with him so he came to see me and asked why I'd taken him off, especially because, in his words, 'My mate told me I'd been the best player on the pitch until then.'

That's the way he is. He enjoyed being in the limelight down there. He ended up going back to Derby and playing for a couple of seasons more under Nigel Clough.

But it was still a case of two steps forward and two steps back. I could have bought myself more time after we reached the area final of the Johnstone's Paint Trophy. We faced Luton Town over two legs. The Hatters were struggling that season. They'd been deducted thirty points and were at the bottom of League Two.

We had meetings at Brighton about how we were going to dish out the tickets for Wembley and how we were going to look after the corporate guests. I was uncomfortable with that, and with good reason, as it turned out.

We hadn't been doing fantastically. Everyone was down and, the fact was, we hadn't beaten a Second Division team over two legs. We didn't deserve to go to Wembley. A goalless draw at the Withdean was far from ideal. It was a poor evening and, with the tie still in the balance, Dave Livermore was sent off in the first half of the return leg at Kenilworth Road. We played well with ten men but no one wanted to hear that. We held on until the end, losing on penalties.

I wouldn't have said that this would be a sackable offence. The match took place on Tuesday and I heard nothing for a couple of days when I received a call to meet Dick at a Little Chef near Hickstead. It was a Friday afternoon. Isn't it strange what you remember? I can't recall what was said exactly other than Dick asked if I fancied a toasted tea-cake! An offer I politely declined. Anyway, once the pleasantries – or pastries – were completed, it turns out that Tony Bloom, who was away in Australia, had demanded my head on a platter.

Dick didn't want to sack me, particularly. I had respect for him, and I'd even signed Jim McNulty, Jason Jarrett and Craig Davies from Stockport on his recommendation as he had heard they were decent. I was uncomfortable with that, but it was the last throw of the dice late in January and, for the first time in my whole career, I'd let a chairman dictate to me what we were going to do with signings.

He told me he was under pressure and that it could result in him leaving the club if he hadn't sacked me. I told him that he didn't really have a choice in the matter. I say we mutually agreed the separation, but he sacked me.

Looking back, I recognise there was a lot of goodwill within the club towards me. But I'm not sure some of the senior professionals helped. I can trace it back to pre-season when we had an issue with Glenn

Murray. I was on holiday and Dick rang saying, 'I need you to come back, we've got a problem with Glenn.' So, I flew back from Portugal and had a chat with him and his agent. I had to persuade him to stay. He was a good player, a goal-scorer and he'd seen a way out to make a few quid more but we managed to keep him.

Could I have done better? I shouldn't have taken the job in the first place. I'd let my heart rule my head but, in fairness, I didn't have any other offers coming through and it seemed like a good idea at the time.

The big issue at the club was this power struggle. Dick wanted to have a season with someone he trusted. I wouldn't ever say he let me down, but he had his idea about players. I did listen to him, and maybe that's where I went wrong. I could see the writing was on the wall with the calibre of players who came in during January.

It wasn't a happy period. Going back to a club where success had been achieved before felt good, yet, the second time around, the same spark wasn't there no matter how hard I tried. It was really difficult to swallow. For instance, there was resentment in the boardroom from the likes of Martin Perry and Derek Chapman, because both of them were fond of Dean. It was always going to be tricky for me.

However upset and disillusioned I was about it, at least Dick honoured my contract. I don't know if he felt a moral obligation or not, but he told me he was going to pay me up. I managed to get a witness to the conversation. It was particularly pleasing when, a few days later, Ken Brown, the CEO of the club, turned up at my house and offered me £40,000 as a pay-off. The settlement on my three-year deal had been met by Dick in full. I had someone to back me up and felt a small victory when I told said director to get out of my house in no uncertain terms.

But the fact of the matter was I was out of work again. I took Claire to New York for her fortieth birthday. I wanted to have a break and spoil her – and I did. We flew business-class and I managed to get myself smashed on the free booze on the way over. Claire knew I'd had too much to drink when she saw me getting emotional at the end of *Marley & Me*.

We landed in New York late morning and, once checked in, we immediately went spending. The next morning she smiled at me and thanked me for a 'great day's shopping'. I had absolutely no idea what we'd bought. I did raise an eyebrow when the credit card statement came through the post, however.

It was Steve Wood, one of my former teammates, who gave me a ring to tell me about the next opportunity. We were just about to go up the Empire State Building when Steve rang. He asked if I fancied going for the Port Vale job. Another door was about to open.

CHAPTER 17

MICKY THE VALIANT: PART I

When the job at Port Vale became available and I knew I was on the shortlist, there was only one course of action to take: to ring Harry.

Harry, being Harry, knew a director and duly dispatched my CV. I quickly received feedback they were keen to talk to me. Unfortunately, however, further news indicated there was a nine-man board of directors and there were others in the frame.

There was, however, a main man. The chairman's name was Bill Bratt, a local businessman. In fact, the process went on for far longer at Port Vale than it had done at many of my previous clubs. I had taken a family holiday and, when I returned, Bill asked me to meet the shirt sponsors, which was a property firm in Essex called Harlequin Property. I believed the owners were on the board too, but I later discovered that wasn't the case – although the fella who ran it, David Ames, would eventually have a big say in who actually ended up being appointed.

The meeting went well and I grew increasingly confident of my chances, especially because I had one other factor working in my favour: I was cheap. Going into the process, I'd decided that cash was not going to be a sticking point. Whatever was on the table, I was going to take. I just wanted to show people I was a decent manager.

I never did discover how much of a factor that was in my appointment. Given what was to happen during what would turn out to be almost five years at the club, I reckon it would have helped the cause. It was also well received when I said I was prepared to work with the existing staff.

Former Vale keeper Mark Grew was the assistant. Ray Williams was the chief scout. Ray was one of those with plenty of knowledge but it was difficult to get an opinion from him.

I decided to go with a player/assistant manager as it gave me two options, and I felt the squad still needed a player or two. The one area of the pitch where we were light was up front, so I gave Geoff Horsfield the chance to go into management. He turned up on his first day knowing he was going to meet the press in ripped jeans, unshaven and looking the opposite of the part. In addition, he seemed to have forgotten everything he had learnt as a top-flight player. He was unable to put a session together.

He didn't want to get involved in confrontations with the players and found it difficult to speak in a group scenario. But get him in the pub with people surrounding him and he was in his element. He was a decent fella, Geoff, but like so many he found it impossible to escape the mode of being a player.

I took Doug Loft and Tommy Fraser, two midfielders I'd known at Brighton. There was limited cash to spend on the squad, so I then got a rather excited call to say, 'Don't spend any more money, there isn't any.' Effectively, with a couple of additions, I'd been left with a group who had finished seventeenth in League Two just a few months before.

Nevertheless, we had to get on with it. At my first meeting with the players, I told them they were going to work hard and that some of them would not enjoy it. But if they worked hard, they could come on the journey with us. If not, we'd rip their contracts up and they could go.

That was my mantra and it was one that the club's supporters bought into. Port Vale is in a real working-class area of the Potteries in Burslem. The punters want to see effort and enthusiasm on the pitch and if they don't get it, they'd let you know. Nowadays they operate in the shadow of their rivals Stoke City, but the older supporters love nothing better than talking about the days when the two competed on a level playing field.

While that love of industry and effort works in a manager's favour, there is one other main characteristic at Vale Park: if there isn't a crisis, then one needs to be created. It's just one of those clubs. It was during the first season that reports of problems with the finances began to surface. There were rumours we were struggling for cash, although in that first season it was pretty much kept away from me. Looking back, it was just the tip of the iceberg, but even above the surface it was fairly clear that all was not well. The fact that Stoke City Council had given the club a repayment holiday on a £2.25 million loan did not ring too many alarm bells. Perhaps it should have done. The fact that there were so many directors was also strange. When pre-season got underway, it was fairly uneventful. Many of the players clearly hadn't done their homework properly. Had they bothered to ring up some of their colleagues, they would have known hard running would be the first order of the day. This was particularly relevant in right-back Sam Stockley's case. He was determined to keep chirping up during the sessions while everyone else was on their knees. I did warn the squad that the more he talked, the more they ran. It didn't take long for the lads to get on his case and, funnily enough, the chatter soon stopped.

There wasn't too much quality in a squad that had changed little and finished a few points off the relegation zone, but that Vale side did have a couple of things going for it. We had a goal-scorer in Marc Richards and a midfielder called Anthony Griffith who was right up my street. He was tough, won tackles and got about people.

Although my style is to play with wingers and get crosses into the box, we didn't have anyone who fitted that brief. One thing you have to remember about Vale Park is the size of the pitch: it's particularly wide. As we had no players capable of providing width, I decided to shorten it by two yards on either side.

I also had a battle on my hands with the secretary, Bill Lodey, concerning away trips. He told me the club would pay for a meal on the Friday night and they'd pay for a pre-match meal ahead of the game. But they wouldn't pay for breakfast. I had to explain to him that he was asking for players to go eighteen hours without any food, and yet we were trying to develop professional athletes. I managed to get that changed quickly. Everyone had to show their face on Saturday mornings. They had to come down, get out of their beds and have some breakfast.

It was similar to Fulham in some respects. It is a friendly club. People have a soft spot for Vale and when you have worked there, you can understand why.

However, I had a few sharp words to say after we kicked off our pre-season with a game against Biddulph Victoria. They were in the non-league and not that far up the ladder. We had more chances than I could count, but ended up losing 1–0. I just thought it was the story of life at Port Vale. We played really well, but couldn't find the net and we'd then lose. It was an attitude that I had to change and that's what I told the players.

When the season got underway, we did reasonably well – until we went to Notts County and suffered our third defeat in one week. I said to the press afterwards that we looked like a woman who had a fur coat on but no knickers, and I put the entire team on the transfer list. All of them. It did make a few headlines. I was calling the players' bluff. No one came in for any of them and I suppose I did it to wake them up a bit. It seemed to work as we had a good season in the end.

We did pretty well in the cup competitions too, winning 2–1 at Bramall Lane in the League Cup. The main reason we managed it was because of the best goalkeeping performance I'd seen in a long time. We had a young lad in our ranks called Chris Martin and he was absolutely outstanding that night. We thought we had a potential diamond on our hands and that he had a real chance of progressing. When I left the club and returned, however, I found that his confidence had been destroyed and he drifted into non-league. It was a shame because the kid had everything.

Anyway, the season ticked along nicely. With Richards scoring goals and the competitive Griffith, who turned out to be the club's player-of-the-season, in the midfield, we had performed above par in the league. Financial demons were always close at hand, so it was achieved in spite of what was going on behind the scenes.

The other issue I had that year was personal. The whole season was overshadowed by the news from my mum that my dad had only six months to live. What could I say? He would never admit he had six months to live. No chance. He'd had two heart operations and come out the other side. As far as he was concerned, he was going to beat this prognosis too. He didn't acknowledge he was dying and nothing changed in his personality. He was bright as a button, but he was still difficult. There were so many times I wanted to say to him, 'You're dying, do you want me to take you anywhere, to see or do anything or is there anything you want to say to me?' But he wouldn't entertain it. He thought he was invincible. On the day he died, he wanted to stay at home and it ended up being a horrible experience.

That evening, I was going to Rotherham for a reserve match at Don Valley so I popped in to see my parents for tea. I knew something was not right. My mum makes a mean meat and potato pie, but my dad had two mouthfuls of food and left the rest. That was all. If he was turning his nose up at that, something really wasn't right.

At the end, I kissed him goodbye before I left. As I did, he grabbed me quite forcibly. He had hold of me and he started talking about Mitchel, my son. He was shouting at me, 'Does Mitchel know how fucking hard it is to be a professional footballer? And what you have got to do?'

I said, 'Yes, yes, he knows.'

'Make sure you fucking tell him.'

And that was the last time I spoke to him.

I stayed our friends Rick and Annette's house that night in Derby as it was on the way to Burslem. I received the dreaded call from my sister early the next day saying that Dad had passed away. I got dressed and rushed to see him. As I raced over, our last conversation stuck in my mind. Once again, it was just horrible. It wasn't 'Take care, son.' No, it couldn't be something like that. I think he knew he was dying. He just wouldn't admit it. Stubborn bastard.

Incredibly, there was a comical element to it all. My mum and dad lived in an old house and the stairs were steep. We couldn't get him down the stairs, so my sister's boyfriend, Charlie, and I had to work out how to do it. It was a right game, taking his body down those bloody stairs.

I look back now and I still wonder why I said the things I said at his funeral, as we did have some good times together. I think he was hard on me because my brother was born handicapped and so he may have been living out his dreams through me. But he was a bully. I didn't see that when I was a kid; I just thought he was a tough man. Anyway, the funeral came and went. And I said what I said.

Professionally, I was in a daze. Towards the end of the season, we played Bury away and I had taken the press interviews but I was in a confused state. Peter Jackson, Bill Bratt and a few of the other directors came to see me. I was grateful for their support.

I really needed the season to end. It's a slog, especially in the lower leagues, but we were still in with a shout of going up so I had to dig deep to see out the season.

Going into the penultimate game of the season we came up against a Bournemouth side that was just beginning to flourish under Eddie Howe. A defeat on the south coast put paid to any hopes of an extension to the campaign, as it meant we could not qualify for the play-offs. They scored the first goal from a corner routine that Eddie still uses in the Premier League. In the end, the campaign tailed off and we finished tenth. Our goals-against record was as good as any of the promoted sides, but we had drawn too many matches.

That, however, was a walk in the park compared to the summer we were about to endure. The board were trying to secure investment as issues over money hit home. After one false start, local Potteries businessman Mo Chaudry went public with his plans to secure control. Unfortunately, that was not well received by the existing board, which rejected it. Other potential bidders – among them, a group of Americans – were similarly put out when the directors failed to take their bid seriously. These rejections gave rise to a fans' group that was effectively a protest movement. It was entitled 'Black & Gold Until It's Sold.'

This was the background against which I was trying to improve on our tenth-placed finish the previous season. Vale Park was hardly a haven of peace and tranquillity at the time. And the first few months of the 2010/11 campaign were particularly testing. At the heart of it were two real factors. The first was the club was in debt to the tune of £2 million. The second was that the directors didn't have that kind of cash to bail out the club.

It seemed that there was one crisis or another to deal with almost every week. If it wasn't people trying to buy Vale, then there were money worries. If we lost a game, it was all exaggerated. Certain individuals were agitating for their own gain – my chief scout being one of them. Even though he used to be a good friend of Peter Jackson (the vice-chairman), he decided he was firmly in the Mo Chaudry camp. None of it was helpful.

Back on the pitch, our pre-season was overshadowed by an injury to Lewis Haldine. It was one of the strangest ones I've come across – even stranger than when I was at Coventry and our full-back, a lad called Andy Whing, managed to pull his hamstring while eating a lasagne! Haldine, the poor beggar, was in pre-season training and was bitten by something. His foot and ankle swelled like nothing I had ever seen before and he ended up in hospital to have major surgery on his foot. He ended up missing a large chunk of the season. It was a blow for us to lose him and all because – the medics think – a spider chomped on his ankle.

Also in our ranks was a lad called Anthony Malbon. He was only an apprentice, but he had something. He really should have enjoyed a successful career but, unfortunately, his off-field habits, the company that he kept and his general attitude meant he never fulfilled his potential.

There are other aspects of being a manager – beyond organising set-plays and dealing with the press – that fans do not hear about. One example of these unseen issues concerned Malbon and our pre-season tour to Ireland. As I explained previously, all players are required to bring in their passports a couple of weeks before a trip. I had explained to all of them what was needed, but Malbon was not forthcoming with his passport. He always answered 'tomorrow' when we chased him up and, when he finally presented his document, it had expired. We told him he needed to get a new one and he assured us it would be sorted in time. When we all turned up at the airport, however, guess who wasn't there? Anthony Malbon.

I couldn't trust him. It was a pity, as he could have taken the next step. He had scored a lot of goals in non-league and he could definitely have done it at a higher level. The fans, not knowing the facts, had a dig at me for 'ignoring the claims of one of the youth team'. The truth of the matter was that, if anyone was being disrespectful, it was Malbon to me, the club and his colleagues – and I wasn't going to stand for it.

However, any issues with the players were trifling compared to what was about to unfold in the boardroom. Unbeknown to me, the club became caught in the crossfire of a bitter battle to take control.

Again, we started that season well. We also reached the third round of the FA Cup and we were in and among the promotion slots all season. I even won the manager of the month award in September and November. Everything was going along swimmingly... until I received a call from a solicitor called Mick Carney. I knew him as he had a few of the Port Vale players on his books.

He was sounding me out about Sheffield United. I was happy at Vale and had no intention of leaving. But, understandably, the Blades were a massive pull for me. I had history with them. I soon realised it was an offer I simply couldn't refuse.

CHAPTER 18

BLUNTED BY THE BLADES

I couldn't ignore the call from Sheffield United. It was my club. My dad's club. My brother's club. Our club. Strangely, however, unlike a lot of people, I didn't have a professional craving to satisfy when I took a call from Kevin McCabe.

I could see the club was in freefall and it was a wrench for me to consider leaving Port Vale. OK, Vale was second in League Two but there were all sorts of issues on and off the pitch, but I felt we were picking up some upwards momentum. And from the outside, it looked as though the Blades were heading in the opposite direction.

It didn't help either that I wasn't the first choice of the chief executive, Trevor Birch. The word was he wanted Andy Scott, who was doing well at Brentford at the time. Ultimately, I knew the actual decision lay with Kevin, so the reality was that it didn't matter what Trevor thought.

Even so, I'll admit I had an uneasy feeling about Trevor after meeting him at his flat. He had made it clear to me I hadn't got the job and there were other candidates. He couldn't wait to tell me that. It was hardly ideal, having to win over the chief executive before a ball had even been kicked, but that was the size of it.

I wanted to make sure Vale would be recompensed for my exit. I told

Kevin that, while I was happy to have an initial chat, any other talks would have to be carried out with my current employer's backing. If he wanted me to simply walk out on Vale, he would have to find someone else to fill my role.

Around 28 December 2010, I received the call I was waiting for: Vale had been paid. I was really sorry to be leaving. Out of respect for Vale, there was no question that I would dismantle my backroom team and take them with me, so I just took Corky. He was something of a cult hero at Bramall Lane with his physical style as a player but, as a foretaste of what was to come, there were complications over the contracts. We both had three-year deals on the table, but there were issues surrounding the termination packages. Alan wasn't happy; he wanted twelve months, like I had. To break the impasse, I told Trevor to take three months off my compensation and give it to him.

With that sorted, we got to work – or tried to, at least. It was an amazing feeling, walking into a club I had supported all my life and being responsible for it. I said in my press conference that I wished my dad had been here to see it. My brother used to come to the games, and you can imagine what he was saying: 'The keeper's rubbish' and 'sack the manager' was about the gist of it. I didn't expect him to alter his stance of a lifetime for me!

However, the glow of actually being in charge of Sheffield United wore off pretty quickly. As a taste of what lay around the corner, I had to have words with the fitness coach on my first morning on the job. He came over to me on the first day and told me that what he normally did was take the boys for a warm-up to get them up to speed. He'd get the ball zipping around and then, after about an hour, he'd pass them on to me.

Corky was looking directly at me. He knew exactly what was coming.

I responded, 'Listen, do yourself a favour. Warm up the lads, leave the balls to the experts.'

That went well.

After the protocol had been laid down for the day, I gathered the first-team squad together and had a chat. I was honest. I told them the club meant a lot to me and that all the fans want to see is effort, enthusiasm and a bit of love for the shirt – and that's what I was looking for.

My first test was at Burnley. We took the lead but by half-time we were 3–1 down, and the fans blamed Nyron Nosworthy for a couple of the goals. They gave him some stick and he gestured towards them, so I had no option but to take him off as we slipped to defeat.

That wasn't the greatest of starts. A few days later, before my first game at Bramall Lane against Doncaster Rovers, the club's media guy, Andy Pack, pulled me to one side.

'Look Micky,' he said. 'There's been a lot of managers through this club. Not one of them has been given any real time. What you need to do is to wave and make a "T" sign to the crowd. You'll be asked about it afterwards and you can say that you wanted the gesture to mean that you needed some time.'

Before the game, Sheffield's 'The Greasy Chip Butty' song echoed around the stadium. I joined in:

> You fill up my senses, Like a gallon of Magnet, Like a packet of
> woodbines, Like a good pinch of snuff, Like a night out in Sheffield,
> Like a greasy chip butty, Like Sheffield United, Come fill me again,
> Na Na Na Na Na... OOOOHH!

I did it every home game, it meant that much to me. I then went onto the pitch, waved to the crowd and made the 'T' sign. What an idiot.

I have to say the fans were very good, even though we weren't doing very well. I was one of them; I was a Blade and I will tell them now that I couldn't have worked any harder. I so wish it had turned out differently.

Anyway, we had a pile of injuries at that stage and things didn't really improve. Darius Henderson, Chris Morgan and Andy Taylor were out for a good while. The fitness guys insisted that Richard Cresswell couldn't play two games in a week.

The weather was horrendous that year. Unbelievably, the club had a fantastic indoor facility but the physio and the fitness guy said we had players carrying knocks who couldn't train inside. If that sounds like the tail wagging the dog, then you are probably right. It is, unfortunately, the way modern football is heading. That unwelcome advice about training indoors meant that, during the week, we would have six or seven players pedalling away on static bikes around the outside of the pitch watching the others train. The lack of bodies made it really difficult to work on any team shape or pattern of play.

I had one other significant issue. The kids were having a great run in the FA Youth Cup and, in itself, that was great, but if you think about it from a manager's perspective – and from the viewpoint of a manager whose team is losing more than it is winning – you see it differently. What's the first thing the fans say in that scenario? Yes, you've guessed it: get the youngsters in the team. The fact was, however, that they were not up to Championship standard at that time. Also John Pemberton, who was in charge of them, had too much influence.

A lot of the lads did actually end up making their debuts under me, but it was a divided club. There was a first-team and a youth team housed in two different buildings; so, effectively, we had two clubs operating under the same banner. There were problems everywhere I looked.

I wanted us to be unified and encouraged a game of football among the staff. I'd done it at every club I'd ever been at but, unfortunately, Pemberton took exception to it and banned his youth coaches from playing. I had to go and see him about it and he said that, if one of them was injured, they wouldn't be able to work. It was petty.

There were issues in the first-team, too. To be fair, there normally are problems if a side isn't playing well. We had the likes of Kyle Bartley, who is now at Leeds United, in our ranks and he made it clear he didn't want to work under me. We sent him back to Arsenal – from where he had been signed on loan – at the end of the transfer window.

It soon became clear I had two options at Bramall Lane. The first option was to keep going the way we were, but that course of action would have ended in relegation. The second was to shake it up and see what fell out of the tree. There were no guarantees that approach would work, either. The problem was that people around the club kept telling me how good these first-team players were, but I was having a problem seeing it. I decided I needed another pair of eyes and ears, so I got hold of Dave Bassett. I asked him to come in on a part-time basis to have a look and see if he could tell me what was missing.

We both decided the opposite was true: they just weren't good enough. We needed a centre-half, but part of my remit was to reduce the wage bill. We looked at taking Danny Shittu and we were quoted £18,000-a-week for him – so that wasn't going to bring down the outgoings. I decided to take Shane Lowry from Villa instead. He was younger and he was available at £1,500-a-week. I also took Neil Collins from Wolves and Micky Doyle from Coventry.

We were competitive in games but didn't get a win for fourteen matches. I kept coming in afterwards and saying the same things both to the players and the press. When I look back now, it's clear the side always came out fighting, but if they didn't take the lead when they were on top, then they always made stupid mistakes. I remember one game when keeper Steve Simonsen punched a ball into his own net in front of the Kop.

And it didn't help that the spectre of the FA Youth Cup was always in the background with whispered suggestions that the kids could be our saviours. As the season progressed, I decided to throw in a lad against Cardiff City called Harry Maguire. He was always going to be a player, but he wasn't ready for it back then when everyone appeared to be howling for the youngsters to be given their chance.

In the first half he slipped while accepting the ball, which resulted in another ball hitting our net. It seemed that, whichever way I turned, I couldn't make any headway. We had two players – Darius Henderson and Lee Williamson – sent off before half-time at Watford. I mean, what chance have you got? Sadly, we lost our championship status at the end of the season.

I always thought that if I could keep them up and that we would have a high turnover of players during the summer. The club itself was, and still is, attractive to players. I threw the likes of Collins, Lowry and Sam Vokes straight into a relegation battle. They needed longer to adapt but I didn't have that time. Towards the end of the season, Dave, Trevor Birch, Kevin McCabe and I had a meeting. The kids were mentioned a lot, but we emphasised again they weren't ready. Dave and I said it would be counter-productive if they had been brought in at that stage.

McCabe said he'd heard seven or eight of the youth team could be in the first-team in a few months' time when we kicked off our campaign in League One. I disagreed with him. I knew it would be a battle and that it was a league for men. I said three or four would be in and around things and he said to me he had some thinking to do as to whether he was going to stick with me as manager. I really wasn't happy with that. If I had listened to McCabe and gone along with his plans, however, I'm sure I would have been at Sheffield United the following season.

At the end of the season, I attended all of the award ceremonies on behalf of the club, despite the fact that I'd not had the whole season to get it right. I was in charge when we went down but I didn't feel like I was chiefly responsible for that. However, I was the manager all the same and so I had to face the music.

Kevin, Trevor and the rest of them were going to decide whether I should stay in a job two weeks after the last ball was kicked. I had to apologise to the supporters and then the ones at the top were going to decide if I was going to be given the chance to carry on.

I spoke to Harry about the situation and we both agreed it was a poor way to treat someone. He phoned up Kevin to make the point that I shouldn't be the focus like this. About an hour later, however, I heard from Harry. The decision had been made – and I was out.

Kevin did phone me to explain the reasons why and promised my contract would be honoured. He advised I was free to join another club. He's a genuine Sheffield United fan who wants the club to do well. In all my dealings with him, he kept to his word.

However, I did feel I'd been sold short. Interestingly, as it happens, the FA Youth Cup side lost in the final to Manchester United. Of all the players who were being talked about, only Harry Maguire and Jordan Slew (another player I put into the first-team and who was transferred to Blackburn Rovers for £1.1 million in 2011) made anything like an impact on the game.

It turned out they couldn't have been that good after all, although it gives me no pleasure to say I was right. I was still out of a job. I understand it's easy to get sentimental about kids. There was some talent and I'm surprised that some have not kicked on, but as far as being in the team to help Sheffield United out of the League One then you can see again that I was right. Everyone was getting carried away, but they weren't quite good enough.

Overall, do I think I had a chance of staying? Probably not.

The problem I had at Sheffield United was that there were too many of them in that dressing room who thought they were players and didn't need to try. I had to have fights with them. I wasn't going to back down. One example of this was John Carver, who stood in for a couple of matches after Gary Speed left for the Wales job. He made people aware at the club that he wasn't happy with me because I'd alleged the squad wasn't fit. One thing I absolutely detest is managers coming into clubs and saying that. I'd thought it, but never said it about the previous bloke's players. I rang John up and told him that it wasn't true. We discussed it and we get on fine now but honestly, it was the least of my problems.

Did I enjoy managing Sheffield United? I've got to be honest: no, I didn't. I felt it put unfair pressure on my mum, my sisters and the family because they lived in the area and they had to listen to phone-ins on the radio and hear me getting battered. In the end, it was probably a relief I left. I can take the criticism, but I didn't want my family to have to hear it anymore. Unfortunately, my dream of managing the club I supported as a boy had turned sour. And I was looking for a job. Again.

CHAPTER 19

MICKY THE VALIANT: PART II

There was only one manager who had a worse time of it than I did while I was at Sheffield United; and that was my replacement at Port Vale, Jim Gannon.

Upon my exit, Bill Bratt had asked me if I would help the board at Vale to find my successor. I was only too happy to offer recommendations and advice, but Gannon was installed before I'd made any suggestions. In fact, upon hearing the news, I phoned Bill up and said, 'I thought you wanted some help', and he said that they'd taken soundings from elsewhere, as was their prerogative. Whoever had given Bill the advice was miles off the mark.

Even while I was managing at Bramall Lane, Geoff Horsfield and Mark Grew – my two former assistants – had kept me informed of what was going on at Vale Park. It did not sound pretty.

I thought I was having a bad time, but it didn't compare to what Gannon was going through. Vale were second when I left, but they ended the season in eleventh place, missing out on the play-offs by quite a distance. It was no surprise when he left, having lasted just three months. He had alienated just about everyone, so Grew had taken over until the end of the campaign. Even so, all that was happening on the pitch was overshadowed by everything off it. If I thought managing Port Vale was difficult at the beginning of the 2010/11 season, then it was nothing compared to what was about to happen twelve months later. To say it was a soap opera was an understatement. As I have hinted at already, there was more subterfuge in a couple of seasons at Vale than I thought possible at a football club. I thought I knew everything about the place. How wrong can you be?

Just before I was due to be unveiled for the second time, I received a call from Mo Chaudry. An EGM had been called and the club wanted me to attend. He had been on the fringes for about twelve months, waiting for his chance to take control, but this meeting had taken it up a level.

If Chaudry got the vote, he would be taking over. He told me not to sign any contract and warned me off putting myself in the camp of Bratt and Peter Jackson. What he didn't know, and I certainly wasn't going to tell him, was that someone had told me he was already in talks with Aidy Boothroyd. Apparently, Chaudry had promised him the job; no wonder he didn't want me to sign. If he had taken over, he would have had to pay me off.

I thought to myself, 'Thanks but no thanks, Mo. I'm signing.' I agreed to become Vale's manager again. So, as I was heading up to the club on the train, I received a call from Bill Bratt to say there was a problem.

The club's constitution stipulated four directors had to be appointed for any decision to retain its validity. On that basis, nothing could be agreed with respect to signing players. No matter who I wanted to bring in, it would be rendered null and void because there were not enough directors to rubber-stamp the move.

He put it to me that Stan Meigh, one of the directors, had a shareholding of £50,000 that he would transfer to me and I would then be co-opted onto the board. That meant we could fulfil the legal duty of the constitution of the company running the club. To me, though, it was a chance for us to sign players.

At that stage, ahead of the 2011/12 season, we had just seven players under contract. I agreed to do it and what I also said to them was if things were going well, I would buy Stan's shares – provided I could see the club was going in the right direction.

I've got to be honest, though. I didn't have a clue what directors were liable for. I was naive. It wasn't until Roger Furnell, the finance director, spelled it out to me that I realised I could be held personally accountable.

I didn't want to get involved in the politics. All I knew was that I couldn't sign any players if I didn't accede to Bratt's request. I had it minuted at every single opportunity that I wanted to step down from the board as quickly as I could. The majority of the punters wanted me back but others made their feelings known quite strongly that I wasn't helping the cause.

'The Black & Gold Until It's Sold' group were at the forefront of this. They let me know how they felt to the point where I had to change my email address to avoid any more abuse on the subject. I could understand their frustration, but what choice did I have? I couldn't start pre-season with half a dozen players.

At the first board meeting it became apparent, very quickly, that we were struggling for cash and that we needed to get money in sooner rather than later. From out of nowhere, however, we had a tie-up with Ameriturf, a company that was sponsoring us and we had a pre-season organised in North America on the back of their cash.

As per usual, it threw up a couple of funny tales. We had a kit man, Mark Cooper, whose nickname was 'Smeagol' after the character in *The Lord of the Rings*. We were playing in Victoria, in Canada, and Mark, who was a decent non-league player, was pestering me to put him on.

Eventually, I caved and said he could have a few minutes during our final match.

The people announcing the substitutes wanted to know his name and we said it was Tommy Cooper. He ran onto the pitch and, no word of a lie, the bloke on the microphone said, 'And coming onto the pitch is Number 31, Tommy Cooper,' before adding, 'just like that...' We were in absolute hysterics in the dug-out.

Twelve months earlier, Mark came within a whisker of having a tragic accident. At the end of every season, I normally went away to my place in Portugal for a few days with a few of the staff for a break. We play golf, have a few drinks. We took Smeagol with us this time.

It was a roasting hot day and we were on the course at Gramacho. The seventeenth hole is tricky. It's a severe dog leg. You chip it down the fairway 160 yards then it's a further 180 to the flag. It's over 300 yards if you fancy at shot at the green, but the green is hidden behind trees and a man-made lake.

Anyway, our kit man fancied himself as a big-hitter, so he had a pop at the green. He fell short and his ball plopped into the water guarding the hole. There was a plastic lining in the water and a sign saying: 'Under no circumstances shall you try to retrieve your ball. Danger.' Unfortunately, he ignored this warning and duly went to retrieve it.

The problem was that his rubber studs caused him to slip in the water and he couldn't get out, no matter how he tried. He was flapping about, big style. Fortunately for him, two green-keepers were nearby and they managed to throw him a life-saving buoy which he gratefully grabbed onto. They dragged him out and bollocked him at the same time. After completing the round, we went and had a well-earned drink outside the clubhouse. Obviously Smeagol's clothes were still wet but we could hardly see him for the steam that was pouring off him!

If that taught him a lesson, then the same could be said of my assistant, Mr Horsfield, after his performance on the flight back from North America. We were flying overnight and the unwritten rule was that if anyone wanted a sleeping tablet, the physio would issue one to enable everyone to get some shut-eye.

Geoff stuck his hand up when asked and swallowed it down. Everyone was falling asleep, however, apart from the former striker who was as bright as a button. He demanded, 'Give me another tablet.' He was being very forceful about it. Don't forget, we were on a plane full of passengers. We weren't on our own.

An hour passed and Geoff was feeling nothing. He had been drinking because he couldn't get to sleep and he was still wide awake. He shouted over: 'Give me another tablet.' He was almost threatening the physio now.

But still nothing: he was still awake. In fact, he was still awake until about five minutes before the captain turned on the 'Fasten Your Seat Belt' sign and told us he was getting ready to land. Our hero was, by now, absolutely out of the game. After having a few beers, three sleeping pills and stayed up half-the-night, he was like a bear in his pit. We couldn't get him to wake up, however much we tried. Have you seen those films when someone is deadweight and they are being dragged along the floor by their heels? That was us trying to get him down the aisle and off the plane. Honestly, he's a size and it was a real palaver. We had to prop him up through passport control as he carried on dozing.

Anyway, the season started well enough. We started with a four-match unbeaten run even though the squad was young and was being bolstered at various times with loanees.

We had to take a few of them pretty much on trust alone, and we wondered what exactly we had done when we signed a striker called Guy Madjo on loan from Stevenage. We saw him in training and wondered if we had actually recruited a pub player. However, the Cameroonian had the last laugh after he scored three goals in his second game for us against Aldershot. The value of that was seen by his parent club and he was returned. We had asked to sign him on loan again but Aldershot took him on a permanent deal, so the joke really was on us.

That season we also signed Tom Pope, a Vale fan who came to us from Rotherham United. He was someone who was going to play a big part in what happened one season later. The stand-out player in the first half of the campaign, however, was a little midfielder called Gary Roberts. He was scouse, a real box of tricks. He was a very talented individual, but he had been to plenty of clubs. He could really play, though. Unfortunately, the spotlight was more on what he was doing off the pitch rather than on it. He wasn't nasty, just ill-advised. Some of it, however, was plain daft.

I remember the landlord at one of the pubs around Vale Park came to see me. He was over 6ft tall this fella, and the first words out of his mouth were 'Gary Roberts'.

He explained, 'Roberts was in my pub on Saturday night. First, he owes me money. Secondly, I want my suit back.'

It transpired that, after having a few drinks, Roberts wanted to go to a casino so he'd asked to borrow the landlord's suit. I looked at him and said, 'You're well over six feet tall; Gary's five feet eight inches – if that.'

With that, the landlord simply replied: 'Yes – and he's got my shoes as well.'

It was just one of the problems you have as a manager that no one sees.

He was just a drinker, was Gary. As a manager, I've always taken a certain approach with players who are producing on the pitch. Within reason, they can get away with a lot and they will be cut a lot of slack. It's unfair, I know, but that's the way it is. However, as soon as their form dips, there's going to be a problem. He turned up the worse for wear on too many occasions and I ended up getting rid of him. It was a real shame because, like I say, he wasn't a bad kid – and he could certainly play.

While that situation was a shame for Roberts, the club and me, it was nothing compared to the bigger picture. Vale were still struggling for cash, big time. It made for a messy campaign, right from the season's opener against Crawley. Five hundred fans gathered outside the ground, making their point. Mike Lloyd, now installed as chairman instead of Bratt, went outside to meet them.

There was talk of serious investment that came to nothing. Perry Deakin, the chief executive officer and Peter Miller, a businessman based in America with a consultancy firm, also joined the board. It later came to light that Deakin and Miller had reportedly not paid for the shareholding that saw them promoted to the board of directors.

Another fan group, the North London Valiants, also got involved and Chaudrey was still lurking in the shadows. The council went public, voicing their fears that a £2.25 million loan would never be repaid, so Deakin and Miller were removed. If a screenwriter had submitted it as a script, it would have been rejected for being too far-fetched.

We were then hit with a transfer embargo. There were more twists and turns behind the scenes than an Agatha Christie novel. It was madness and, all this time, I was trying to motivate a group of players to achieve in League Two.

One particular fixture from this season springs to mind. We were due to play in Hereford on Boxing Day, so we travelled the night before, on Christmas Day, to prepare properly. I left Claire and the kids in Market Harborough at 3 p.m. and was joined on the coach from Burslem by the physio and the players. I gave Geoff Horsfield and Mark Grew the day with their families.

We were still in and around the play-offs at this stage. We were playing well. The reason I'm talking about this moment in the season specifically is because Vale went into administration later in the season after a whole string of creditors stuck their hands out for cash – only to find there wasn't any. The club sponsors, Harlequin Property, began legal proceedings over an unpaid loan of £125,000. More worryingly, the club was hit with a wind-up petition by HM Customs and Revenue.

On the day when we went into administration, we played Crewe at home. We drew 1–1. I received a call immediately after the game to ring Mike Lloyd. There weren't any directors at the match – which was unusual because it's a derby fixture.

Anyway, we were due to be paid, so I almost fell over when Lloyd said: 'Sorry, Micky, but I regret to inform you that neither the players nor you are going to be paid this month.'

I was furious and I said to him, 'You're telling me this after a game, are you? We've still got a chance of the play-offs and the lads have worked their nuts off and you are now telling me they are not going to be paid.'

'Not only that, but why couldn't you have told them this at the start of the month because like everyone else, they've got commitments. If we could have given them time to pay bills it wouldn't be so bad but now they have possibly spent money they could have put to one side. It is cowardice of the highest order.'

I had to call a meeting there and then in the dressing room to break the news. As you can imagine, it went down badly.

The fans were happy, however, because it meant the probability of a change of ownership might be around the corner. But I was seriously pissed off I had a group of players who had given their all and, with the ten points we had deducted, it effectively meant the season was over.

The next day Joan Whalley, the local MP, comes into the club. She is a proper supporter and she's a massive Vale fan. She approached me and said, 'Micky, Micky, what great news. With the administration we can get rid of the old board of directors, we can start afresh…'

I looked at her and said, 'Great news, eh, Joan? Where were you on Christmas Day?'

She looked at me quizzically. 'Er, Christmas Day? I was with my family…'

'Can I tell you where I was? I left my family at 3 p.m. to travel for an hour and a half to meet the team coach. I then travelled down to Hereford with the physio and the team.'

'I had one pint, got the players into bed and tucked up nicely. I then got up in the morning. Fed them some breakfast. Took them for a walk and prepared them for a game because we want to be professional.'

'We won. I came back home. I saw my family again at 8 p.m. on Boxing Day… And you are telling me that administration is good news? We've lost ten points. The whole season has been a sham. We can't get promoted. Don't give me, good news. It's a load of bollocks as far as I'm concerned…'

The board meetings before administration were horrible. The directors were so paranoid that they refused to meet up in Stoke. They thought the rooms were bugged. Honestly, you couldn't make it up. We ended up going to Uttoxeter.

I sat in these gatherings with little idea of what was going on. Every single board meeting I said, 'I want to step down' and they promised me that, as soon as they could get someone else on board, I would be replaced. But what used to happen was I would get excused and they would carry on afterwards; they never left the same time as I did. It was as if they were going through the motions when I was there and then waiting to speak behind my back once I left the room.

When Roger Furnell told me to get out of it as soon as I could, I took his advice and resigned my position.

In the meantime, Begbies Traynor had been appointed as our administrator. We needed to sell someone as quickly as we could, but the only player we could off-load for any immediate cash was Lee Collins. Before we went over the edge, Keith Hill at Barnsley had spoken to me about him and we were haggling over a fee. Keith was aware we needed money. I was trying to get £100,000; they offered £50,000. I told Begbies Traynor that we might be able to get more, but the administrator took the £50,000.

The fact was that we weren't being paid. Before the PFA eventually stepped in, the community rallied around unbelievably. They had collections, and a burger van even turned up after training every day to feed the boys.

This had happened to me twice now, once at Leicester and now here. And, by now, I'd learnt that the one person who is vulnerable in these circumstances is the manager; the players' deals are always protected. The administrator is within his rights to clear out the manager and the coaching staff but, fortunately, I must have been held in some esteem because I kept my job. My job, as promotion was now out of the question, was to keep the players motivated. To be fair, we did pick up some decent results.

When you consider some of the lads were living maybe an hour away, the players did well to get in and concentrate on their football. One player, however, said he couldn't make it in. He said couldn't afford it, but that was strange because he had a flat two miles away. That was Ryan Burge… and the less said about him, the better.

We then heard the administrator, after some very quick work, had a preferred bidder: a fella called Keith Ryder. He first turned up as the 2011/12 season was drawing to a close. He had hired a room at Crewe Hall so that he could meet everybody. When I was finally introduced to Keith, I couldn't even tell you to this day what his business was. He told me his plans and said he'd like me to stay on as manager, but he was going to make his mind up after he'd interviewed me, as he was going to do with all the staff; I didn't see why he needed to do that as my CV already answered all his questions.

I was pissed off about it. I had to come over from Market Harborough to be interviewed by him on my day off; he didn't need to do it on a Wednesday. But, since the rest of the staff had to go through it, I kept my mouth shut. The interview was bog-standard stuff. He appeared genuine enough. But later on, he turned up at a supporters' meeting in a chauffeur-driven car. I've never bought into that; anyone can hire a big car for a day, but the fans seemed impressed. My doubts about him kept coming towards the end of the season. He turned up at games and he talked about it well enough, but no one could still work him out.

Our penultimate match of the season was against Swindon Town. Leading up to the game, the chairman asked me who we would like to keep and what contracts they would be asking for. So I advised the players during the week to ask their agents to give me an idea about their deals for next season, because the new owner wanted to know about it. We formalised a list with information from the agents. We'd also had a couple of trialists in and one was a lad called Paul Marshall. He worked well in training, so I decided to offer him a contract for the next season.

I announced the team before kick-off and the talk went something like this: 'In goal, Kasper Schmeichel, right-back Kyle Walker, centre-half John Terry and Rio Ferdinand...' Eighteen blank faces stared back at me. I continued, 'Surely we have these players in our squad, the amount of money you lot are looking for...'

I told them to go out and make sure Swindon didn't enjoy a party at our expense. That fell on deaf ears, however. They did a real job on us and we were thumped by five. I was hopeful when Paul Marshall came off the bench for the last quarter of the match, but he just strolled around. He didn't want to get on the ball and he didn't look interested. I thought to myself, 'I've dropped a bollock here' and I decided there and then to withdraw his contract offer. Maybe I was out of order.

Anyway, after the match Keith Ryder came down to see me. Swindon boss Paolo di Canio was being presented with the trophy for the best manager award, which was an absolute load of bollocks. They'd bought the league that season, but fair play to them; it is won on the pitch. Ryder's first question was 'How do we do this next year?' I asked him if he was serious. He was, so I answered in earnest: 'It's straightforward. You bring in the best players that are offered to you. You pay the agents and you pay the players more money than anyone else is offering.' We hadn't paid an agent since I'd been at Port Vale, and that was quite significant. An agent's fee is normally about five per cent of the value of the contract. He said, 'Right, let's do it.' I came away from the County Ground that night thinking, 'Great, we're going to have a go next season.'

That summer there was a large turnover of players. I signed Jennison Myrie-Williams; we took Ashley Vincent from Colchester; we signed Chris Neal, a goalkeeper from Shrewsbury, David Artell, a centre-half from Crewe and Richard Duffy. I had Tom Pope in on a permanent deal from Rotherham United.

We lost Marc Richards, sadly. We were willing to fork out for him but he was offered £3,000-a-week at Chesterfield. Otherwise, we were pushing the boat out and Keith Ryder was behind it. He asked the players into the office and told them that he had big plans; he sold his club vision to them. It worked well and we were spending some money, not massive amounts, but enough to be competitive.

For pre-season, I'd organised a trip to Ireland; yes, back to Ballygar. Strangely, the trip itself somhow passed without incident, but it sticks in my mind because it was the last time I ever clapped eyes on Keith.

The day before we left, there had been an issue. I was due to meet Keith and pick up the money to pay for the hotel, the transport and all the food at Vale Park. In total it came to £14,000. I wanted it in cash. I'd told Keith about this and I knew that we needed it before we stepped onto a plane. He was due to give me the money twenty-four hours before we flew, but I couldn't get hold of him. I started to smell a rat.

After spending all afternoon chasing him, I eventually received a message from him at 6 p.m. asking me to wait for him. But he didn't turn up until 8 p.m., looking completely dishevelled and holding a plastic bag. Inside it was £14,000 in loose notes. There were just hundreds of fivers, tenners and twenties in there.

I asked if he was coming over with us as I could get someone to meet him at Dublin Airport if he fancied it. He said that he had some business to deal with and that he would try to make it over for a few days. And that was the last time I ever saw him. Try as I might, I couldn't raise him – not in Ireland or back in England. I just couldn't contact him. We all left messages and tried everything – but nothing. It remains one of the strangest episodes of my life. He vanished. It was a con.

The Football League returned all the contracts one week before the season started. Keith had signed them, but they were now all invalid. I arranged for all the players to meet me in the dressing room. 'Boys, I don't know how to tell you this,' I said. 'But Keith Ryder has done a runner. All of the deals you have signed are not worth the paper they've been written on – which means you are all free transfers. You can leave, for nothing, today.'

The squad were shocked. I was embarrassed and annoyed because I'd bought into Keith Ryder as well. Not only that but I had talked some of these players into signing. I had to explain it to the supporters too, via the press.

After my speech, David Artell, our centre-half and one of the more senior lads in the team, stood up and gave one of his own. He said: 'Boys, we're still being paid. The administrator will find a new buyer. We have got to stick together. We're one week away from the start of the season. Let's just see it out.'

It was a great moment. A real Churchillian rally. But the next day we had another pre-season friendly; everyone turned up – apart from Artell. So I called him. Eventually, he answered. 'I'm a bit embarrassed, boss,' he said. 'I'm going to sign for Chester.'

He signed a two-year deal but, thankfully and ironically, he was the only one who left. I was surprised that Artell was the only one who quit. In one way it was quite good timing, because almost every other club had assembled their squads and Keith had injected some cash to keep it going. Every club probably had done their budgets and it was true, they were still being paid – so they stayed put.

As it was, we got off to a decent start. I was surprised at the amount of possession visiting teams had when they came to Vale Park. I was openly criticised for that, but the reason for it was missed by a lot of people. The visitors played an extra midfielder and we stuck to our formation of 4–4–2. We weren't bad and we had a new and revitalised Tom Pope in our side. Popey was a striker and a Vale fan, which I'm sure earned him slack with the supporters.

I wasn't surprised after watching him for a few weeks. If there was a channel run to be made, Tom made it; if there was a knockback to a thrower-in in the last third of the pitch, Tom did it. But he was no-where near goal. No wonder he never found the net.

We worked at it during pre-season. I told him I wanted him to work the width of the eighteen-yard box. I wanted him in the middle, and if the others didn't get crosses in, it was up to him to tell them. I didn't want him anywhere near the wing.

Pope ended up getting thirty-three goals that season. His team-mates loved him, and no wonder. It went so well that I received my ninth manager of the month award in September.

Shortly after that we played Oxford United one Monday night shown live on Sky. That evening the administrator said Paul Wildes was going to be the new owner. The story has it that Norman Smurthwaite, who was in his villa in Portugal, almost choked on his gin and tonic when he heard me say afterwards that I didn't know why anyone in their right mind would buy a football club. As we were to later find out, Norman was Paul Wildes's business partner and would be my boss too less than twelve months later.

My relationship with the supporters was tested shortly afterwards. Sam Morsey, one of our young professionals, was red-carded for a poor challenge when we were two-up against Rochdale. There was a quarter of the match still to play and Morsey went into a stupid tackle and was dismissed. I criticised him in the press and in the changing rooms. We were comfortable, but games like that change your season. Some of the fans weren't happy, but I remain convinced it was justified.

However, the boot was on the other foot when we faced Sheffield United in the second round of the FA Cup. It was a big game for me. We were one up going into added time. They put a cross into the box and one of their players put it out for goal-kick. Unfortunately, the linesman said it came off our defender. Suffice to say, they scored from it. Then, a couple of minutes later, they scored again.

I know now what goes on behind the scenes in referees' rooms, but at the time of that tie I didn't. For some reason I waited thirty minutes to see the referee. 'Where did you get the decision from? Not one of their players appealed for it...' and he replied, 'It didn't cost you the game. You're just making excuses for your poor defending...'

Decisions like that change games. It's really important the officials concentrate for ninety minutes. On that day, they got it wrong.

As we headed into the New Year, we decided to strengthen our side and the player being thrown our way was Lee Hughes. I'm not going to go into his past as it's been well-documented elsewhere. I took my chance with him. He was a voice in the dressing room but he wanted the position that Tom Pope had. And, fair play to our leading scorer, he ended up doing the work for Hughes to profit.

Our results from then on were steady. We had a threat with two goal-scorers in the side. But, unfortunately, the wheels started to come off slightly and matters came to a head after a defeat at Bristol Rovers. What people have to understand is that there is a time during the season when form dips, players' confidence gets knocked and the crowd, who are used to seeing the side win, get very disappointed when losses start coming in. It becomes a struggle, and that's happened at some stage in every single one of my promotions.

We were beaten at Bristol Rovers and to say that I was abused by my own fans, situated behind the dug-out, is an understatement. We were well in control of our own destiny but I'd kept a fans' favourite out of the team, we'd lost and we were on a bad run.

But I had good reason for leaving Ryan Burge out of the line-up. He'd failed to show up to our pre-match meal and he'd been criticising the club on social media, despite us having an agreement that none of us would air our grievances in a public way.

After the game Paul Wildes was waiting for me. He was fuming. He said, 'Have you lost the players?' That grated me. I challenged him to go and ask them. I then asked him what he wanted to do. There was no way I was going to resign; we were third in the table. We agreed to go home and think about the situation. I called a meeting in the changing room and told them I'd had the chairman down. The reaction was 'Typical Port Vale. If there's not a crisis – let's create one.'

But it also created a siege mentality. Bizarrely, the next day I received a call from Norman. At that time he didn't have any executive powers but he told me I had his backing. I heard nothing from Paul. I just went in to see him and he merely said it was business as usual.

After that, we didn't lose between then and the end of the season, the highlight being a 7–1 thumping we dished out to Burton Albion. Everything clicked. Hughesie got a hat-trick when we were five-up ten minutes after half-time – and all this in front of a bumper crowd of over 10,000.

We just needed a win at Rochdale to get promoted. We went 2–1 up in the eighty-ninth minute and thought we'd done it. But, remember, this is Port Vale we are talking about. They equalised in stoppage time. And then, in the next game against Northampton, Lee Collins, who I had sold to Barnsley, had scored a spectacular own-goal to secure us promotion. Thanks for that, Lee! And with that, we were up.

Given everything I'd dealt with – administration, players being able to leave one week before the start of the season and the total turmoil of the past twelve months – I started thinking about my dad. I did get emotional afterwards. He'd not long been dead and I could not help but think about him, and even now I just wish he would have been there to see it.

Nothing had been planned after the game. Strangely enough, it was Claire's birthday again (just like it had been after the final game at Leicester), so she had booked us all a room near Burslem so we could have a night out locally after the game. Norman came in to see me afterwards to tell me that Paul Wildes had offered me a new deal. I thought he was coming in just to talk through the new contract. I was to find out later that I was miles off the mark.

I felt great; not just for myself, but also for those players who had taken a chance. I was so grateful to people such as Hughes and Darren Purse who had helped us over the line, and others such as Doug Loft,

Jon McCombe, Anthony Griffiths, Adam Yates and Louis Dodds who had been there when I first arrived.

I was also indebted to the people at the club who the supporters don't see, such as Estelle, my PA, Kerry, Barbara, Jo Lumani, Joan, Tracey, Andy Burgess, Dave Johnson, Steve Speed, the groundsman and Bill Lodey. When clubs go into administration, you, as a manager, have the spotlight on you, but there are unsung heroes in the background, good people there who keep you going.

Going into Burslem after the game was bedlam. We couldn't get into the pubs, so we ended up going for an Indian. The fans were banging on the windows and the restaurant manager had to lock his doors. He was having kittens, thinking the windows were going to be smashed through. During the evening, Louis Dodds came in for a quick drink and a chat. My daughter Madison was so chuffed to see him as, although she was only eight at the time, he was her favourite. I'm not sure why, although my wife seemed to agree for some reason!

All in all, it was a great season – one I look back upon now with a great deal of pride and satisfaction.

I would just like add a quick footnote about Keith Ryder. After seeing him with that bag of money – it looked like he had been in a fight to get it – no one has clapped eyes on him since. Quite bizarre. I am still gobsmacked by how that all happened. Would my time there have happened without him? Maybe not. He did keep the club going for a few months.

But, as ever at Port Vale, I was to receive a rather rude awakening one month later.

CHAPTER 20

A VALIANT FINAL EFFORT AND ROTTEN AT ROVERS

By the time thoughts turned to the 2013/14 season, Vale had a new owner: Norman Smurthwaite. He had bought out Paul Wildes and he asked me to meet him at the Hilton at Leicester, just off the M1. I had no idea what happened to Paul; I didn't have any reason to ask. He was chairman one day, the next he wasn't.

All I knew was that I had a new boss and the club had a new owner, and I wanted Norman to make good on the promise that Paul had made about a new contract as I had one year left on my existing one. Unfortunately, however, I wasn't going to get it. The meeting didn't go exactly how I thought it would. It was amicable to start with, but then he dropped a bombshell.

He told me that any contract offer would not be forthcoming, and he was shelving any talk about fresh terms and that we should continue as we were. I'll be honest, I was seething.

He then he hit me with another verbal right-hander: 'I need your help.'

So, he took away the contract I was supposed to be getting and now he's saying that he needs my help!

He went on, 'I don't know how to run a football club.'

I replied, 'So let me get this straight. You aren't going to give me the contract that the club indicated I would be getting and now you are asking me for my help. You are talking bollocks.'

I got up and walked out. Our first meeting did not go according to plan and I'd put myself in a position where he's going to sack me. I expected a call within a few days saying they were going to terminate my contract, but it never came.

I thought to myself, 'I'm not putting myself out of work.' So I went to the club and started planning the pre-season. However, Norman had issues. He wasn't happy with the kit deal we had with Sondico and decided he was going to end it. He didn't have a shirt sponsor, either. A bit of background for you: all the kit manufacturers talk to each other and Norman couldn't secure a deal for love nor money. So the club has no kit. And no shirt sponsor.

I introduced Norman to Paul Kenny at the GMB. They thrashed out a shirt sponsorship deal and Paul also agreed to put the union's name on one of the stands at Vale Park. I then introduced him to Fabrizio at Errea, a friend of mine from my Brighton days. We travelled out to Italy to sort out a deal for the kit, too.

So, just to reiterate, Norman's taken my contract away, and I've got him a kit deal, a kit sponsor and a sponsor for the stand. He has done all right out of me, has Norman.

Everyone thought we had a fractious relationship, but that wasn't the case. As our relationship has developed, we became friends. I could talk to him differently from other managers. For instance, I'd give him a knock early in the morning in his office. His hair would be all over the place. He's one of those blokes who just can't seem to manage to look smart, even when he has to. I'd say: 'We're going to Southend this weekend. Can you sanction a pre-match meal please?' He'd reply, 'Nah, no, no, no.' So I'd tell him that I'd come back later when his twin brother was in. I used to walk out and, half an hour later, he'd come down and we'd have a proper conversation about it.

We had a decent pre-season and I'd brought in a number of players – people such as Chris Roberts from Preston, Gavin Tomlin from Sheffield United and Carl Dickinson, formerly of Stoke City – who were to have an impact that season.

The main problem was with me. I had a problem with my left hip which came on when I was running the line for my son's junior team. I just felt something click. I couldn't get to the bottom of it and struggled through pre-season in pain before having an operation in September.

It meant I had to take a break. I wasn't doing myself any favours on the training ground. So I handed over the reins to Rob Page just before we played Tranmere. I thought it was a good step for Rob as he was already coaching Wales Under-21s, and Norman was insistent that he took over instead of Mark Grew. I told him I wouldn't interfere and he got off to a flier at Prenton Park. Three weeks later, however, I was back. But I wasn't fit enough and, sure enough, we lost our next match to Peterborough United.

In the FA Cup we were drawn against Shortwood United, a little club situated not too far from Forest Green Rovers in deepest Gloucestershire. It was selected for television on Monday night. The cameras were there for BT Sport, no doubt hoping for an upset.

In the run-up to the game I took a call from my old mucker, Neil Moxley, from the *Daily Mail*. There's only one reason why the national newspapers are interested. They want a drama. And, more specifically this time, Mox wanted to write a fly-on-the-wall piece about Port Vale's potential embarrassment at the hands of the part-timers. He asked if he could come on the coach. I don't think he expected me to say yes. Effectively, I had granted him access all areas. In many ways that is dangerous for a manager because there was no way I could stop him reporting it as he saw it.

He did receive prior warning that something might be up on the coach as we travelled down. But I don't think even he expected to be at the centre of the pre-match chat we had in our dressing room. Five minutes before we were due to go out and just as the players were going to sit down to listen to the final instructions, I asked Rob Page to go and find our intrepid hack and escort him to the away dressing room.

'Any idea who this is?' I asked a group of puzzled faces.

'No? Well, this is a reporter from the *Daily Mail*. There's only one reason this wanker is here tonight. He, like hundreds of thousands on television, is tuning in to see you lot fall flat on your fucking faces. Do not give him, or that lot out there, the satisfaction because they will like nothing better than to rub our noses in it if we do not go about our business properly.'

It was an easy team-talk and we won 4–0.

Shortly after that, we found ourselves in a spot of bother for a very unusual reason. We had a young centre-half, called Joe Davis, who was the son of Crewe boss Steve Davis. Now, to the outside world, Port Vale versus Crewe Alexandra may not be El Clasico. But it is to the people involved. And in the build up to the derby, the staff and I had long conversations about whether to play Joe against his dad's team. My main concern was how it would affect Davis Jnr if his dad's side were struggling. I wasn't questioning his integrity. I just wondered how he would take it from a mental perspective.

Anyway, we went with it, but Davis Jnr cost the team the first goal with his over-excitement early on and then he picked up a booking. A few minutes later, he committed another foul. If I wondered how the Davis family was approaching the match, I needn't have bothered. I looked over at his dad in the other dug-out and he was pleading for the referee to send him off!

A bizarre situation, I thought to myself. He'd cost us one goal, got booked, trodden a fine line and then his dad is calling for him to be dismissed. So I substituted him after thirty-three minutes. It was the subject of some chatter after the match but I felt it was the only option available to me. Joe only needed to commit one more foul and they'd have been screaming for the official to pull out his red card.

I had a drink afterwards with his dad and said, 'What a twat you are, trying to get your son sent off.'

He just looked at me and said, 'It's football, isn't it?'

I knew exactly what he meant.

It was another good group. Tom Pope was scoring goals, and by this time we had signed, on George Foster's recommendation, a teenage striker called Jordan Hugill, who I think will have a big future in the game. Back then, though, George plucked him out of the non-league ranks. Jordan was, however, the unlikeliest footballer you have ever seen. He was miles behind in terms of fitness, but he kept on going. He did well in his first full season with us; so much so, in fact, that there was very strong interest in him from Preston North End.

He refused to sign a new contract and had got himself an agent. It was obvious he was going to leave, with his representative threatening to take him either up to Scotland or abroad. That meant we wouldn't be able to earn any money out of him, as he was under twenty-three years old. Due to an administrative error, we had missed the deadline to offer him a fresh deal as well. Obviously, that didn't go down too well with the chairman. Everyone knew the score. Preston did, and so did we.

I was happy enough to leave Norman to deal with it, until I received a call from Peter Ridsdale who I knew from my days at Leeds United.

Peter, as everyone knows, is a massive Leeds fan and was, in a former life, involved with menswear retailers Burton. Back in the day the man-of-the-match at Elland Road used to receive a £200 voucher to spend on clothes. I won the bonus so often I was like a walking advert for Burton at times. Actually, people have commented on my dress sense and wonder now if I'm still spending them in there...

Anyway, Peter picked up the phone to moan to me about Norman. He said the deal was off unless someone else dealt with it, so I had to step in and negotiate a sale that looked to be heading for the rocks. A deal, incidentally, that might still benefit Vale if Jordan goes on to bigger and better things.

That campaign will be remembered by Vale fans, however, because it turned on a training ground bust-up between Doug Loft and Dan Jones, two players who wore their hearts on their sleeves. The incident that caused so much angst towards the end of that season actually came out of nowhere.

We were having a competitive five-a-side and they both went in for a challenge. Dan Jones was the first up and I don't know whether there was a tangle of legs or not but, out of nowhere, he lifted Doug off his feet with an upper-cut. It fractured his colleague's cheekbone and jaw.

I've seen fights on training grounds all around the country. I've even been involved in a couple myself. But this one really was out of the blue. Honestly, it came out of nowhere. And it was a shame because on his day, Dan was as good as anyone in the division. Lofty was having a great season. He'd been with me since day one and he was the club captain.

Anyway, Doug went to hospital and Dan was sent home. It was another incident that you find yourself dealing with that has sprung up out of a moment of madness. The approach the club took was to sack Dan. The general consensus was that we had little option. He had done a lot of damage, but it didn't sit entirely right with me. When we told Dan, he understood. Lofty also left the club at the end of that season. It had been a solid campaign but left a sour taste.

Once again, we had performed pretty well. My contract was again on the agenda as the campaign came to a close. Norman kept saying he wanted me to 'go on to bigger and better things' and I took that to mean he wanted to get rid of my wages and earn himself some compensation at the same time. Perhaps I was just being cynical.

I honestly thought the final game of the 2013/14 season would be my last at the club. We'd finished ninth and reached the Fourth Round of the FA Cup. I didn't really think we had a budget that would see us challenge in the play-off spots. There was a story during the season that the chairman had pleaded poverty over the club's finances to a variety of agents and that he had been forced to meet a £1 million deficit on the budget out of his own pocket. The chairman was doing what a chairman should. Look after the club as best he could.

But there was an average set at 7,900 fans. They'd not been pulling in gates like that at Vale Park since the days when John Rudge was packing them in during the club's brief stay in the Championship. Even with a decent cup run, we were struggling to make that one stack up. But, after all of that, I signed a rolling twelve-month deal with the club.

That summer we sold Gavin Tomlin to Crawley, lost Hugill to Preston, Lofty joined Gillingham and Jennison Myrie-Williams went off to Scunthorpe United, which was a blow. Ahead of the 2014/15 campaign, we went down to HMS *Raleigh* in Portsmouth. It was George Foster, the chief scout, who came up with the idea. He travelled down there to make sure the facilities were up to scratch. They were fantastic.

The only problem was that every time we wanted to walk around the base, we had to have a chaperone with us. The services could not afford to have thirty non-naval people wandering around their site. It was totally understandable.

After five days' solid training, we decided to let the lads off the leash and allow them to go out for a drink. It was off-site, nowhere near the base. The idea was that they could go out for a drink and get back to Raleigh in time for their curfew.

What the boys perhaps did not appreciate was that on the ferry back over to HMS *Raleigh*, the navy police it themselves. The footballers being footballers, and not caring about regulations, decided to get lairy. The two keepers Chris Neil and Sam Johnson are nearly arrested getting back to base!

I was hauled before the commander of the naval base and told that the conduct of my players was unacceptable. If it had been one of his personnel, they would have been arrested – but they decided to give the pair the benefit of the doubt. I apologised and promised it wouldn't happen again. They looked after us brilliantly, and it was a real eye-opener for everyone the manner in which the recruits are beasted and organised.

As the season got underway, I wasn't really sure I was in the best frame of mind for it. The budget was similar to the year before and I was disappointed that we were doing everything on the cheap. The chairman had said he was disappointed with season-ticket sales, given what he had invested.

I was looking for players who could make a step up. Ryan McGivern, a left-sided player at Hibernian, came in. I also snared a lad called Mark Marshall, who had served a two-year drugs ban for taking performance-enhancing drugs when he was younger. I'd looked into his character and he seemed a nice kid. He eventually became a crowd favourite and is currently doing really well at Bradford City.

For me, the final piece of the jigsaw was a player called Byron Moore who I signed from Crewe. I will never forget his transfer as long as I live. He'd turned down a contract at Crewe and I nipped in. I signed him at 4 p.m. and I was busy congratulating myself on it. Four hours later, however, I received a call from member of the media who said that Moore's brother had committed suicide and that my player had found him. You can imagine the devastating effect that would have on anyone. They don't teach you how to deal with that on the Football Association's Pro-Licence course, let me tell you.

That aside, I was excited to get going again. We started the campaign well, but it started to turn when we played Notts County. Former Manchester United keeper Roy Carroll was chiefly responsible for it. He had an absolutely magnificent game against us.

I had a fall-out with my opposite number Shaun Derry at the final whistle. He was celebrating – and he had every right to do that – but I did feel that it was a little over the top. I went over to him at the final whistle to shake his hand and whispered in his ear, 'It's only three points.' He was a first-time manager and he didn't much like it. We had to be separated in the tunnel and again upstairs. Roy actually came over looking like he fancied a bit of trouble. Big bloke, Roy. Fortunately for me, someone got between us.

After that, our form dipped. We lost at home to Cardiff, Chesterfield and against Peterborough. When we faced Crewe, we never turned up. The grumblings started. I felt I still had the backing of the players, at least. If the fans thought differently, well, it's easy to throw at a manager under pressure. The only way a manager can show he still has them onside is by winning a few games of football.

We then had a home game against Bristol City, who were flying that season under Steve Cotterill. We were in it until the first goal went in but we were soundly beaten. Once their third went in, I just had a moment. All I could hear was the visitors' support; nothing was coming from the Vale supporters. I wasn't getting much stick. But it was one of those moments where I just felt tired again. And I just had a moment where I thought to myself, 'This has run its course.'

I remember Dean Glover asking me afterwards, 'What are you thinking?'

I said, 'You don't want to know, Dean.'

I went home and couldn't sleep. When I'm emotional and I can't sleep, I make stupid decisions. I got up and said to Claire, 'I've had enough. I don't want to go to training anymore.'

I rang Norman and asked for a meeting, ironically in the same hotel where we first met. I said it was time for me to step down. He wanted me to take one week off. To be fair to him, he was – and remains – very supportive. Maybe I could have held on for a few more matches. But this is the thing about me. There was no turning back; my mind was made up.

I had a rolling contract so, after a bit of negotiation, we came to a settlement. No one will be surprised to learn it was more beneficial to him than me. Having said that, I think he appreciated what I had done for Vale. But it was time to step aside.

If you are going to be a top manager, you have to have the hide of a rhino. You must be so thick-skinned. I had that when I was younger – that drive and ambition. I wanted to leave Port Vale with the fans saying good things about me. I was trying my best, but some of the supporters thought I was lazy. A lot of managers don't go out and about watching matches. I did.

I had deals on the table for a couple of players. Sam Clucas was one and he's gone on to play in the Premier League. Andre Gray was another, but I couldn't get the money – it wasn't there for whatever reason.

I do believe my personality changed during my managerial career. I honestly think I became soft. Not that I ever let players get away with murder; if you ask anyone to look at the characteristics of my team then I think they would say they were always fit and organised. Standards were maintained on the training ground. Dressing rooms were always clean, tidy and looked after. That was the way I had been brought up. Those were the values Gerry Summers had instilled in me down at Gillingham all those years ago. I don't think managers care about it anymore. They don't get involved in it.

When I left Port Vale, I was on a good contract. But in my heart of hearts I knew I had missed the opportunity to get to the top because I think I fell out of love with the game.

It's the day after you make a decision to leave and you see the reaction of people to you leaving that it hits home what you have done. I had created a family atmosphere at Vale Park. I think that's the one good thing about me. The unheralded people at the other end of the operation – the kit ladies or the canteen staff, for example – they were always as important to me as the players. I like to think that's why people were sorry to see me go. I treated everyone with respect and I would mix with anyone.

I did 249 games for Vale over the two spells – I'd given good service. But after losing six games, which is fuck all these days, I wasn't thinking rationally. Maybe top managers shrug off defeats. In the Premier League you can go more than six – perhaps seven or eight – matches without a win.

But, the thing is, as a manager, you don't get a break and you end up making sloppy decisions. You can have the best budget in the world, but you've still got to go and sign players who gel and who are committed to both you, as a manager, and the cause in general. Maybe I should have taken a week off at Port Vale, and Leicester beforehand, and I would have been right as rain.

Perhaps I was fed up of getting in my car and travelling 180 miles every day – although I know it is an explanation that does not appear to hold much water given the location of my next club! To be honest, there's no rationale to it. The only explanation I can offer is that Tranmere got me a flat up there, so I didn't have to put up with any travelling. Anyway, I needed a break, so I took a break. And then the Tranmere Rovers job came up. On the face of it, they didn't have much going for them. Yet, even though they were bottom of League Two, I did think they were a big club for that level. But it was arrogance to think I could turn around a club that had been relegated twice in two seasons. They were bottom of the table. Why would I touch it? I shake my head now. I have to apologise to the Tranmere fans. What the fuck was I doing there? Was I thinking straight?

I went to meet owner Mark Palios and his wife Nicola, who are spot-on people. He was ambitious for the club but everything depended on staying in the division. For me, unfortunately, it didn't happen. What I don't want to do is point the finger at everyone else without looking at myself – that would be wrong. But I do have to ask questions about the Tranmere players. Were some of them giving it their all? Debatable.

They had the cult hero, Jason Koumas, who the fans loved. But he had seen his best days – and that's being kind to him. He was always injured and did very little training before he announced he should be joining the squad. That didn't sit kindly with me.

Anyway, I decided to take the job on, with the aim to get through to the end of the season and then give it a kick-start. I was confident about getting through to the end of the season and my spell started very well.

For some reason, I decided to take an unknown assistant with me and asked Chris Shuker, one of my players at Vale, to help. He had not long retired and had never coached at any level. Maybe his personality didn't help. He wouldn't say boo to a goose, Chris. He was quiet and I needed someone to get my juices going. But also coming into the club was a fella called Alan Rogers, who had played at Leicester and Forest. Alan was hanging around the club, coaching in the centre of excellence and I eventually got him on board with me as a coach.

We needed players in. I went back to Port Vale and signed Steve Jennings who had been at Tranmere before and then I signed a big centre-forward called Armand Gnanduillet from Chesterfield on loan.

The first game I saw them play was Oxford at the Kassam. They had this system but it seemed muddled to me. I couldn't work out if they were trying to pass it or hustle. So I went down at half-time to introduce myself and tried to get them going. It didn't happen on that particular day. However, after that we went on a run of five games without defeat and played some reasonable stuff.

The season changed when we travelled to Morecambe. On the face of it, a goalless draw away from home isn't too bad. We had been playing three at the back but Marcus Holness did his knee ligaments in and was out for the rest of the season. Despite reuniting myself with Jordan Hugill, who wasn't really fit, and Jennison Myrie-Williams, who started well but lost confidence and form as the season progressed, we couldn't get going and were trying to scrape through to the end of the season.

But I have to hold my hands up: I brought former goal-scoring legend Iain Hume back to the club and he was the worst signing I've ever made, anywhere. He'd been playing in India and to say he had developed a problem with his eating habits was an under-statement. He was fat and unfit, yet believed himself to be far better than he was. It's a deadly combination. And when your team is struggling, it's not what you want.

I also had an issue with a player who appeared on an American gay porn site. He stood there as naked as the day he was born and he was distraught. We had to call the lawyers to ask them to take it off the site.

Even once it was sorted, the stress of it all meant that his form tailed off horribly.

We brought in two local Liverpool lads, Lee Molyneux and Adam Dugdale, but their form was horribly erratic. There was some jealousy in the dressing room. Even so, we somehow had some decent results. After the draw with Morecambe, John Coleman and Jimmy Bell, Accrington's managers, come to watch. In the manager's office afterwards, John was telling everyone that we'd need two balls one week later when our two teams met. The gag is that we would need one for ourselves because we wouldn't be able to get it off them. I could see Jimmy Bell's face thinking 'Shut up, John.' We beat them 3–0.

But those highlights were few and far between. It all fell to pieces at Portsmouth. We were two goals up going into the last fifteen minutes but ended up losing 3–2.

I couldn't really knock them until the last five or six matches of the season. They were having a go for me, but we were losing matches by the odd goal. Someone has to carry the can and it's usually the manager. To be fair to Mark, he never questioned me. Looking back, I should have resigned just after Christmas after getting them out of the bottom three. I wasn't to know that Hartlepool, under Ronnie Moore, would go on a great run.

My final game in Football League management was Oxford at home. We had two games left. We were still in with a shout of staying up. But after the final whistle, fans were making their way down the stands to give me a mouthful. I'm not going to criticise them; it was understandable, to a degree. They were, however, quick to get on the back of certain players.

If you are going to be a footballer, you need to be able to deal with unhappy fans, but there were a few at Tranmere who couldn't deal with it. When we got back into the changing rooms, I could hear a crescendo of noise. 'We want Adams out' was the gist of it. I went upstairs to do the press and the chanting kept going. The fans were demonstrating against me and, as the players were leaving, they were throwing eggs at them.

Mark Palios wanted a chat. We went into the away dressing room and you could still hear the chanting. I said to him: 'Do you know what, chairman, if we go a goal down then this will all start up again. It might give the players an excuse to chuck it in. You don't really want that. If you go a goal down, you want the crowd to give them a lift. What you don't need is them concentrating on me negatively.'

I don't know if I was bottling it. I probably was. We only had two games left, but we agreed that to give us the best opportunity of winning at Plymouth next week, it would be best if I stood down. The problem we still had, however, was how to get me home. My car was outside the main stand in its normal spot. The punters knew that. We came up with the idea for someone to get my car and I would go out of an exit further down the stand. The fans would then have had to race around the ground to egg my car.

I was upset. I had never left a club through the back door, but it would have been dangerous to go out of the main exit. It was a really poor end to a career that had started so promisingly at Fulham. I was disappointed, angry and upset with both myself and some of the players. It was the lowest of the low for me, the way it ended. It was a horribly long two-and-a-half-hour drive home.

I was disappointed with the way I was treated, but I could understand it. The thing to remember is that it's not always about the manager and it isn't always about the decisions he takes. I think it's more about the players. It's about taking responsibility. Certain people needed to look at themselves.

Even though it was the third year the club had gone down, it's a good club with a decent infrastructure. There were good people behind the scenes, but a lot of bluffers. And they'll be back.

But me? I was gutted. It was the first time I'd failed at that level and I left feeling as low as I'd ever been.

CHAPTER 21

FINDING MY HEAD WITH THE LITTLE BIT O' RED

I fully accepted my share of the blame for what took place at Prenton Park. I say that quite openly, but I still wanted to get back in.

After I left Tranmere, I almost jumped back into the game immediately. Shortly after the season finished, I heard Crawley Town were looking for a new manager after John Gregory had left. I applied and I was chosen for interview, so I went down to meet them. They were interviewing a few people so I wasn't really expecting a response. But it ended up being the quickest interview I've ever had. If it lasted more than four minutes, I'd be amazed.

I walked into a room at a hotel which they had set aside for interviewing the candidates. There was one of the part-owners, the club secretary and John Gregory waiting in the room. John had just had heart surgery, so I understood why he had stepped down. He had been at the sharp end, was reasonably successful at Aston Villa and I like and respect him.

To start with, they had obviously done their homework and reeled off my win percentage as a manager. Then the secretary took over.

The budget, I was told, was being reduced from £1.1 million to £700,000. I asked how many players they had under contract at the moment and they said they had ten players under contract, which currently cost the club £750,000. It didn't take a genius to work out they were already over-budget. They told me they were looking to off-load striker Izale McLeod and that the transfer fee received would cover the signing of three or four additions to the squad.

That took the net figure up to twelve players. I was told by John I'd have to do some wheeling and dealing. Unfortunately for him, I'd seen the circulars he'd sent out the season before. Obviously, he'd had no success generating any cash, and I was expected to get some with the same group.

The wages were also being reduced for the manager. I was told I could employ one member of staff on £25,000. The secretary enquired, 'Do you want me to continue?' I replied, 'Listen fellas, I appreciate you inviting me down here but I don't think there's a need for you to go any further. This isn't for me.' That was it. I shook their hands and it was over.

I felt guilty about not being in work and apologised to Claire. But even if I had been offered the job, there wasn't any way I could have taken it in those circumstances.

Four weeks later, around mid-July, I received a call from Jimmy Bell, who had been over to Sligo Rovers with Jon Coleman. The club was struggling and they invited me over for a chat ahead of a game against Longford with a view to taking over. Unfortunately for me, they won that particular game and so, as I was leaving for our discussion, they contacted me to say that they had decided to stick with their man. I had a call from their secretary, Brendan Lacken, breaking the bad news. All I could do was wish them good luck.

It was difficult for me. Sligo had just turned me down and I had nowhere else to go. I was down; really down. It was the lowest I'd ever been in football: a whole new low. You can't imagine what I was like that week.

As it happened, during the course of the next few weeks, Sligo lost to Bohemians, St Patrick's and Limerick. The latter of that trio had been cast adrift at the bottom of the table. In the last match, they substituted the captain, Gavin Peers, who left the stadium at half-time after a dressing room row and caught the train back to Sligo.

I subsequently received another phone call asking if I was still interested. Brendan Lacken apologised, then apologised again, and asked if I would come over again.

I wasn't working. I wasn't doing anything. I told them I couldn't promise anything but, truth be told, my situation hadn't changed – so I agreed to go over to see them.

Sligo is a beautiful part of Ireland. The stadium, the Showgrounds, has some fantastic mountain scenery of Knocknarea as its backdrop. It's on the wild Atlantic way and is famous for its surfing community. It really is a picturesque place.

As I got on the plane I wondered to myself what I was doing but, on the other hand, I had nothing to lose and it was a day out if nothing else. When I arrived, I was faced with a five-man committee. I'm not sure they knew who I was, although they had my CV in front of them. They were fund-raising to raise a few euros for their campaign 'Rally around Rovers'. The club is owned by the people of the town and they were second bottom with only eleven games to go.

I knew I needed to have a look at the squad. I'd had a word with Jon Coleman who'd told me there were lads still playing for Sligo who had won the League of Ireland title three years previously. Surely they couldn't be that bad.

They needed someone with the Pro-Licence as well. I asked if I could bring in a member of staff to work alongside me and they said I could but his wages would eat into the money available for players. They asked if they could give me a decision in the morning and duly offered me the position that morning.

I got on the phone to Alan Rogers and explained everything to the silly Scouser. He didn't have a clue where Sligo was. I told him it was a twelve-week gig to start with. I also told him there was hardly any money in it for him. 'I don't care, I'll do it,' was his response.

I was still in two minds on whether it was for me, but his enthusiasm persuaded me to give it a go. So I gave Sligo my answer and travelled back home to Market Harborough where I grabbed some gear before duly going back to Ireland with Alan.

I had a proper look at the players when we returned, and we had some interesting fellas. One was called Rauri Keating, who is Ronan Keating's nephew, and we also had the brother of Westlife singer Markus Feehily, Feo, who dedicated his life to being Sligo's kit man once he realised he wasn't good enough to play for the team.

It turned out I even knew a face in the dressing room: goalkeeper Richard Brush, a kid I had at Coventry. He was also someone I gave a free transfer to when I was in charge of the Sky Blues. I had no idea if he was pleased to see me or not.

I went in there with a simple plan: I was going to enjoy these three months and hopefully rescue the club. I didn't want to fall out with anyone. Alan also had one simple aim, and that was to treat these twelve weeks like a stag do.

What I quickly came to realise was, unlike in England, here was a squad who wanted to listen and learn. I remember the first team meeting we had. I told them I was there to help get them out of the mess they were in.

I picked on Peers first, the one who had got the train home. I told him not to do it again. The club wanted me to discipline him and fine him, but I knew I needed him. I was told he was a leader and a winner, so what was the point of alienating him? I also Alan Keane back into the team.

After the first match, which we lost 2–0, I was asked what I thought. I told the committee I was genuinely heartened by the response. The players had a go. In the meantime, I managed to get Jennison Myrie-Williams over from England. That had a massive effect because he was playing for his own future and he was on fire.

The club had decided to house us in place called Castlebaldwin, about ten miles outside of the town. There were about fifty houses there, a garage and one pub. They thought we couldn't get into any bother stuck out there. That was their first mistake – but more of that later.

The results picked up. We beat Drogheda and Derry and then we played Dundalk. That's when I came across Stephen Kenny for the first time since the battle of Longford with Brighton. It was satisfying to take a point out of that one. We beat Bray. The outlook was improving.

I stayed for two and a half weeks before going back to see the family. I could get a return flight for €50, so it wasn't an issue if I left Ireland for just three days at a time. When I was at home, Alan was left in charge. By this stage, results had improved but we weren't totally out of the woods and Alan had been asking me for a couple of weeks if he could take the lads out to 'build team spirit'.

While at home, however, I received a call from the chairman, which was unusual in itself as the club usually left me alone. To say Joe Burns was angry was the biggest understatement of all time. It transpired my rental car, supplied by the local garage, had been written off after being smashed against a wall. When I left Sligo, it was fully functioning. Not a scratch on it. I advised the chairman I thought Alan was doing a weights circuit with the young professionals. In my absence, he had been allowed use of the vehicle.

'You need to chase him Micky,' said the chairman, 'because the police want to speak to him.'

In Ireland, if you have an accident you have to stay with your car until the Garda turn up. So I managed to get hold of him. 'Alan, the chairman has just rung me because my car has been smashed up,' I said, waiting to hear the story. I didn't get one.

'There has been a problem,' came the reply, 'but I'll deal with it later.'

'Look, Alan, don't deal with it later. Deal with it now. The police are after you. Are you with the lads? You are? Right. Tell the lads to go home and get your backside to the police station.'

No one was any the wiser as to what happened other than an animal came out into the middle of the road and my assistant swerved to avoid it. The result was that a Volkswagen 4x4, worth £24,000, ended up losing a fight with a wall.

When I returned, the committee wanted me to do something about the situation. Joe Burns, Robbie Fitzpatrick (who is a top bloke) and Brendan Lacken took me out for a nice meal near Strandhill, another lovely part of the world. There, they announced, 'He's gone out, we suspect he has had a drink and he's smashed your car up. We can't have that. We need you to get rid of him.'

I replied, 'I brought him in, but I'm not sacking my mate. I understand you are angry and upset, absolutely I do. But if he goes, I go. I'm not holding a gun to your head, but that's where we are.'

I wasn't bluffing; I would have walked. I didn't want to, but I would have gone if it had come down to it. Fortunately, everyone saw a little bit of sense and Alan escaped with just a slap on the wrist from the club.

He didn't get off so lightly at the police station, however. They made him sweat – and rightly so, as they hammered home the seriousness of the situation. He didn't realise that he was supposed to stay with the car, in his defence – if, indeed, there was one.

After that, we lost a derby at Galway. I was annoyed after the game but, for once, I managed to keep my cool. Now, perhaps at this stage I should tell you that, while the supporters and committee members were pleased we had arrived, the same could not be said of the opposition coaches and managers. To put it bluntly they hated us. They resented our presence. It was the same story everywhere.

In one of our first matches against Derry, their coach was threatening all sorts. 'You English bastards, fuck off back to England, what are you doing over here? Fucking taking people's jobs, fuck off home.' Charming.

Before the next game against Shamrock, I said to Alan, 'Right, one thing that is happening today is we won't be taking any of that shit. From anyone.'

Their manager was a fella called Pat Fenlon. Anyway, Fenlon kicked it off with Alan. I wasn't helping the situation by saying, 'Don't take that shit off him Alan.' It only served to wind him up some more. Then, all of a sudden, Alan reacted. It exploded. He called Fenlon a leprechaun and chaos ensued. People were threatening all sorts.

Alan got sent to the stand and eventually was served with a three-match ban. As he was dismissed he claimed he was defending himself – with justification, I might add – as they had been hammering him all game. He'd said one thing in retaliation and now he was the one watching the match from the seats in the stand.

Anyway, we managed to get the club safe with a win at St Patrick's. The job had been done. But one of the most bizarre episodes of my entire managerial career was about to unfold. Coming back from that win in Dublin on the Friday night, a lad called Patrick Nzui – one of our players who wasn't in the squad – went out on his own in Sligo for a few drinks. The story goes that, as he was leaving a club that night, a young lady bent down in front of him. I think he slapped her on the backside. She didn't take too kindly to it, giving him a right-hander in return.

Unfortunately for Patrick, the police saw the incident, said he assaulted her and gave him a night in the cells as a reward. And even more unfortunately, what Patrick didn't realise was that the young lady he'd touched was the niece of one of the local heavies. And when I say 'heavy', I mean 'very heavy'. Interestingly, however, the family did not want to press charges. On the face of it, that was good news for Patrick and he was released on Saturday morning with no more questions to answer. Or so he thought.

On the Sunday morning, I received a call explaining what had taken place with the added twist in the tale being that the reason the family didn't want to press charges because they were going to sort out Nzui themselves. The advice, and it came from one of the natives in Sligo, was to get the player out of the country as quickly as possible, because the family were going to make an example of him and deal with him severely.

So on the Monday, I called Nzui into the office and asked him what had happened. But all he had to say for himself was: 'I can't remember', so I refreshed his memory. I ran through the story with him, but he denied everything.

'Well, let me tell you something Patrick,' I said. 'The word is that you have assaulted the wrong person. The word is that these people are going to sort you out. Properly. Look, you're not in my plans. You need to leave.'

At this point, he decided quitting the country was the best course of action. Taking the threat seriously, we told him to lie low until Tuesday until we could get him a flight back to England.

Having ironed out that issue, we went out to training. We were about fifteen minutes into a crossing and shooting drill when I noticed a shady character standing in the corner of the stadium. It was unusual because no one ever watched us practise. It was a lad with his hood up, looking suspicious, clocking the players. I said to Alan, 'Go and see what he wants.' But as soon as Rogers went to confront this lad, he bolted.

A couple of the players said to me, 'I don't like the look of this, gaffer. They're looking for Patrick, aren't they?'

Bear in mind there was only two black lads in the squad, Nzui and Jennison, and the former was now back at his house, packing his stuff and getting ready to leave.

We resume crossing and shooting until, all of a sudden, a person appeared from the left-wing area. He had his hood up and a balaclava across his face, and he was marching across the pitch. Oh, and he was holding a gun. Yes, you read that right. He was holding a gun.

You have never seen players move so fast. All I could see were backsides scrambling over walls, people disappearing into the distance. My tough Number Two, Rogers, was screaming at the gunman that the player he was heading towards wasn't Patrick.

All I could think to myself was 'Someone's going to get killed. And I'm going to see it.'

Then, I thought, 'What am I going to do here?'

The gunman started walking up to Jennison and ordered him to get on his knees in front of him. Jennison did as he was told. I opened my mouth to say something but I was a bit worried that the gunman would turn his attention to me. But I managed to shout that he had the wrong man.

It's just as this situation was about to unfold into a scene of carnage on Sligo Rovers' pitch that the gunman pulled down his mask and started laughing. It was one of the injured substitutes, John Russell. He'd been missing from the drills because he was supposedly having treatment but, instead, he'd popped into town and bought himself a balaclava and replica gun. He had set the whole thing up with the physio and she had recorded the whole incident on her phone. I still have the footage. Jennison, it goes without saying, is still alive.

To be fair, it was a brilliant stunt. So good, in fact, I had to cancel the training because the players were still shaking twenty minutes later.

Following matches, we always put on receptions where we would share a pint with the board and the players. Even away from home we'd have a drink, so we had built up a connection with them. There really was a feeling of camaraderie, so we wanted to take them out to say thanks after the last game of the season. The final match was against Limerick and Alan bought a couple of bottles of Sambuca. He was pictured with his arms around a couple of the young lads and, as happens nowadays, a picture ended up on Facebook and the committee had another reason to have a go at him.

The day after this night out, Alan was going back home. As he was getting ready to go home, he decided to have a bath. He started running it and then his mobile rang; it was his missus. He took the call and I decided to nick his hot water and have a soak myself. Obviously, when his ended, he saw me in the tub, took off all his clothes and decided to get in. I wasn't having that, and began to get out. It was at that precise moment, when I was getting out and Alan was getting in, that my mate ran in and took a picture with his camera phone. We were effectively snapped in the bath together.

Anyway, we were having a farewell drink on the Saturday in the pub in Castlebaldwin and Alan was showing the picture to the locals and threatening to put it up on Twitter. Only then, someone reached over and pressed the 'send' button and, all of a sudden, it was out in the Twittersphere. I told Alan to get it down sharpish, but it was too late. All I could hear was 'Bing, bing, bing' as people were re-tweeting it.

The picture was taken down, but not before the committee had seen it. Bear in mind that they had also seen Alan out and about with two bottles of Sambuca and a couple of the young professionals.

Twenty-four hours later, I was due for a meeting to discuss the finances. By this time both Alan and I had verbally accepted new deals to stay on for another year. I turned up to Costa Coffee to meet one of the committee members. This fella turned up. He was nice as pie.

'Micky, what a job you've done. You've rescued us this season. We were dead and buried. I'm so pleased you're staying.'

But all of a sudden his mood changed. 'But fucking Alan Rogers. He's got to go. You've got to get rid of him.'

I said, 'Whoa, what's the problem? You've started off with "great job" and then all of a sudden you're attacking my mate.'

He replied, 'Have you seen Twitter? No? Well you might not have, but the committee has. Have you seen what's on there?'

He showed me. Alan with the Sambuca and me and him in the bath.

I held my hands up. 'Look, I apologise for that. Alan's his own man. I'm the more serious partner of the duo. He's a bit more carefree.'

'Well, whatever Micky, but how am I supposed to go around the general public in Sligo asking them for funds to run the football club, when there's a picture of you and him in the bath together? He's got to go. You can stay. He's got to go.'

I replied, 'If Alan goes, I'm going. I came here to talk about our finances. I'm happy to spend my time doing that, but you are attacking my pal. I'll talk to you when you are in a better mood.'

And with that I left.

I started thinking about things properly after that, and realised that I hadn't seen Claire or the kids very much at all, or my mum and brother, or my grandkids or daughters. I came to the conclusion that I simply couldn't do it anymore. I told Sligo it wasn't fair on my family and I left.

Even though I left, I'm so glad I went there. The people at the club were first class. Sligo Rovers' players restored my faith in footballers. They were genuine kids who wanted to listen and learn. They all wanted to cross the Irish Sea and test themselves.

They even put me, Claire, Mitchel and Madison up in a hotel when they came to visit. The visit was all the more sweet as I was able to take them to Ballygar and catch up with Mary and Emer O'Keefe once again. We also paid our respects to the wonderful late Art O'Keefe at the local cemetery.

But I do think there's a reason why they don't succeed. It's a small stretch of water between Ireland and England, but kids get so homesick. It's a massive gulf for them and they need more support. That's why a lot of Irish boys don't succeed in England. The likes of Keane, Russell and Peers could have played Championship in their prime, but they never got the opportunity. And it's a shame.

I look back on those twelve weeks with a great deal of fondness. If that's my last job in frontline football management, and it looks like it will be, then I have to say: 'Thank you, Sligo Rovers.'

I left there a more contented man with a lot of great memories.

CHAPTER 22

TODAY AND TOMORROW

I had agreed to stay on at Sligo for another season but, due to the problems Alan had created, it meant that I would be going back on my own, and I didn't want to do it.

There were a number of reasons why I wasn't keen. My mum was in her seventies and was looking after my brother, whose mobility is now very limited. I also have three grandkids – Jake, Grace and Elliot – in Gillingham and Southampton. I wouldn't have seen them for a while, so it didn't sit right with me to accept the job. From a personal perspective, my life is complicated and, by committing to a managerial post in Ireland, life would have been doubly hard.

I know I'm sounding like a broken record by now, but at this point I was thinking: 'what next?' I clearly need to learn that you always need a job lined up when you turn one down!

Fortunately, my salvation came in stages.

Firstly, my old skipper at Fulham, Simon Morgan, was working for the Premier League by this stage and he asked me if I was interested in a role as a match-day delegate. The job involves protecting the integrity of the game and to be the eyes and ears of the Premier League. I have to protect the brand and the competition and make sure the rules and regulations are followed. The main focus is assessing the referees. I'm there to offer advice to the referee from a manager's perspective, which is different from a referee assessing another referee.

While there are ex-footballers, scouts and administrators now working as delegates, I think I'm one of the few who has managed in the Premier League, so I do believe I offer something different. I watch my one-time colleagues get upset and irate on the touchline, and because I've been in their shoes I know what it is like. While referees don't always agree with my opinion, I would like to think the officials respect my judgement. But, as is the case in all walks of life, some people appreciate the feedback and others don't.

Contrary to general opinion, referees aren't daft. I suppose I do have more respect for them now than when I was a manager. Their fitness levels are excellent, and so are their communication skills. And they care.

I think video technology will play an increasingly important part in the future of refereeing. I believe it's inevitable, although I don't see it becoming like American football where the game is stopped for an advert while the officials make a major decision. I do think it's good to have another set of eyes and ears watching a monitor and give decisions off the pitch. The goal-line decision system in particular has been a success. It takes the doubt from major decisions. I remember playing days scoring at Maine Road for Leeds against Manchester City in my playing days. It went over the line but wasn't given. It would have come in handy on that occasion!

So that keeps me busy at weekends. I also do work with two friends of mine that used to play with me at Southampton, who are now partners in Midas Sports Management. Steve Wood and David Hughes brought me on board as a football consultant. I'm not a registered intermediary but I watch games and players and highlight talent for them. Their agency is slightly different from others. It isn't all about doing deals; it takes a more rounded look at a player's career and provides a service to suit. All the people involved have played the game to a professional level. That goes for the likes of Dave Beasant, Gary Peters and Andy Reed, too. Don't they say that you have to walk a single step in someone's shoes to find out what it is all about? Well, I was released at the age of sixteen; I've been dropped, moved on, suffered lengthy injuries. I know what it is all about. As do the others.

I've also taken a position as a football consultant at Brooke House College in Market Harborough. It is a multi-cultural college and I can find myself either coaching or mentoring the coaches and talking to parents or students who want to join the college.

I've also been over to the States recruiting and coaching for the college. Andy Thompson, based in North Carolina, has also invited me out there on a couple of occasions to coach for his company PUK. The game over there is really taking off at grass-roots level, particularly among girls. The only downside of the trips is listening to Andy bleating on about how bad Sunderland are.

To be honest, the one thing I've missed since leaving Sligo isn't dealing with chairmen, players and the press. The thing I've missed the most is coaching because I think that's where my strengths are. Coaching is about painting pictures for players. Even if players don't speak the same language as you, you can still show them what you want. The language is universal on a training ground. My job at the college allows me to keep dipping my toe into the things I enjoy the most. The principal is a fella called Giles Williams, and he's been first-class to me.

I'm now in talks with a football club local to me, Harborough Town, who want me to be involved with starting up an Academy. That appeals to me. I'm not interested in the educational side and I've got no ambition at all to be the Harborough Town senior boss. My focus will be entirely on youth and putting a bit back into the game, trying to put kids on the right path to fulfilling their dreams and ambitions.

I must also mention Harry Price at UK Trials. The organisation offers players from the age of eleven upwards the chance to showcase their talent to scouts at Football League clubs, which I think is terrific. A lot of people will be sitting at home and thinking 'I can be a footballer.' If there is someone out there who thinks he deserves a crack, then UK Trials will give you that platform. If you are good enough, you never know, do you?

One question I'm asked all the time is would I ever consider going back into football management? Well, after twenty years, nearly 800 games as a manager, four promotions, nine Manager of the Year awards, two LMA Manager of the Year awards, the simple answer is yes. But I think I've learnt more about the game in the last two years outside it than I ever did managing in it.

I'm sure many people will way that I've had more than enough opportunities and that I've been very fortunate to have managed some fantastic clubs. And, while they're right, I think I have unfinished business in terms of management.

Will I get another crack?

Watch this space.

CHAPTER 23

MICKY IN THE EYES OF OTHERS

SIMON MORGAN (FULHAM & BRIGHTON)

When Micky arrived at Fulham, we'd just been relegated. We were crap. With a capital 'C'.

As a player he had Premier League quality, but everyone in the dressing room knew that he also nursed ambitions to become a manager.

To be absolutely fair to Ian Branfoot, Micky's predecessor had started the process of clearing out several players and bringing in new faces. We had bottomed out under Ian.

There wasn't a lot of money sloshing about. However, the club slowly became populated by good, seasoned professionals – people like Terry Hurlock, Kevin Moore and, of course, Micky – and the negativity gradually disappeared. And, indeed, cometh the hour, cometh the man. He was the hero of the day.

The pace of the change was accelerated under Mick. His mantra was: 'I'm taking no more nonsense.' And he didn't. In one of his first sessions as boss in his own right, I remember him saying, 'You lot are a danger to yourselves both with the ball and without it.' His solution was to make us run.

The first run we went on was from the Fulham training ground to

Epsom, which is a distance of about two miles. We hadn't gone too far when Micky Conroy pulled up lame. He moaned at the gaffer and got absolutely nowhere for his troubles. I don't know if Fulham's striker was trying it on with his new manager but, muscle problem or not, he was told that he could walk there and back. It was a taste of things to come.

It was about that same time that we went to Newquay on tour. It was bang in the middle of summer and for the rest of the population, it's a time for rest and relaxation. It wasn't for us. It just so happened that it was scorching hot, too. We worked our wotsits off one day only to be told that we had four hours to refresh ourselves before the next training session. Obviously, we did what everyone else was doing: we went and had a few ales. We were merry without being too drunk because we were mindful of what might happen on our return. When we eventually went back, a game of young versus old was organised. It lasted about fifteen minutes before Micky, who must have known where we had been, let us off.

But that was tame compared to what went on in Ballygar. There was one road, one church, five pubs and one hotel. We were treated like absolute royalty from the moment we arrived until the minute we left.

Having said that, it was pre-season and we had to put it in. Micky's philosophy was: 'I'm going to treat you like adults. But I'm telling you that if you are not fit for work next morning, there is going to be trouble.' Obviously, footballers can drink and sweat it out the next day, although it is not a pleasant experience.

One morning, there was a right commotion taking place. A plastic horse that had been standing outside one of the pubs for years had gone missing. The Irish police, the Garda, were called and it was pretty clear that this was a big deal in such a small place. The locals were not particularly happy with whatever had taken place.

Anyway, everyone was hunting high and low for this horse when the priest from the church came running down the road saying that it must be a miracle. He had been praying for divine intervention and had found the horse sitting in the front pew! Divine intervention? Or some half-cut footballers from south-west London?

When the season kicked off, we found that the team Micky had assembled could, incredibly, score a few goals. Conroy found his feet and, with players such as Richard Carpenter and Darren Freeman, our season snowballed into a successful one.

I can say honestly, hand on heart, that it was my most enjoyable promotion in the game. Sure, I had other promotions with the club, but the one under Micky was, frankly, worth all the effort and heartache that goes into a career as a professional footballer. It wasn't all champagne and caviar, but it was massive fun that season.

One of the highlights for me came at Darlington, of all places. We had been warned that it was going to be a feisty encounter. When our centre-half, Terry Angus, was the butt of racist abuse, the game turned into a real battle on the pitch.

We ended up winning 2–0. But that wasn't the full story. There had been allegations that one of our lads had assaulted a ball-boy. It was rubbish. But the police and chief steward made a mistake trying to barge their way into Micky's dressing room. They came in and started saying their piece. Micky shouted at them: 'Get out of my dressing room. How dare you come in here? Where were you when our centre-half was being racially abused?' And with that, he tried shoving the pair of them out of the door.

The only problem being that he couldn't quite manage it. He was trying with all his might. Half of us were pissing ourselves with laughter and the other half were shouting out such helpful tips as: 'Little legs, you need to get on the weights...'

He was given some serious stick for that. But not quite as much as he received when we were allowed on an end-of-season tour to Majorca. Obviously, having won the league, this was something everyone was looking forward to. The only problem was that the club decided to send us on a late-night flight over to the holiday island. It was after 2 a.m. when we reached our hotel and it was a case of throwing our bags in our respective rooms and heading straight out into the town and towards whichever bar was still serving. There was but one instruction from the manager: having won promotion, we were welcome to have a drink – we had earned it – but under no circumstances were we to draw attention to ourselves.

Five or six hours later we headed back to the hotel for breakfast. Apart from a few footballers who were obviously the worse for wear, the restaurant was rammed full of holidaymakers. The manager was up and about and grabbing himself some toast. However, it was the first time that he had seen one of those continental toasters where you place the bread on the conveyor belt and the machine toasts it for you and he didn't quite understand this new-fangled toasting equipment. He's struggling and, the next thing we know, flames were jumping out of it. The situation was not helped by Micky attempting to extinguish the blaze with the use of paper napkins. Smoke was pouring out of the machine while waiters came flying from all angles to sort it out before the fire got out of hand. Every pair of eyes in the place was on Micky as he sheepishly made his way over to us – at which point someone piped up: 'Under no circumstances draw any attention to yourselves...'

Of course, we all knew what was going to happen when the club was taken over. Although we had been on a fantastic journey together, it was unlikely to last. I think if he's being honest, Micky probably knew the writing was on the wall.

When it happened we were all under direct instruction from Kevin

Keegan not to have anything to do with Micky. We ignored it. We had to go for a final drink with him. So off we went to the pub, only to find that he was trying to flog a load of Fulham clobber that he had pilfered in the car park!

It was such good fun and I'll never forget one of his team talks which contained the following sentence: 'Everyone was put on this earth for a reason. And maybe I'm here to get Fulham Football Club promoted.'

I've ribbed him mercilessly over the years for that. But do you know what? Perhaps he was right. And I, for one, wouldn't have missed it for the world.

PAUL ROGERS (BRIGHTON AND HOVE ALBION)

It was April 1999 and I was nearing the end of my contract with Wigan Athletic. At thirty-four years of age, my best footballing years were behind me. But I had been brought up in Surrey and was desperate to get back down south as that was where I saw my future.

I didn't know Micky Adams. I did, however, know Alan Cork from the time we had spent together at Sheffield United. It must have been Corky who suggested to Micky that he should have a look at me when he took over as manager at Brighton.

Micky probably would have taken Alan's word on it, but in his own words he 'wanted to take a look to make sure your legs haven't gone.' So there was no pressure as I went into a game at Northampton Town with the Latics still in the mix for a place in the League One play-offs.

It wasn't a good afternoon. I was sent off eight minutes before half-time. Not the greatest thirty-seven minutes of my playing career, to put it lightly. And, to make things worse as I trudged off towards the tunnel, I could see my potential new manager mouthing the words 'fucking wanker' and making the appropriate hand gesture in my direction. That appeared to be that.

But the next morning, Micky was on the phone, saying: 'It's taken me two and a half hours to get to Northampton and two and a half hours to get back. And you lasted all of thirty-seven minutes. How on earth am I supposed to make a judgement and recommendation to my chairman based on that?' But, even so, he was as good as his word and tried to push through the signing.

I'd been on good money at Wigan – something like £105,000-a-year – and, originally, Micky wasn't even offering half of that. His thinking was that he was 'doing me a favour' by getting me out of Lancashire, but the first offer just wasn't good enough. He said, 'Leave it with me, I'll get you some more cash.' And he did. My basic was pushed up to £65,000 and there was another sizeable chunk due on appearances that season. He wanted to look after me as best he could and, in the end, I played about forty-five times for him in the coming campaign.

However, he could be a massive pain in the arse. We used to call him 'Little Legs' – behind his back, obviously. It was either that or 'Francis Benali's understudy'. Did he know? Probably not, or else we would just have had a load more running to do. That was one of the hallmarks of his sides: they could always run.

When I joined Brighton it was pretty clear that we were going to a) win at all costs and b) be the strongest and fittest team in the league. We did pretty well, too. But I remember the night when he got us up at the crack of dawn after we'd got back from Scunthorpe at some horrible hour and he got us to line up in a park at 8 a.m. We'd made the mistake of shipping two goals in the final few minutes to lose 2–1 and he properly lost his temper. He said, 'First half, all right. Second half, shit.'

Micky had just had knee operation and was hobbling about with the whistle in his mouth as we rode around this pond. We'd had a session on the bikes and his number twos Bob Booker and Dean White had grassed us up to the manager – so we chucked their bikes in the water as a way to let off a bit of steam at the end of it. I don't know how but that wake-up call did the trick and we didn't lose for the last thirteen matches.

He was properly loyal to the players. That was one of his big characteristics. And he was a proper grafter, too. He didn't ask any of us to do work he couldn't do or hadn't done himself. It was always competitive and always fun.

The result was that Brighton team was one of the most enjoyable I played with. Possibly not in terms of the quality, but in terms of the heart, drive and will to win. Micky harnessed it all and pushed us forwards. Special times with a special set of blokes. That was Brighton at the time. And Micky was obviously at the heart of it. I still keep in touch with him now which, I suppose, speaks volumes for the respect I have for him.

JAMES SCOWCROFT (LEICESTER CITY, COVENTRY CITY)

When Micky arrived, the club was in turmoil. Leicester were going into a new stadium, there were issues at boardroom level and, before he took over as boss in his own right from Dave Bassett, we had just been relegated. If history teaches us anything, it is that unless the situation is managed correctly, then clubs the size of Leicester City can go into freefall. There was the very real prospect of the club spiralling out of control.

At the time, there was a complex mix in that dressing room. We had a good number of well-established players on big money alongside a few players who weren't on as much money but were still hungry for the chance to play for Leicester, and there were those he had brought in on free transfers. But what Micky did brilliantly was knit all of them together. There were a lot of strong characters but his people management skills were exceptional.

He was straightforward. He was honest. He had a vision of where he wanted to go and how he wanted to do it. And he galvanised that group. As far as I'm concerned, it was a shame Micky's time at the club didn't last longer because, at the time, he was as talented a manager as there was in the game. Some managers can manage. Others can coach. Not many can do both. But Micky could.

I'll be honest; I wasn't sure about him at first. We were two completely different characters. I was from a sleepy corner of Suffolk. He made no secret of the fact he was working-class stock from Sheffield.

I'd been at Ipswich a long time and I'd had more than my fair share of injuries. I went to see him and he just said, 'You're not fit, are you?' I didn't know what to say, but he continued, 'I will get you fit to play football.' I went away from that meeting thinking, 'I'll believe that when I see it.' But that is exactly what he did. I had a spell playing under him for three seasons and I can count the number of matches I missed through injury on the fingers of one hand.

The other reason why I wished I'd met him sooner is that he was made me stronger mentally. That's a difficult concept to convey to someone who isn't in sport, but I know that if I'd met Micky when I was eighteen rather than a few years later, I'd have been a better player for it.

The other area where he stood out was during the time of the administration. There was a lot of scaremongering going on. Don't forget, this was one of the first occasions that any club had gone into administration in the Premier League era. People were going to lose their jobs – that much was obviously well-known. But Micky refused point-blank to allow anyone to feel sorry for themselves. He kept us all on an even keel and made sure we were focused. We went with him and earned promotion.

If Leicester City needed a manager at that time, then Micky was the perfect fit. Everything was kept in perspective. How can I put it? Micky just 'got' the situation and understood what was needed to put it right. Like I say, it was unfortunate that Micky chose to call time on his stint at Leicester City.

But if I was to pay him one compliment, then I think it's best to use my actions rather than my words. When the time came to leave Leicester City, I had the choice of a few clubs. By this time, Micky had moved on to Coventry and was in the process of stabilising that club, too. When I heard he was interested in working with me again, then it was an easy decision for me to make.

As a footballer, you don't choose to play for a manager for a second time if you don't have the utmost respect for him. And any manager can't ask for much more from his players than that.

TOM POPE (PORT VALE)

It was very difficult for any of us players to get one over on Micky. I've got no idea how he did it, but he was always one step ahead. And if he wasn't one step ahead, then he made sure you didn't get too far in front of him.

It wasn't long after he turned up at Vale that the club went into administration. I don't know if it was his grand plan or if it was necessity, but he soon brought the best out of me.

I'd found a niche for myself in as much as other strikers liked playing with me and that's probably because they scored goals. I suppose it couldn't have been a coincidence that Nicky Maynard at Crewe Alexandra, Adam LeFondre at Rotherham and Marc Richards at Vale all posted some of their best returns when I was alongside them.

But Micky saw that there was more to my game than doing the donkey work for others to profit on. He thought I could finish. Well, it was either that or else he didn't have much by way of an alternative up front. Very early on in our relationship, he took me to one side and said, 'I will get you some wingers, so stop running after midfielders and stand between the two posts. You will score goals.'

I got a lot of confidence from our pre-season in Ballygar. I wasn't one of the lucky ones; I stayed in digs rather than the penthouse at the hotel. It was in the middle of nowhere, but it had six pubs and Micky obviously trusted us because we ate our food in the boozer, and after 8 p.m. we had ninety minutes to have a drink.

Some of the opposition in Ballygar wasn't the greatest, however, and one day as a treat he said that we could all stay out for an extra hour if we won the game and put fifty passes together. We managed to get a few goals ahead and then dropped the two centre-halves on the goalkeeper's toes. By this time, the opposition had been given a run-around. They didn't want to come and get the ball back off us and we passed it between ourselves seventy times before losing possession. Micky was going mad on the side-lines, calling us all the names under the sun because we weren't really going anywhere, just knocking the ball about between ourselves. Still, we managed to get our additional sixty minutes on the curfew…

But I think it speaks volumes for him that we stayed to work with him, even though we hadn't been paid for a couple of months during administration. I mean, it takes a special person to have us all running around like headless chickens and yet we were all willing to go the extra mile for him.

It was difficult, however, to get one over him. And, like I said at the top of this piece, I have got no idea how he got to know about half of the stuff that went on. For instance, we used to have Wednes-days off if there was no midweek game. It just so happened that my birthday fell on a Wednesday. I didn't have anything planned but Chris Lines phoned me up and asked if I fancied a pint. We headed off into

Newcastle-under-Lyme and one turned into two, which turned into ten. I staggered home at 3 a.m. and turned up for training absolutely steaming seven hours later only to be called into his office by the manager.

'You are in no fit state to go out training anywhere, are you?'

I replied, 'How on earth do you know? I only went out for a couple of pints.'

'Well, you've got your teammates to thank for that.'

'I can't believe Chris has grassed me up.'

To which Micky went, 'He hadn't. But now I know it was you pair, you can do some extras.'

I had to go back into the dressing room and confess to Linesy that I'd let it out to the manager that he was out with me. And he made us pay that day. He properly ran us.

To be fair, he was what I needed. I needed a manager to push me. I remember that I had gone on a ten-game run without scoring, and in the week before we played Cheltenham, he called me into the office. He sat me down and put on a DVD showing clips of all the goals I had scored that season. I then went out and got a hat-trick.

I was feeling pretty pleased with myself, but in the last minute I gave the ball away and it almost resulted in us losing a goal – and two points. I walked back into the dressing room and got one of the biggest bollockings I'd ever had. Never mind the goals I'd scored – it was all about losing possession in the last minute.

He really got the best out of me and I think he also got the best out of the squad. He was dealt a hand and I don't think anyone but Mick could have played it better.

I run a Sunday team myself, and while players are quick to acknowledge praise, some of them are less keen on criticism. In fact, you just can't tell some players anything constructive. But Micky was always straight with the players. I think you can be at that level. Once you start moving upwards, it's more difficult because the people he would be speaking to are earning a lot more money. I'm convinced he would have got it right at Sheffield United, but he was dealing with a different set of players there. Some of them were on big money.

In the end, I felt like I let him down. I got involved in a dust-up and hurt my hand. I couldn't even bend my fingers back. I was in agony. As a frontman you need your arms to get yourself up in the air and it undoubtedly restricted my movement.

Micky might have dropped me, but he stuck with me and we never won a game in six. A lot of other managers would have booted me out and got someone else in. But he stood by me and I couldn't find a goal that might have kept him in a job.

I've never told him that – but I'm sure he knew. As I've said, he always had a way of finding stuff out.

He's comfortably the best manager I ever played for. It's very rare at any club for all of the players to be onside with a manager. There's always at least one who has an issue. But if you look back to that Port Vale squad, none of us did. It's hard to keep twenty-odd players happy and all singing off the same hymn sheet, but Micky did that constantly at Port Vale.

ACKNOWLEDGEMENTS

Firstly, I want to say thanks to all the players I've managed. I hope they know that while, at times, decisions I made might have felt personal, as a football manager you have to make some tough decisions. I feel like this because I'm not one of those managers who talks behind people's backs. If I've ever had anything to say, I've always opened my mouth and said it. I know some will not want anything to do with me if they were to see me somewhere later on in life. And that's OK. Honestly, it is.

I also want to thank all the coaches that I've worked under. You learn – good and bad – from the managers you work for, particularly Howard Wilkinson, Chris Nicholl, Bobby Gould, George Curtis, Billy Bremner and even Alan Ball who, for whatever reason, didn't fancy me.

The people who have influenced me the most include Ian Branfoot, a great coach and friend, especially in those early years at Fulham, and Dave Bassett. What can you say about Harry? If you've ever seen him on the telly talking ten-to-the-dozen, you have to realise that isn't an act. He's like that in real life, as well as being a good friend and mentor.

Thanks must go to Alan Cork, Bob Booker and Dean White: you really should be still in the game. I mean, what Alan Cork can't teach a centre-forward really isn't worth knowing.

At Port Vale, thanks to Mark Grew and Geoff Horsfield, Jack the kit man, Andy Foster, the physio and Steve Jordan, the masseur. I could go on. A special mention must also go to Jo Lumani, my press officer at Coventry and Port Vale

Thanks to the secretaries, Derek Allan at Brighton, Andrew Neville at Leicester and Bill Lodney and Estelle Baggley at Port Vale. Thanks to Tim Stevenson, the club doctor, and Malcolm Stewart, the physio at Brighton. Thanks to my good friends Sharon Duce, who I met at Fulham, and Danny and Sam Hubbard in Market Harborough.

Thanks to some of the chairmen I've known, especially Dick Knight at Brighton who stood by me when others were happy to abandon me. The much-maligned Bill Bratt, Graham Mudie and Peter Jackson at Port Vale are strong people who gave me their 100 per cent backing. Norman Smurthwaite, too. He has broad shoulders and has made a huge impact on the club.

To all the supporters at every club I've ever played for or managed, I've got to say that I gave it my all; even at Tranmere. Thanks for all your support.

To Paul Kenny, a huge thank you. He's backed me at Fulham, Brentford and Port Vale, but I have to call him 'Sir' now. I bet his wife, Pat, doesn't address him like that! They are great friends.

Thanks to the late and great Art O'Keefe, too. What a man.

Lastly, I must thank my family from the bottom of my heart. It's been an emotional rollercoaster for all of them, particularly for my three girls, Steph, Stacy and Lauren. They had to see the break-up of their mum and dad as I spent more and more time away from them because football eats away at all of us who work in it. You have to give it your all. Seventy per cent isn't good enough to reach the top. It probably affected them more than me. I also want to thank Mandy, my first wife. Believe you me, she put up with some shit.

Thanks to my mum. What a strong woman she is. Rock-solid. I don't know how she does it. Thanks to my sister Jill and my nephews Joshua and Joseph (even though they are Wednesdayites), and Charlie for their support.

To Mitchel and Madison, my two kids with Claire. They are having the best of their dad. I'm not as uptight as I was and I'm so privileged to see them develop into fantastic young adults.

To Neil 'Mox' Moxley. He has the patience of a saint. All football managers are paranoid about sports writers, but from day one of meeting Neil, I knew he was a genuine guy. Without him this book wouldn't be in existence, and I consider him a good friend.

That leaves the two most important people in my life. Thanks to Claire, the one solid person in my life. Through good and bad, she never changes. I do not know what I would do without her. She loves me unconditionally, I hope, and I know it isn't easy at times. I'm really looking forward to spending the rest of my life with her. The trappings of success in a football career have treated us pretty well, all told, and so hopefully we will enjoy some of them together for many years to come.

Finally, I want to thank my dad. In reality, this book is about him. I know you will be thinking to yourself, 'Why is he even talking about this man?' But without him, none of this would have happened. He was the driving force behind my career. I suppose a lot of people would say he bullied me in lots of ways, but I don't think that's true and I don't want people to feel sorry for me. The truth is that my life and career has been shaped by him and not one day goes by that I don't think about him. And, do you know what? I don't think about the bad. I only think about the good.

I would give up all the success tomorrow just to spend one more day with him. Just one more day.

AUTHOR'S NOTE

The call came out of the blue.

'I'm thinking of writing my book? Do you fancy helping me?' said the voice at the other end of the phone.

First of all, it's flattering to be asked. But there were conditions. If we were going to tell Micky Adams's story, we were going to do it, warts and all.

I didn't want to pen a fairy-tale. I wanted the nitty-gritty and the real low-down on La Manga. I wanted to get underneath the skin of my pal – and tell it the way it was.

That's why you will find testimonials from players who worked under Micky at his clubs in these pages. He hasn't necessarily chosen players who will be sympathetic to him. He could have done. But he hasn't.

That way, I hope, you will get a different perspective of a man who has overcome a fair few obstacles in his life to enjoy the career he has in our national game.

We don't – unless it is an integral part of the story – talk about matches which happened thirty-five years ago. Unless it was one that sticks in the memory – such as the Coventry City v. Leeds United FA Cup semi-final in 1987 – we have tried to steer clear of such banalities.

I believed, and still do, that this book will have to stand and fall on its honesty, and the sheer weight of stories across the broad spectrum of clubs Micky has worked for and characters he has come across.

It's taken the best part of eighteen months to get to this point and, having heard him speak candidly about his life and the relationships within it, I have a new-found respect for Micky Adams.

He's led a life, one most of which he can be proud of. I hope by the time you put this book down you understand why I hold him in such high esteem. He's not perfect. Who is?

But above all, I hope he considers me a friend, because I had a lot of time for Micky Adams. And, having heard his story, I have even more time for him now.

Neil Moxley, September 2017

INDEX

Stone, Steve 138, 140
Summerbee, Nicky 187–8
Summers, Gerry 11, 297
Sutton, Alan 39, 40–41
Swansea City 114–19
Swindon Town 279–80

Taggart, Gerry 179, 193, 195
Taylor, Andy 264
Taylor, Gordon 215
Taylor, Paul 14, 15
Taylor, Peter 15–16, 122, 172, 175
Thelwell, Kevin 241
Thomas, Glen 81
Thomas, Rod 159–60
Thompson, Andy 317
Tigana, Jean 112
Le Tissier, Matt 49, 50, 51, 63–6, 74
Tomlin, Gavin 289, 293
Tottenham Hotspur 15, 16, 183
Tranmere Rovers 298–302
Turner, Ben 238
Tydeman, Dick 14–15

UK Trials 318

Vincent, Ashley 280
Vokes, Sam 266

Walker, Ian 177, 187, 206, 213, 218
Walker, Len 85, 86, 113–15
Walker, Pat 202, 203
Wallace, Danny 48–9
Wallace, Ray 48–9
Wallace, Rodney 48–9
Walsh, Tony 'Banger' 231
Walton, Mark 93, 108
Ward, Elliott 235
Warhurst, Paul 176
Warnock, Neil 193
Watson, Paul 92, 98, 99, 124, 158, 161–2
Webb, David 119–20, 126–7
Wenger, Arsene 141, 221–2, 224

West Bromwich Albion 235
Whalley, Joan 276–7
Whing, Andy 231, 258
White, Dean 166, 245, 324–5
Widdrington, Tommy 51
Wigan Athletic 323–4
Wildes, Paul 283, 284–5, 287
Wilkins, Dean 244–5, 249
Wilkins, Ray 72–3, 107, 114, 128
Wilkinson, Howard 36, 38–45, 49, 57, 66
Williams, Gareth 224
Williams, Geraint 'George' 241, 242–4
Williams, Giles 317
Williams, Ray 252, 257–8
Williamson, Lee 266
Willis, Dave 73–4
Winkelman, Pete 227–8
Wise, Dennis 185–7, 232–3, 235
Woan, Ian 133, 138
Wolverhampton Wanderers 196–7
Wood, Steve 75, 250, 316
Woodward, Alan 148, 149
Wycombe Wanderers 155–6

Yorke, Dwight 143

Zabaleta, Pablo 246
Zamora, Bobby 160–62, 163, 166, 171, 172